Conversations with
Nalo Hopkinson

Literary Conversations Series
Monika Gehlawat
General Editor

Conversations with Nalo Hopkinson

Edited by Isiah Lavender III

University Press of Mississippi / Jackson

The University Press of Mississippi is the scholarly publishing agency of the Mississippi Institutions of Higher Learning: Alcorn State University, Delta State University, Jackson State University, Mississippi State University, Mississippi University for Women, Mississippi Valley State University, University of Mississippi, and University of Southern Mississippi.

www.upress.state.ms.us

The University Press of Mississippi is a member of the Association of University Presses.

Any discriminatory or derogatory language or hate speech regarding race, ethnicity, religion, sex, gender, class, national origin, age, or disability that has been retained or appears in elided form is in no way an endorsement of the use of such language outside a scholarly context.

Copyright © 2023 by University Press of Mississippi
All rights reserved

First printing 2023
∞

Library of Congress Cataloging-in-Publication Data

Names: Lavender, Isiah, III, editor.
Title: Conversations with Nalo Hopkinson / Isiah Lavender III.
Other titles: Literary conversations series.
Description: Jackson : University Press of Mississippi, 2023. |
    Series: Literary conversations series | Includes index.
Identifiers: LCCN 2022042581 (print) | LCCN 2022042582 (ebook) |
    ISBN 9781496843678 (hardback) | ISBN 9781496843685 (trade paperback) |
    ISBN 9781496843692 (epub) | ISBN 9781496843708 (epub) |
    ISBN 9781496843715 (pdf) | ISBN 9781496843722 (pdf)
Subjects: LCSH: Hopkinson, Nalo—Interviews. | African American women
    authors—20th century—Interviews. | African American women authors—
    21st century—Interviews.
Classification: LCC PR9199.3.H5927 C66 2023 (print) | LCC PR9199.3.H5927 (ebook) |
    DDC 813/.6—dc23
LC record available at https://lccn.loc.gov/2022042581
LC ebook record available at https://lccn.loc.gov/2022042582

British Library Cataloging-in-Publication Data available

Books by Nalo Hopkinson

Brown Girl in the Ring (Warner Aspect, 1998)
Midnight Robber (Warner Aspect, 2000)
Skin Folk (Warner Aspect, 2001)
The Salt Roads (Warner Books, 2003)
The New Moon's Arms (Grand Central Publishing, 2007)
The Chaos (Margaret K. McElderry Books, 2012)
Report from Planet Midnight (PM Press, 2012)
Sister Mine (Grand Central Publishing, 2013)
Falling in Love with Hominids (Tachyon Publications, 2015)

Books Edited by Nalo Hopkinson

Whispers from the Cotton Tree Root: Caribbean Fabulist Fiction
(Invisible Cities Press, 2000)
Mojo: Conjure Stories (Warner Aspect, 2003)
So Long Been Dreaming, coedited with Uppinder Mehan (Arsenal Pulp Press, 2004)
Tesseracts Nine: New Canadian Speculative Fiction, coedited with Geoff Ryman
(EDGE Science Fiction and Fantasy Publishing, 2005)
People of Colo(u)r Destroy Science Fiction, coedited with Kristine Ong Muslim
(Lightspeed Magazine, 2016)
Particulates, coedited with Rita McBride (Dia Art Foundation, 2018)

Contents

Introduction   ix

Chronology   xiii

Nalo Hopkinson: Many Perspectives   3
    Charles Brown / 1999

Speaking in Tongues: An Interview with Science Fiction Writer Nalo
Hopkinson   12
    Gregory E. Rutledge / 1999

Interview: Nalo Hopkinson   30
    Mary Anne Mohanraj / 2000

An Interview with Nalo Hopkinson   37
    Christian Wolff / 2001

Interview with Nalo Hopkinson   46
    James Schellenberg and David M. Switzer / 2001

Nalo Hopkinson: Winging It   60
    Charles Brown / 2001

An Interview with Nalo Hopkinson   68
    Dianne D. Glave / 2001

A Conversation with Nalo Hopkinson   84
    Jené Watson-Aifah / 2001

viii CONTENTS

"Making the Impossible Possible": An Interview with Nalo Hopkinson 95
Alondra Nelson / 2002

Breakdown or Breakthrough: A Conversation with Nalo Hopkinson on
Race and the Science Fiction Community 111
Isiah Lavender III / 2005

Conjuring Caribbean Moonbeams: An Interview with Nalo Hopkinson 131
Michael Lohr / 2007

"Happy That It's Here": An Interview with Nalo Hopkinson 138
Nancy Johnston / 2008

AE Interviews: Nalo Hopkinson 151
Paul Jarvey / 2011

"Correcting the Balance": Outspoken Interview with Nalo Hopkinson 157
Terry Bisson / 2012

Interview: Nalo Hopkinson 176
David Barr Kirtley / 2013

Somehow Déclassé: Interview with Nalo Hopkinson 189
Gary K. Wolfe and Jonathan Strahan / 2013

Writing from the Body: An Interview with Nalo Hopkinson 201
Jessica FitzPatrick / 2015

Interview with Nalo Hopkinson 211
Tiffany Davis / 2017

Waving at Trains: An Interview with Nalo Hopkinson 216
Avni Sejpal / 2017

CONTENTS ix

SLF Portolan Project Interview with Nalo Hopkinson Los Angeles,
California, 2019   224
Mary Anne Mohanraj / 2019

"Fresh": A Second Conversation with Nalo Hopkinson on Life, the
Academy, Race, and the Science Fiction Community   232
Isiah Lavender III / 2021

Index   241

Introduction

When Jamaican-born Canadian Nalo Hopkinson burst on to the science fiction scene with *Brown Girl in the Ring* in 1998, she seemingly single-handedly reinvigorated interest in Black science fiction (SF). Afrofuturism had not caught fire at this point, but Hopkinson *did*. She grabbed the attention of the SF community with her Caribbean-inspired science fiction, fantasy, and magical realism. Hopkinson represents the obvious first link in Octavia Butler's legacy. Now a professor of creative writing at the University of British Columbia and a frequent instructor at the Clarion Workshop for Science Fiction writers, Hopkinson is well placed to influence the emerging generations of speculative fiction writers.

Arguably, among her six published novels, three short story collections, six edited collections, and one comics series, the best known remain *Brown Girl in the Ring* (1998) and *Midnight Robber* (2000). The first excitingly mixes Afro-Caribbean folklore, organ theft, gangs, and a single, Black teenage mother protagonist within a dystopian Toronto, and the second features an entire Black Caribbean planet named Toussaint, interdimensional travel, and a cyberpunk feel interwoven with Caribbean myth as a young Black girl comes of age. In both novels, if not all of her work, Hopkinson strongly critiques the dilemmas of modern Black life and empowers Black people, specifically women, to create their own futures.

Hopkinson has won multiple awards for her writing and editing achievements beginning with The Astounding Award for Best New Writer in 1999 for *Brown Girl in the Ring* as well as the Locus Award for Best First Novel. Her first collection of short stories, *Skin Folk*, won her the World Fantasy Award in 2003, featuring dark fantasies and haunting technologies as Hopkinson pondered modern existence through speculative modes. Her third novel, *The Salt Roads*, won the Gaylactic Spectrum Award in 2004 for exploring queer issues within speculative fiction in a positive way. In recent years, Hopkinson has turned her attention to writing for an ongoing comic book series in Neil Gaiman's *Sandman Universe*, specifically *House of Whispers*. All of Hopkinson's singular fictions reflect her interests in raced,

xii INTRODUCTION

gendered, and queered identities from a Caribbean perspective permeated by the folklore of her youth.

As one of the founding members of the Carl Brandon Society (1999), an organization devoted to Black indigenous people of color (BIPOC) speculative fiction started at WisCon: The Feminist Science Fiction Conference, Hopkinson has always had a vested interest in expanding racial and ethnic diversity in all facets of speculative fiction from its writers to its readers. Her editing work demonstrates her abiding support of BIPOC writers by providing opportunities for readers to engage with the Caribbean legends inspired by African belief systems and postcolonial future visions as seen in her anthology *Whispers from the Cotton Tree Root: Caribbean Fabulist Fiction* (2000). Further, Hopkinson breaks critical ground with *So Long Been Dreaming: Postcolonial Science Fiction & Fantasy* (2004), coedited with Uppinder Mehan, as the first anthology featuring the stories of multiethnic authors who imagine futures from a third world perspective where the natives are colonized. Hopkinson also coedited, with Kristine Ong Muslim, the *People of Colo(u)r Destroy Science Fiction!* collection (2017), in response to the far right's perception of the genre's decline because of its increasing diversity, which led to the various Sad/Rabid Puppies voting campaigns at the Hugo Awards to deny awarding such emerging BIPOC excellence, to deny the colored wave of science fiction.

Although Hopkinson has been the guest of honor at multiple academic conferences, her appeal clearly goes beyond the realm of academia in that she was also the guest of honor at the Seventy-fifth World Science Fiction Convention in Helsinki, Finland, in 2017. In fact, the Science Fiction & Fantasy Writers of America bestowed the ultimate honor in naming Nalo Hopkinson the Thirty-seventh Damon Knight Memorial Grand Master for lifetime achievement in science fiction and fantasy in 2020. Hopkinson is the first Black queer woman so honored by her creative peers, only the second Black person, following living legend Samuel R. Delany, to win the award, not to mention the youngest. Indeed, Nalo Hopkinson *is* a dynamic writer, teacher, and speaker who engages issues of race, gender, technology, science, and the occult in her body of work.

Because orality is an important feature of Hopkinson's work, I will take a minute to highlight its importance to her creativity. Two pieces immediately come to mind: "Code Sliding" (around 2005) and her guest of honor lecture at the International Conference of the Fantastic in the Arts (ICFA), "A Reluctant Ambassador from the Planet of Midnight" (2010). In "Code Sliding," Hopkinson discusses the importance of language and the ability to switch between linguistic registers. In other words, she utilizes the power of language to affect the nature of reality with the concept of hybridity and puts it on full display in *Midnight Robber* by delving into Caribbean Creoles to resist forces of oppression and to claim space for Caribbean cultures by referencing history. Hopkinson recognizes that knowledge is coded in the construction of languages and she provides us with the key to understanding the differences in values, perceptions, and behaviors that create racialized worldviews in her short essay. With her forty-five-minute ICFA guest of honor address in a largely white-attended banquet hall in Orlando, Florida, Hopkinson tackled the difficult subject of translation, about what people mean when they say "I'm not racist" by performing her talk as an alien ambassador. The power of her performance will never be forgotten by those in attendance; her chin bounced off her collar bone, her head lifted, and the alien ambassador emerged, channeled through her body, possessing her mind as a translator, grappling with racial constructs. Hopkinson educated white people on how erasure feels, challenged perceptions of a monochrome future peopled by whites alone, and demanded BIPOCs create futures for themselves to annul the lingering effects of a fading colonialism and slavery. That particular audience in mass rose up on its feet for a standing ovation! Truthfully, Nalo Hopkinson's powerful influence helped to make possible science fiction's present and ongoing colored era.

In this respect, Hopkinson's work, by far, has garnered the most scholarly acclaim of the new Black generation with many academics classing her stories on par with both Butler and Delany while also insisting on her inclusion as a member of the big three Black science fiction writers at the beginning of the twenty-first century. There are roughly 860 articles and book chapters on Hopkinson's work, but only two published monographs where she is a primary subject—Ingrid Thaler's *Black Atlantic Speculative Fictions: Octavia E. Butler, Jewelle Gomez, and Nalo Hopkinson* (Routledge, 2010) and Sonja Georgi's *Bodies and/as Technology: Counter-Discourses on Ethnicity and Globalization in the Works of Alejandro Morales, Larissa Lai, and Nalo Hopkinson* (Universitätsverlag, Winter 2011). Likewise, fourteen published dissertations featuring Nalo Hopkinson exist which have not yet become books. By comparison, there are four dissertations featuring Nnedi Okorafor and none with respect to N. K. Jemisin as of yet. I mention Okorafor and Jemisin in passing because they could be thought of as the new "big three," with Hopkinson herself completing the triumvirate. This sample size of Hopkinson's importance might seem small at first, but the books are coming.

At least thirty-five published interviews exist of which I am aware. Not only does this number inform us of Hopkinson's popularity, but also suggests

xiv INTRODUCTION

to me that she is a writer in demand because she simply fascinates people. This fixation, perhaps, begins with the early *African American Review* interview from 1999, where she provides insight on code-switching. Furthermore, I think of the 2002 *Social Text* interview as an obvious choice because of how she saw herself contributing to the conversation on Afrofuturism. Likewise, her 2008 interview in the *Queer Universes* collection offers us a glimpse of her thinking on the subject of sexuality. Also, Hopkinson's 2013 *Paradoxa* interview illustrates the importance of her thinking on postcolonial science fiction written by people of color. Fortunately, you can read all four of them in this collection and decide for yourself! But for me, no other Black science fiction writer, not even the legendary Delany himself, has been more concerned with projecting complex futures for people of color than Nalo Hopkinson. Consequently, I have undertaken this project to help the world know Nalo Hopkinson a little bit better, a little bit more in her own words—from her interests in collecting drift glass on the shores of Lake Ontario to making great food to crafting mermaids to designing her own clothing, among other things—as well as her time as a professional writer, with its struggles and triumphs, across twenty-one interviews. I have gathered together these interviews, from the earliest I could find in the pages of *Locus: The Magazine of the Science Fiction & Fantasy Field*, to the most recent one I conducted for this volume, to simply help others see this incredible human being through her own thoughts, to see her intellectual curiosity, resourcefulness, and humor.

As with all of my academic pursuits, I'd like to acknowledge God's hand in this project in terms of putting the right people in my path beginning with Nalo Hopkinson herself. I could not have completed this project without the love of my wife, Heather (the newest Dr. Lavender), and sons, Kingsley and Frazier. Likewise, I am grateful for the resources I am afforded as the Sterling-Goodman Professor of English at the University of Georgia; to my "seminar" crew (Amy, Kensie, Nate, and Josh) for listening to my struggles over lunch and drinks, usually at Ted's Most Best; to Becky and Ro Martini, at other locations in Athens; as well as to my mentors, John Lowe (a saint in my household) and Barbara McCaskill. A special thanks to Mary Heath at the University Press of Mississippi for believing in this project. Finally, my part-time research assistant, Chanara Andrews-Bickers, deserves all kinds of praise on this project in terms of establishing who the rights holders were for the various interviews, making first contact with them, and smoothing things out for my negotiations.

—IL3

Chronology

1960	Nalo Hopkinson is born in Kingston, Jamaica, on December 20, 1960, to Slade Hopkinson, a poet, playwright, and actor as well as a teacher, and Freda Hopkinson, a library clerk.
1960–1976	Moves around the Caribbean, particularly Guyana and Trinidad, during her adolescence, absorbing the richness of Caribbean folklore from her parents and their friends, like the world-renowned Barbadian poet the Honorable Edward Kamau Brathwaite, CBH, as well as classics of Western literature.
1977–2011	Immigrates to Toronto, Canada, with her family at the age of sixteen and spends the majority of her life here.
1982	Earns a bachelor's degree from York University in Toronto with a double major in Russian and French.
1993	Father dies of kidney cancer.
1995	Attends the Clarion Science Fiction and Fantasy Writers' Workshop, where Samuel R. Delany is one of her instructors, and publishes first short story, "Midnight Robber," in *Exile: The Literary Quarterly* 18, no. 4.
1997	Wins the Warner Aspect First Novel Contest for *Brown Girl in the Ring*.
1998	Publishes her first novel *Brown Girl in the Ring*, which wins the 1999 Locus Award for Best First Novel.
1999	Hopkinson is one of the founding members of the Carl Brandon Society that sprang into being at WisCon, the feminist science fiction convention held annually in Madison, Wisconsin. She also wins the Astounding Award for Best New Writer.
2000	Publishes *Midnight Robber*, which is short-listed for both the Hugo and Nebula awards for best novel, and edits first short story collection *Whispers from the Cotton Tree Root: Caribbean Fabulist Fiction*.
2001	Publishes first short story collection, *Skin Folk*.

2002	Earns a master's degree in writing popular fiction from Seton Hill University in Greensburg, Pennsylvania; *Skin Folk* wins the World Fantasy Award for Best Collection.
2003	Publishes *The Salt Roads*, which is short-listed for the Nebula Award for Best Novel; edits short story collection *Mojo: Conjure Stories*; wins her first Sunburst Award for Canadian Literature of the Fantastic for *Skin Folk*.
2004	Coedits, with Uppinder Mehan, *So Long Been Dreaming: Post-colonial Science Fiction & Fantasy*; wins the Gaylactic Spectrum Award for Best Novel for *The Salt Roads*.
2005	Coedits with Geoff Ryman *Tesseracts Nine: New Canadian Speculative Fiction*.
2007	Publishes *The New Moon's Arms*, which is short-listed for the Nebula Award for Best Novel.
2008	Wins her second Sunburst Award for Canadian Literature of the Fantastic for *The New Moon's Arms* as well as the Aurora Award for the best Canadian Science Fiction/Fantasy novel.
2009–2010	A period of homelessness in her life.
2011	Moves to Riverside, California, to take academic position as a tenured professor of creative writing at the University of California, Riverside.
2012	Publishes *The Chaos* and short story collection *Report from Planet Midnight*.
2013	Publishes *Sister Mine*; the book wins the 2014 Andre Norton Nebula Award for Middle Grade and Young Adult Fiction.
2015	Publishes short story collection *Falling in Love with Hominids*.
2016	Awarded an honorary doctor of letters from Anglia Ruskin University in the United Kingdom; coedits with Kristine Ong Muslim *People of Colo(u)r Destroy Science Fiction* (Lightspeed Magazine, 2016).
2017	Guest of honor, World Science Fiction Convention, Helsinki, Finland; wins British Fantasy Award for Best Collection for coedited *People of Colo(u)r Destroy Science Fiction*.
2018	Coedits, with Rita McBride, *Particulates*.
2018–2020	Lead writer on the twenty-two-issue run of *House of Whispers* comic for Neil Gaiman's *Sandman Universe*.
2020	Named the Thirty-seventh Damon Knight Memorial Grand Master by the Science Fiction and Fantasy Writers of America.

2021   Awarded an honorary doctor of letters from the Ontario College of Arts and Design University in Toronto, Canada. Leaves Riverside to take her current academic position as a tenured professor of creative writing at the University of British Columbia in Vancouver, Canada.

**Conversations with
Nalo Hopkinson**

Nalo Hopkinson: Many Perspectives

Charles Brown / 1999

From *Locus Magazine* (January 1999). © *Locus Magazine*. Reprinted with permission.

"Writing is something I just absorbed at the knee, because we were surrounded by writers, by artists of various kinds of story-making. We went to the theater a lot, we went to dance performances. There were books everywhere, my dad being a teacher, my mother a library worker. And a lot of the stuff I was drawn to was the fantastic. I was reading Homer's *Iliad*, *Gulliver's Travels*, as a tot, so what *I* got was the fantastic element. There was no political commentary in *Gulliver's Travels*—I didn't figure that out till much later! When I found Dad's copies of Carlos Castaneda, from the point of view of a nine-year-old, yeah, yeah, that *is* how the world works! Dad had just been lying to me, and here's someone telling me the truth. The world *is* that damn weird.

"When I was around eleven or twelve, we were living in Kingston, Jamaica. My mother was working in the big library, and I would go meet her after school and wait for my father to finish work and pick us up. She would give me her adult library card. So that was where I discovered the science fiction section. I'd already been reading stuff like that, so it seemed in some ways a natural fit. But when you're a young girl from Kingston, Jamaica, and you're reading Harlan Ellison's 'Shattered like a Glass Goblin,' it's very difficult. Then discovering people like Samuel R. Delany and Elizabeth Lynn, the New Wave writers and feminist writers—finally SF was beginning to talk to me about things that also were reflected in my own world.

"I never thought to write for the longest while, because my Dad was the writer. In the Caribbean writers' community—many of whom live in Toronto—*his* name is known. I am Nalo Hopkinson, Slade Hopkinson's daughter. As an artist, my father's education was very much Euro-classical. He wrote sonnets. But he did one particular poem about a homeless woman who lived outside the grounds of the University of the West Indies, about

4 CONVERSATIONS WITH NALO HOPKINSON

her madness and her tantrums and her sucking blood from the air. And then he suddenly turns and talks about the Caribbean setting and the university—he called it 'the latitudes of the ex-colonized.'

"I think in some ways it was easier to wait, because he died in 1993, and it wasn't until then that I applied for Judith Merril's writer's workshop through Rice University. I entered that, not ever having written any fiction, except a really bad vampire story when I was about eleven, which my Dad read and said, 'This is good. Is there anything bothering you now?' I think that was when I put the pen back down—I wasn't about to answer that question!'

"You had to have some writing in order to apply to Judy's course, because she wanted a bunch of people who were more or less at the same level of competence, so I had to churn out something. And what I did was six pages of something I knew was unfinished, about a young woman in a city, who's having visions of things she doesn't understand. I had no idea whether it was bigger than a short story, no idea where it was going. But it showed I could string a sentence together, so I got in the workshop—which then didn't run because there weren't enough registrations! But Judy had done this quite a few times. She just got a handful of us together, we met at her home in Toronto, and she said, 'You don't really need to pay someone money to do this. I can show you how to run a workshop, and then you'll just go off and do it.' So she showed us how to do the critiquing.

"The writing group we formed, the core was three of us, one of whom had been to Clarion West. And the other two of us were very interested. The opportunity came, we both applied to Clarion, and we both got in, so we went together in 1995. The teachers were Joe and Gay Haldeman, Nancy Kress, Pat Murphy, Samuel R. Delany, Tim Powers, and Karen Joy Fowler. A wide spectrum! One writer would come in one week and say, 'Here are the rules,' and another one would come in and be completely different.

"Clarion *is* boot camp for writers. By the time I got done with six weeks of writing at that speed and at that level, that nakedness, I could produce hallucinations on my computer terminal, out of a clear blue sky! I made my first professional sale, of a story I wrote at Clarion. Pat Murphy helped me pull it together, then Chip Delany read it and said, 'Send it to Ellen Datlow.' That was for *Black Swan, White Raven*, in 1997. And 'Precious,' which I also wrote at Clarion, also sold.

"I came back to Toronto, and you go through this funk, because now you have to write full-time! The six pages I produced for Judy Merril developed into the beginning of *Brown Girl in the Ring*. While I was working on them, I heard about the Warner Aspect contest for new writers. I knew I

CHARLES BROWN / 1999 **5**

was nowhere near to a finished novel, but I had two chapters, and that was the first stage of application, to send the first couple of chapters. I sent it out way early—the deadline was January 31st, and I sent it out in August, figuring if there was any kind of interest, I'd probably have done a lot more on it by the time I heard. Two weeks later, I got a letter back which said, 'It looks good. Send us the whole novel for a second-round reading.'

"I took a few deep breaths, said, 'OK, I sent them a letter that said I'll write it. I'm just going to heat it up a little!' Luckily, I had a few months off work. I'd gotten a writing grant—Canada has this. I had two months off, so I wrote night and day. Workshopping with my writing group every two weeks, and I wrote the last two pages on January 30th! Six months later, I was at work and got a phone message asking me to call them back. I've gone through sending out stories and getting rejection letters, and I put myself in that mindset: 'This is a no.' When she said, 'I have good news,' I still said, 'And what would that be?' I didn't figure on winning. I think I managed not to screech in her ear when she told me. The Warner Aspect First Novel Contest was judged by C. J. Cherryh and Warner Aspect. I found out later they had nearly a thousand entries from all around the world—from Qatar, from Australia. I also found out much later, they had so many entries, they had to hire a supplementary reader to do the first round, and that was Josepha Sherman. She was my ghost reader!

"I work for an arts council as a grants officer. It's a peer assessment model which I think comes out of Europe and England, where the people who make the decisions about who gets grants are other artists. I'm the person who facilitates the jury process, keeping it moving along, sending out the letters afterwards. So I'm sort of in the arts environment all the time, which can be energizing.

"*Brown Girl in the Ring* started when I was doing research for a nonfiction article on health risks that tend to hit Black communities more, and I stumbled on a piece of research that had been done in the UK, where they had looked at incidences of schizophrenia in various populations, and found the highest rates were in male immigrants from the Caribbean. They had no real theories as to why, but part of their idea was that the imbalance that caused schizophrenia was probably impelled in part by the culture shock of coming to such a different land and, being male, having fewer social resources.

"The image caught me. And because I usually start with a female protagonist, I started with a woman who had some of those symptoms, but had no idea how to explain them. I put them in terms of her culture, and the more I started to do research into what in her own culture would make

6 CONVERSATIONS WITH NALO HOPKINSON

sense of what she was feeling, the more I started finding out about *orisha* worship, which takes different names on different islands, but can be traced directly back to West African belief systems. *Orisha* worship was something I had grown up in the Caribbean knowing about, but from the outside. My parents made it seem like a version of Christianity, a more charismatic one, because that's what they thought it was. I was brought up very middle class—I am very middle class!

"There is a lot of supernatural stuff in Caribbean folklore, but the connection between it and other tracebacks to African culture isn't always made. I started doing more and more research into it. The more you know, the more coherent the whole thing becomes. So I had this young woman, and the person who was originally her mother—later her grandmother—and when I started to think about how they were making a living, the story and the setting clicked into place. Which is really gratifying, because I went to Clarion a little bit afterwards, and one of the things Chip Delany said was, 'Think about how your characters are making their money, because if you don't you'll end up with something that just seems to hang in space and doesn't really make any sense, and even if it doesn't show in the story, intuitively your readers will know,' and I *did* that!

"The other part of the story was the whole organ-selling thing. I saw what was supposed to be a documentary that claims that people in Third World countries are cannibalizing and selling organs, and in the new Russia, surgeons are actually selling organs to supplement their income. The more research I did, the more I was getting contradictory reports, and finally I whittled it away until I only had a few little 'pig' organ-donor farms.

"The herbal lore the grandmother uses to heal people is very powerful. At one point in Haiti, they were using herbal lore to poison the water. It was chemical warfare, and they closed Haiti down. People would import water in steel casks, and by the time they'd broached the casks, the water was poisoned, and nobody knew how it was being done. The Africans who were doing that called it 'science.' You can't talk about one thing people do, and then sort of hie off from the belief systems, so I didn't see it as blending genres.

"I also didn't see it as horror! Though there is one scene. . . . I needed to make it believable, and it was being seen through the eyes of someone in the medical profession. I walked across the hallway to my neighbor's door, because she's a medical technician, and I had that dazed look I get when I'm in the middle of writing something. She opened the door and said, 'Hi,' and I said, 'If you were going to cannibalize, what tissues would you seek?' And she said, 'You need my *Gray's Anatomy.*'

"The drug in the book comes from reading *The Serpent and the Rainbow* by Canadian writer Wade Davis, who went to Haiti and did research into the herbal medicine. When they started to realize that the lore of zombies is based on reality, and they were finding people who had been made into zombies and come back, they started to do research into it. It's the drug from this fish, and there are other things in it, depressives, etc. It's a form of punishment, Davis says, for someone who just totally offended everyone. When I started reading, it seemed that it was a quite popular drug! It had ramifications in medicine too.

"I'm trying to create systems in SF literature that still use the tropes of the literature but that come from my context. There are things you can say, and you'll get an immediate reaction from people as their connections are made. You say 'vampires' or 'Anne Rice.' . . . Coming from a context that's magic Caribbean, those elements are all there. Also, in the eastern Caribbean islands, you've got a girl's game, a challenge game. There's one girl in the middle, the others in a ring around her, and the challenge is, 'Show us something you can do that we can't.' The person in the middle has to come up with something the others then try to do. The one who's closest to it gets picked to be next brown girl in the ring. And I thought that also was an apt metaphor for a young woman who's just coming into adulthood, kicking and screaming, not very happy about it, and wants to figure out really quickly what she can do, what she *must* do in order to have a life.

"I left the setting in Toronto partly because I was writing so fast, it's set where I live. I didn't have to make up an environment. And partly because I don't know a whole lot about how people live in the suburbs. If I have to describe somebody surviving in a hostile environment, that's one I know. And it's a fascinating city. I love it during the warm months—June until the end of August, I'm there! It's a historically rich city, and it's got so many communities, it's one of the most culturally diverse in the world.

"And it occurred to me that most post-holocaust novels happen outside the city. I wondered about the people who stayed—because people *will* stay; they always do. I wondered what would be keeping them there, what they would be doing there, what would they have the opportunity to do there? So I came up with communities of people who were opportunists. I came up with people who were too damn ornery to leave—the grandmother is one of those. And people who can now *form* communities in ways that seem right to them. That was also sort of an opportunity to re-link things in a fashion less citified.

"When I had my book launch, that was a trip! There were about eighty people in the audience, basically the SF community in Toronto, and my friends. The Caribbean artistic community, if they know SF, it's in terms of Jules Verne and George Orwell. So these people say, 'I've never seen anything like this before.' The SF community knows the tropes and the conventions and the language of SF but to have it written from within the Caribbean community is new to them. So I'm getting lots of interesting reactions. And the African American community, from the few responses I've gotten so far, is from an American context that's not mine. *Emerge* magazine did a wonderful review, but they talk about the novel in terms of it's speaking out against Black-on-Black violence. I guess you could take that from it, and that's how it works for them. They're very curious about it in the Caribbean—it's just a matter of distribution. I know my friends are taking copies down, so I'm beginning to get reviews.

"Convention-going is hard, and it's a completely Other space for me. I came to Worldcon, and apart from the shift I have to make because I'm in another country, I'm constantly shifting communities. At Worldcon events, I'm in that great SF fan community where a Wookie will walk by me on one side, an author on the other. I step outside, go to the local restaurant, and the people who connect and say hi, the people who make a point of coming over and asking, 'How're you doing?' are the Black people. I'm having to shift back and forth—and probably most of them can do it too. The dissonance is huge, when you're talking about shifting from the SF community to a community that is not mine but where I recognize enough of the language.

"They talk about Canada being two solitudes, English and French. I don't see that so much in Toronto because it's mostly English, but I come here and there are two *nations*. The overlap seems really tiny. And the way other Black people greet me here is, 'I've got to connect with you, because we're under siege here and we need to let each other know that we are allies.' So how do you move from that mindset, take two steps over, and go to a panel?

"This was my first Worldcon, and there seem to be more Black SF readers than you'd think. In the Caribbean, science fiction was in the libraries, and I didn't have a whole lot of trouble finding people who were out there reading it. The readership is smaller. Science fiction, in North America particularly, is traditionally a literature of colonizing, and we've had a problem with that. Part of it doesn't really seem to speak to us. But there's so much being done in the field that *does*. The literature is changing, it's evolving, and there are people who are tackling things like that head-on. But I think it's still very much a literature that does not really include us, except as window dressing. The overall impression you get from the book covers is that the humans are the white people, and the aliens are people of color.

"At some convention with Delany, the issue of race came up, and somebody very helpfully said, 'I don't see races. I just don't make it a problem in my life,' and he responded very gently, "If you don't see something that can be life-threatening to me, I'm not going to be very comfortable in your company." I find that when people from other communities do get written into SF, it's with a gloss that says, 'Yes, but we're all the same.' In a way that's true, but it totally ignores the actual social issues that do make a serious difference.

"I'm working hard to finish the book that was mostly finished before I started finishing *Brown Girl*! The title I'm working with is *Midnight Robber*, which is a masque from the Trinidad Carnival. This book is bigger. I'm challenging myself more. There are things I'm trying to do that may be beyond my grasp, and I chose not to enter the Warner contest with this because it's more complex, and I needed to get prepared for it. The only similarity to *Brown Girl* is that I am writing from a Caribbean context, but this one is set on a planet far, far away, a world that's been colonized by people from the Caribbean.

"In some ways, I'm taking on really old tropes of the genre: degenerate diseases, colonies, another galaxy. Those have been worked and reworked to death. Partly it's because I'm still groping for my own system of dealing with the tropes, but partly it's reinterpretation in a different context. If you talk about it from where I live, you end up with something very different. When you talk about people who have a history of *being* colonized going on to colonize things, that gets very interesting.

"The Midnight Robber is a character we meet at Carnival, who dresses in elaborate bandito costumes with huge gun belts and a hat that goes out to *there*, and baubles and flashing lights, and big flashing guns. He waylays people at Carnival, supposedly threatening them with the guns—which are *so* big there is no threat there. The big part of the Midnight Robber masque is the speech he writes beforehand. The gist of it is the man claiming to be the son of an African prince, who was kidnapped from Africa, brought to the New World, and has had to go through all kinds of adventures, which he relates, in his quest to get back home. (He never does.) So he has gotten to the point where he now waylays passengers, and the way you get him to *stop* telling you the story is to give him money. In my version, it's a battleship fleeing to another galaxy, and the Midnight Robber will be female—which it's only ever been once in the histories.

"Marcus Garvey's big thing was, 'Give me enough money. I'll buy us a bunch of ships and those of us who want to leave can get out of here.' I'm using that metaphor too, that whole thing of 'Swing Low, Sweet Chariot'—the ship that will come and take you away someplace better, when the ship's already brought you to someplace pretty scary.

"I recently performed in a dance piece that my friend, who's a South Indian choreographer, did. His whole training is Indian classical dance, but he's coming from a more contemporary take on it—he was raised in the suburbs of Toronto. The piece was about the divinity of water, choreographed on my body. What dance training I have is ballet and Afro-Caribbean, so the movements are completely different, but I was trying to get those confluences, that sense of jumping from one context to another that we have to do, as 'hybrid people'—I heard someone once refer to himself as a hyphenation. We're *all* hybrid people, but I hear people who like to think that isn't so. Jewish communities understand that it is. That's where the word *diaspora* comes from. But when someone says to me, 'Oh, I like your culture, because we white people don't have that,' I think, 'Oh, give me a break! Do your damn reading!'

"It's the same thing with writers of color writing SF as with women in SF. We'll pick up the stakes, widen the envelope. That's another wonderful thing about SF: I can do something with it, and people like new stuff. They'll be curious, they'll be interested, they'll be intrigued. It has the potential to be a very welcoming community.

"I come from the Caribbean. I am African in appearance—that's obviously most of my ancestry. But I have a great grandmother who was Jewish. I have native Indian from the Caribbean. There's so many different communities that have to coexist, that to me 'Black' means something different, 'Caribbean' means something different, when I'm in Canada from when I'm in the States. The Toronto perspective is, 'Leave it to them whether they want to do the sensible thing or not.'

"I go into an SF context, a con context, and the goodwill is there, but at every turn it's pretty obvious to me that there's not a whole lot of understanding. There's a little nexus of us, people who get together, and it tends to be queer people, people of color, the women, who understand what it's like to be on the fringes.

"Somebody asked me why I chose to write the dialogue of *Brown Girl* in Creole. I said, 'I wonder if anyone asked Jeff Noon why he chose to write *his* book in Creole.' It's my default position, like choosing to write Black characters. Whenever I pick up a pen, before I put the character on paper, I have to figure out what color they are. White writers tell me they don't have that experience, unless they *choose* to have it. I don't choose to have it. I have to find some way to signify, because it's important, what my characters look like. And I'm still working on that one!

"Science fiction has so much about it that I love, that is about being able to put on the person you'd like to be, about exploring, pushing the boundaries between things that people for so many centuries have taken as unchangeable—like gender, like race. There's so much there I find so tasty, and it *can* go across communities. I want to see more communities involved in it."

Speaking in Tongues: An Interview with Science Fiction Writer Nalo Hopkinson

Gregory E. Rutledge / 1999

From *African American Review* 33, no. 4 (1999): 589–601. Reprinted by permission of Gregory E. Rutledge.

Gregory E. Rutledge: Why are you a writer of Black fantasy?

Nalo Hopkinson: Because it's better than being a writer of purple prose? I'm a writer. I'm predominantly Black. I write fantasy (actually, I say "speculative fiction," because my work can include elements of science fiction, fantasy, dark fantasy, horror, and magic realism). I'm not a writer of Black fantasy. (I go into that more below.)

Rutledge: How long have you been interested in Black fantasy? What do you know of your predecessors like Butler, Delany, Saunders, Barnes, and others?

Hopkinson: I think perhaps we're using the word *fantasy* in different ways, so I need some clarification. Are you using it as an umbrella term for all the genres of fantastical writing? I'm accustomed to hearing it used to name one specific genre. According to the classifications with which I'm familiar, Butler writes science fiction, not fantasy. Delany has written both. Saunders's *Imaro* trilogy was sword and sorcery (i.e., a subgenre of fantasy). Barnes writes futuristic action adventure as well as having cowritten hard SF with people such as Larry Niven and Jerry Pournelle. Tananarive Due has been dubbed a horror author. I don't know Virginia Hamilton's work very well, but she has published young adult science fiction as well as collections of African American folktales.

I've read some form of fantastical literature since I was a tot, be it folktales or Homer's *Iliad*, so I gravitated naturally toward the SF shelves. Some time in my twenties I saw a photograph of Chip Delany, with whose work I'd fallen in love on first encountering it, and realized that he was Black. I'd never heard of such a thing before. I wept. It felt as though my universe had just doubled in size. Though my life was surrounded with Caribbean writers of color (my father and his friends), none of them wrote SF. I'd only met one other Black person who read the literature.

I began to wonder if there were any other Black writers of speculative fiction. I was working at a public library at the time, and used that resource to research the question. I found and devoured all the Butler novels I could get, and got books by Saunders and Barnes on interlibrary loan. A colleague pointed me to the shelves where Virginia Hamilton's novels were. For the past few years, I've been haphazardly collecting works of fantastical fiction by Black and Caribbean writers, and some by other people of color. This comes in handy when I'm on yet another SF convention panel on why people of color don't write SF. Black people don't write a lot of science fiction, but we are well represented in magic realism. And though we don't *write* a lot of science fiction, it's in our other artistic forms: our music (remember P-Funk's *Mothership Connection*?), our visual arts, our comics. African UK filmmaker John Akomfrah made a documentary on Black expressions of science fiction in music. It's called *The Last Angel of History*.

The long tradition of science fiction out of which came works such as Mary Shelley's *Frankenstein* and Karel Capek's *R.U.R.* has on this continent been overshadowed by the pulp era, which produced a lot of, well, pulp, as well as some fine literature. But it's left Western SF with a stigma about being adventure stories in which white people use technology to overpower alien cultures. Small wonder that Black writers haven't been drawn to it in large numbers—we've been on the receiving end of colonization, and for us it's not an entertaining adventure story. I believe it's Chip Delany who pointed out in an interview with Mark Dery that science fiction is a literature about how our technological creations affect our lives. African cultures have been made into consumers of technology, not its creators, and Western technology at that. How then are Black people to feel a buy-in to science fiction? Come to think of it, this seems largely to be a problem for writers. I worked for a while at an SF bookstore, and the patrons came in all shades and colors. I think there's an invisible readership of people of color. You rarely see them at cons, so it becomes easy to think that they aren't there.

I think the dearth of Black writers of science fiction is changing, and hope that Walter Mosley's recent call to arms in the November 1998 *New York Times* will speed it up. I know that my publisher, Warner Aspect (the

SF imprint of Warner Books), was pleased to discover after they accepted *Brown Girl in the Ring* for publication that I am Black. They are very much aware of that particular gap in the field and were happy to be publishing a new Black author.

The thing is, that notion of colonizing alien races has only ever been one theme of science fiction; it's as varied a literature as any other. And even within that topic, many writers have been hugely critical of the assumption that human culture (which for much earlier SF meant white, Western, privileged humans) would be "superior" to other intelligences. It's just that the discourse is only slowly coming from other experiences: the working class, women, writers of color, queer writers, disabled writers. But science fiction has always been a subversive literature. It's been used to critique social systems well before the marketing label of *SF* got stuck on it. And that's when I find SF compelling. When Chip Delany writes about fetishized desire and power games through the eyes of an ex-slave who doesn't talk a whole lot about why he finds sub-dom play arousing, I'm forced to think twice and thrice about a whole bunch of things in relation to each other: sexuality, race, class, color, history. I think that a speculative literature from a culture that has been on the receiving end of the colonization glorified in some SF could be a compelling body of writing. Look at the work of the Jewish speculative fiction writers, like Jane Yolen's novel *Briar Rose*, which uses the elements of the folktale as a lens into the horrors of the Holocaust, and never once allows readers to romanticize the experience. It's brilliant. Or the wickedly incisive and funny work of First Nations writer Sherman Alexie.

Rutledge: How would you characterize what you write, if Black fantasy isn't acceptable?

Hopkinson: English is a very flexible language, but sometimes that flexibility makes meanings muddy. When I say "Black SF writer," the adjective *Black* is modifying the word *writer*, not the word *SF*. I'm a Black writer of SF. It's easy for someone to take the phrase *Black SF writer* to mean that a Black SF writer is someone who writes something called "Black SF." I write speculative fiction. I am Black. I wouldn't say that Jeff Noon writes "white Manchester men's SF," that Ursula Le Guin writes "women's SF" (though I'm sure some would say the latter). It's very important to me to be a voice coming from one flavor of Black experience, and Caribbean, and Canadian, and female, and fat, and from feminist and sex-positive politics. But what I *write* doesn't have those identities; *I* do. My writing won't appeal to everyone, but I don't want to wave a flag over it that says, "This is written only for Black people" (or Caribbean, or Canadian, or female . . . you get my drift).

It isn't. I'd like readers to discover for themselves if my work resonates with them or not. Funnily enough, it is important to me to be identified as a writer of speculative fiction, perhaps because it feels like claiming my share of space in a literature that has largely not represented me. I recently heard from a Black woman my age who said that she stopped writing SF when she was younger because people told her that Black people don't write the stuff. Now she's sticking to her guns and getting back into it.

Rutledge: How do you see your work as reflective of that by "standard" fiction writers who are Black, and how different?

Hopkinson: I don't think my work is reflective of the work of Black writers of mimetic fiction. The body of work being created by Black writers in all genres is precious and valuable. Yet I don't see what I'm trying to do as being in relation to realist writing styles. I'm going to try to paraphrase part of the Mosley article and hope that I capture it accurately. He says that access of Black writers to the mainstream has only really happened in this century, and there is still a barrier there: "excellence" in the work of Black writers is judged by how well we write about "being Black in a white world," which is obviously only one part of our lived experience. "A limitation imposed upon a limitation," he calls it. His words really struck me. They concretized for me some of what I'm trying to do in my writing.

I was born in a part of the world where people of African origin are in the majority. Racism most emphatically exists, but my early experience of being made aware that my dark skin, round ass, and tight-curled hair made me devalued coin did not come from being part of a minority community. And in fact, being middle class, I had more access to privilege than many. Nor was it a simple issue of Black and white, not when there are African, European, Asian, and South Asian people there, all with centuries-long histories of being in the Caribbean—not to mention the aboriginal cultures whose people were there even before Columbus got himself lost and they found him. And all of those races and cultures have undergone and are undergoing a certain amount of mixing. My experience of being "raced" (that's not a word, is it?) is a complex one that has to take into account the cultures and histories of many races, not to mention class and economics. It cannot be a simple binary, and it is nowhere close to being the only issue that frames my writing.

I have an early short story about a young Afro-Caribbean woman living in Canada who exchanges her body for one which is white and slim with straight hair. She diets rigorously, and she hates it when her parents talk in Creole and when other Black women dress in ways that celebrate their bodies and their cultures. I took the story to a writing retreat to be critiqued. Some people said I had to decide what my protagonist's problem was. Was it internalized racism, or female body image problems, or the problems that the child of immigrants faces when she tries to adapt to a new culture? They felt I had to choose one, that my story would lack focus if I didn't. But the themes were all interrelated; it wouldn't have made sense to me artificially to disentangle them. It may be a weaker story as a result of my stubbornness, because I'm still developing the skills to portray all those complexities, but I'd rather keep trying to do that than simplify my writing.

When I read the work of African American realist writers, there's always the awareness of the white world in which the characters live; there *has* to be, if the fiction is to be representative of the real world. The realist work of Caribbean writers must reference the effects of hundreds of years of colonialism. It's there in the work of African writers, too, although my sense is that it's a little less all-pervasive, perhaps because it wasn't possible to reave people on the continent from their pre-slavery histories and cultures to the extent that you could when you removed them from their homelands. The experience of slavery is a huge cancer in the collective consciousness of African people all over the diaspora. The ripple effects of it (if you'll bear with a mixed metaphor for a moment) still continue, and they touch the past, the present, and the future. People recognize that about the effects of the Holocaust on Jewish people, but we don't get the same recognition. We're supposed to have "gotten over it" by now, even though its domino effect still very much straitlaces our lives. Speculative fiction allows me to experiment with the effects of that cancerous blot, to shrink it by setting my worlds far in the future (science fiction) or to metonymize it so that I can explore the paradigms it's created (fantasy). I could even choose to sidestep it altogether into alternate history. Mosley says that SF makes it possible to create visions which will "shout down the realism imprisoning us behind a wall of alienating culture."

I don't want to write mimetic fiction. I like the way that fantastical fiction allows me to use myth, archetype, speculation, and storytelling. I like the way that it allows me to imagine the impossible. Mosley also said something to the effect that human beings first imagine a reality, then figure out a way to make it manifest. When women SF writers first began imagining women in positions of authority, the idea seemed risible to many. Not anymore. I don't see science fiction and fantasy as being just wishful thinking. I like to believe that they can also be more like, I dunno, guided imagery. Societal biofeedback? If Black people can imagine our futures, imagine—among other things—cultures in which we aren't alienated, then we can begin to see our way clear to creating them.

Rutledge: What do you see your writing doing, if anything? That is, do you construct your stories with an agenda in mind other than the craft of telling a good story?

Hopkinson: After all I've said in the previous answer about what I see SF by Black writers doing, I'm now going say something that's apparently contradictory. No, I don't have an agenda when I write, unless you count it as an agenda that I want the story to be a compelling read. Story themes come to me in later drafts, when I've figured out what the story's about. I start with a word, a phrase, or a snapshot image. I try to marry it with another image and see what comes out of the tension between the two. I wordsmith as I go—constructing my language in ways that are pleasing to me, figuring out the "voice" of the story. I write until I have the semblance of a story, then I take it to my writing group, where people ask all the questions that hadn't occurred to me: "Why does she find oranges nauseating on page 17 when she loved them on page 2?" "He's obviously trying to overcome his terror of dogs: How come you didn't write more about that?" I think, *He's afraid of dogs? She hates oranges?* then I realize that they're right, those two facts are the crux of the story, but I didn't see that when I wrote it. So I figure out what happened to make him afraid of dogs and her revolted by oranges, and I finish the story. Or maybe I disagree with my writing group completely, but something that someone says sparks my own thinking, and I figure out the key to the story and write that.

Every time I've set out to write a story with a message in it, it's died on the vine. I have to write about images that fascinate me. It doesn't work if my fiction is really veiled lectures on what I think people would be doing if they knew what was good for them. That's another reason I say I don't write "Black" fiction. Sometimes I write about Black experience, sometimes not. I have a short story that, if I imagined it in any cultural context at all, was set among the English peasantry of a previous century. It's about how difficult coming of age can be for young girls.

Rutledge: Who are your literary role models, past and present?

Hopkinson: How many years do you have? Chip Delany, as is probably obvious by now. I like that his work is transgressive, that it talks frankly about things like sex and queerness and fetish behavior, which are all still so taboo to name in so many Black communities. I also like that he's such an amazing stylist that you can *smell* his worlds; he can construct layered, intricate sentences that please me so to have read. Pretty much the whole

18 CONVERSATIONS WITH NALO HOPKINSON

canon of feminist SF writers—Tiptree, Le Guin, Tepper . . . there are many, and many newer ones springing up. Octavia Butler, who is not realist, but firmly realistic. She refuses to take the pleasant way out in her writing. And she writes every day, which is still difficult for me. Candas Jane Dorsey and Ronald Wright, for first novels that rocked. Kelly Link, whose work is quirky and gorgeous and funny and often vaguely disturbing. Gene Wolfe and James Morrow, who can make me read about organized religion and love it. Elizabeth Lynn, whose characters represent a range of sexual identities and who was one of the first writers I read who explored alternative relationship models and intentional communities. Shani Mootoo, another rocking first novel. I like its masked, magical Trinidad and the way it explores gender roles. Ray Bradbury, who writes with such breathless enthusiasm and from an obvious appreciation of beauty. Kim Stanley Robinson's *Pacific Edge*, for an appealing utopia with warts, and for writing that is exquisite in style. Every so often I pick it up and reread a passage or two, for its word craft, world building, and characterization. Keri Hulme for *The Bone People*. Shakespeare, Charles Johnson, for his magic realist novel *Middle Passage*. This is a game I could play all day.

Rutledge: Ti-Jeanne embodies many of the concerns of contemporary society faced by Black women in the Americas (e.g., unwed motherhood, poverty, conflicts between self and tradition). Is this character, as Edana Franklin from *Kindred* seems to be Butler, very much like yourself?

Hopkinson: Have you asked Butler? I wonder if she feels as I do. This is becoming one of my least favorite questions, to be asked if my characters are thinly veiled autobiographies. No, I make them up. My life has been very different from Ti-Jeanne's. My family was often short of money, sometimes acutely so, but I never had the experience of living in extreme poverty. We were middle class; it was a given that I'd finish school and go on to university somehow. Between my parents and me, we worked and paid the cost of my education. I have never lived in what is in effect a ghettoized war zone. I never had children, never been pregnant, was never a medical professional. I hope that my portrayal of Ti-Jeanne rings true, but only some of her experience is anything like mine. I know what it's like to be a green girl, to feel somewhat aimless in life. I know what it's like to be overrun by events. I've also had boyfriends who were really bad for me. I know what it's like to be scared and unsure of myself.

As I do more talks and interviews, I'm getting very curious about why people always ask me if the characters are people I know. The one person who put the question differently wanted to know if a particular short story was a recounting of a dream I'd had, which is another way of saying, "Did you experience this?" (And no, I didn't; I made it up.) Someday I'd like to turn the question back on the audience. It's as though people believe that fiction doesn't exist, that it's all real people's experiences with the serial numbers filed off, a kind of mask. But it's more like a quilt; there are bits and scraps of real people in there, but they are recombined to suit the story, and there's at least as much whole cloth there, in the backing and the stuffing and the binding. Maybe people have gotten distrustful of fiction. So many people still parrot that fiction is at best worthless, at worst evil, because it's *lies*. So perhaps if a fiction resonates with some people, they decide that it can't be deception—as if it ever were—that it must be truth? And truth means it must have really happened to someone the author knows?

Rutledge: What nonliterary influences are most prominent in your creative efforts?

Hopkinson: By *nonliterary*, you mean everything that isn't writing? Food. I love writing about it, describing it, particularly the foods with which I grew up. Caribbean history. I'm doing more and more research into folkways that operated in the previous century and the beginning of this one. Language, which I talk about more later. Folktales. I love the way they portray archetypes as stories that can resonate on many levels.

Rutledge: How long have you known you wanted to be a writer? Do you have expertise in any other field? Did you publish anything before your novel?

Hopkinson: I wanted to be a writer at a very early age. My father was a writer and so were many of his friends, and I loved reading. But I didn't believe I had any talent for creating fiction, and it was the only form of writing that drew me strongly to want to attempt it. I won an essay-writing competition at age ten or so (there's a picture on my web page of a young me in my school uniform, accepting the plaque). I wrote a few nonfiction articles for local papers. But it wasn't until 1992 that I took the plunge and started taking fiction-writing courses and sending my short stories out to magazines. As to expertise in other fields, I facilitate a mean arts grant jury, and I probably still have the skills, though not the wind, to teach a funk aerobics class. I learned to sew because very little ready-made clothing fits me well, and I type between seventy and eighty words a minute.

I've published short stories in journals and anthologies, and I've had short stories produced for radio broadcast. In the science fiction field, it's rare to publish a novel before you've published a number of individual short stories in magazines or anthologies. Once you've built up a portfolio of

20 CONVERSATIONS WITH NALO HOPKINSON

short-story publications and have a novel manuscript to shop around, it's easier (but by no means easy!) to get the attention of an agent or publisher.

Rutledge: Do you write any book reviews or do any kind of literary criticism?

Hopkinson: I have published a few nonfiction articles, mostly brief book reviews and one opinion piece, but nothing from an academic point of view. I write reviews mostly of speculative fiction, mostly for popular magazines. They are short and usually don't go much beyond a summary and a sentence or two of critique. I hope to be able to do more critical writing about the field at a later date, though the more I discover how difficult it is to write fiction, the less I'm willing to lambaste anyone's efforts. I do enjoy reading literary criticism when I can wade through the unfamiliar vocabulary. Sometimes it gives me a glimpse of some of the greater issues to do with writing, and that's inspirational and helpful.

Rutledge: What's your educational background, both formal and informal?

Hopkinson: Elementary school in the Caribbean. Took my "O" Level exams, but not my "A" Level (Ordinary and Advanced Levels—British system). Four high schools in four different countries: Trinidad, Jamaica, Guyana, and Canada. Was good at biology, literature, and languages; indifferent at geography, history, civics, and art; horrible at math, physics, and chemistry. Now I have to study it all in order to write what I do, and it's much more fun this way. Studied Russian and French in university, graduated with a combined honors. I went to college for a diploma in recreation management. (In Canada, colleges are very specifically for vocational training; they are not degree-granting institutions. Those are all called universities.) Tried the sciences again at the university level. Was good at biology but horrible at math, without which I couldn't take physics or chemistry. Whew. I dropped out and abandoned plans to become a chiropractor. Took a few silversmithing courses, plan to take more. In 1995, I attended the Clarion Science Fiction and Fantasy Writers' Workshop, a graduate course through Michigan State University (Octavia Butler is a Clarion graduate, and Samuel Delany was one of the writers-in-residence the year I attended). I guess you don't want to know about the aerobics instructor training courses.

Informally, my father was a poet, actor, and playwright who taught English and Latin at the 6th Form level (senior year of high school). My mother is a library cataloguer. Books were everywhere, and I had pretty much free rein of them. My parents took me to theater, dance, readings, visual arts exhibitions. And I worked for nine years in a large public library system, with access to everything it had to offer. I am a voracious reader. I also worked for six years as a grants officer for a local arts council. That was a great education. I got to see what projects other artists were undertaking and what issues were important to them, and to hear how they described their artistic vision and creative processes, and hear how other people assessed their proposals. Then I got to see the finished work. It's made it much easier for me to conceptualize and communicate what I'm trying to accomplish—and to read rejection letters. I have a sense of what goes into the decision-making process, and I don't take "no" so personally.

Rutledge: Why did you move from the Caribbean to Canada?

Hopkinson: Daddy had chronic kidney failure, and there was no treatment available in Guyana, where we were living at the time. Canada had excellent treatment, and with that and his own determination, he was able to extend his three-year life expectancy to nineteen years. But we had always moved around. I was born in Jamaica. My family left there when I was eight months old for Trinidad; left there when I was, I think, five years old for the US (Daddy had been accepted into the graduate theater program at Yale University and subsequently dropped out); went back to Jamaica, then to Guyana, then Trinidad, Jamaica, Guyana again, to Canada when I was sixteen. I've been here twenty-two years now.

Rutledge: How has the publication of *Brown Girl in the Ring* and its success as the winner of the Warner Aspect First Novel Contest changed your life?

Hopkinson: It's meant that, for now at least, I'm working full-time at my writing, not at a nine-to-five job. It's a precious thing (I was going to say "luxury," but I live month to month). I've had some longtime dreams fulfilled. I've seen my name in print, for one. I've learned that, yes, I can write something as huge as a novel. I met Chip (which first happened before I started writing fiction, when he came to Toronto to give a reading from *The Madman* and I got to interview him for a local paper). My mother now has some notion that at least some of my weirdness is in service of a pursuit of which she approves. My father never saw my fiction in print. He died in 1993.

Rutledge: Where do you see problems with your first novel in terms of structure, artistry, characterization, and things that go into making a novel successful?

Hopkinson: If I were to do it again, I'd do more in-depth characterization of some of the secondary characters, particularly Rudy, but also the Premier and her assistant. I think the structure works well. I'd probably be less melodramatic. People have correctly pointed out that the dystopian near-future setting is nothing new. That was deliberate on my part. It was my first novel, and I was wrestling with a host of skills that were new to me and elements that would be plenty new to readers. I had my hands full. It was pretty astonishing just to get to the point of typing the final sentence. The rest has been a bonus.

Rutledge: What goals do you have as a novelist?

Hopkinson: To finish novel #2 by the publisher's March 1 deadline! Creatively, I'd like my work to get more layered, more subtle. I want to work on characterization. I want to learn how to handle more complex ideas.

My second novel is now at the final draft stage. I have ideas for two more and a very dim notion for another after that. As I accomplish those, I'll get ideas for others. I'll continue writing short stories. It's a form I really like, because every word has to count, and you can explore one idea nicely in a short story.

I want to bring a new voice to the field, and perhaps some new readers. The speculative-fiction community is alarmed by the fact that the readership is aging. We hear that younger readers aren't coming to the field in the same numbers. If that's so, part of it might be because the corporate film that bowdlerizes SF tropes has become so popular. *Star Wars* and the like don't have much to do with why many of us read the genre, but they're fun to watch and a lot of people would rather do that than try to figure out words on a page; we're taught in school to hate reading. Part of the reduced readership may be because of the way speculative fiction is marketed. There is genre writing (SF, mystery, romance, etc.) and then there is "literature." Under the genre labels, there are thousands of books churned out every year that are fairly formulaic brain candy. I don't see too much wrong with that—sometimes comfort reading is just what you want, and I think it can serve to disseminate and diffuse issues that were previously radical. And to be realistic, publishers have to sell books to survive. But I think that genre labeling has led to people who are unfamiliar with the genre assuming that SF on a book spine automatically means a lightweight read. I'm flabbergasted when people tell me that *Animal Farm* and *A Handmaid's Tale* aren't speculative fiction, that they're "real literature." And really, much non-genre fiction that is published each year is also entertaining brain candy; that's not the sole province of genre fiction. But work with genre labels on it gives the snobs something to point at when they say, "I don't read *that* stuff; I only read 'literature.'" I think people forget that realism is as much a convention as any of the genre tropes. I recently read an article by a local author in which he chided a local science fiction writer for calling his characters "guys." He said they weren't guys, they were talking lizards. Well, a guy in a realist fiction isn't a "guy" either. It's a fabulation into which the author has crafted the illusion that you're perceiving a human. One doesn't deem a Picasso worthless because it doesn't look like a landscape. Why, then, the conceit that only realist fiction can be good fiction?

I think some of the way to solve the shrinking market may be to entice in whole new communities of readers. I'm hoping to be a writer who can do some of that. When my novel was launched, people who wanted to support me bought it and read it even if they normally didn't read anything they thought of as science fiction. Some of them have told me they were pleasantly surprised, that they didn't realize science fiction could be like that. I hope that at the very least it got a new bunch of people into our local SF, Black, and women's bookstores. If so, I'll be happy if any of those people return to those bookstores in search of other writers. When I give readings at African History Month events and literary events, I'm being introduced as a science fiction writer. I don't look like many people's conception of an SF writer, and since my work is coming from an experience that many have never thought of in terms of science fiction and fantasy, it's making people curious. People are taking copies of the book to friends in the Caribbean, because it has no distribution there yet. I'm getting favorable reactions back. Educators are beginning to include it in their courses, graduate students in their theses. Because the protagonist is a very young woman, the book is also reaching a youth audience. I gave a reading a year ago to an auditorium of high school kids, and their questions were illuminating: "You live in Toronto? *This* Toronto, right here?" They were only familiar with contemporary urban expression from the US. Afterwards a few of the Caribbean kids came up to me to tell me how much they'd enjoyed seeing me on the stage and hearing their urban Canadian environment described in a Caribbean Creole. And they liked hearing the folktale elements. It gave them a sense of ownership and pride. I think that's how the readership in a genre starts to expand.

Rutledge: What kinds of hobbies do you have? Are you, for example, a Trekker?

Hopkinson: Can watching TV be a hobby? I think of hobbies as more doing/making things than passive spectatorship. I watched *Star Trek* through childhood, up until a few years ago. I started to lose interest somewhere in the middle of *DS9*, and *Voyager* never really grabbed me, which is fine, because my television broke in 1996 and I've not replaced it. The one I had was a donation of someone's old clunker. I haven't been able to bring myself to fork out hundreds of dollars that could be feeding me on an object that sucks my energy and free time but gives very little satisfaction in return. I saw the last Trek movie—sort of a nostalgia thing—but will probably not see the one that's just been released, though I kind of liked Jonathan Frakes's

24 CONVERSATIONS WITH NALO HOPKINSON

work as a director in the last one. I'm a bit addicted to email, but that's not a hobby either. I like to sew, but haven't had much time for it with the writing. I still love reading, and I buy a few new books every week when I can afford it. But reading's also more of a pastime than a hobby. I recently resurrected an ambition to be a dancer when a friend who's a choreographer created a solo dance work for me. We just finished a four-day run, and he's talking of staging it in 1999. I like dancing for fun too, though I have to be in the right mood for the club atmosphere. I loved the silversmithing courses I took; I will eventually learn more silver- and iron-smithing. I've taken up city bicycle riding; it's good for generating high levels of adrenalin as you duck cars that are trying to mow you down. I have dreams of getting back to pumping iron, but I'm not good at sticking to the regime.

Rutledge: Do you have any other creative projects in the works?

Hopkinson: CBC Radio recently made a recording of me performing one of my short stories to an original musical composition by William Sperandei, a local jazz trumpeter. It was so much fun! I'd like to do more of that, perhaps release a spoken-word recording with music. I'll think about it more once I have this second novel to the publisher. And I'm working on a collection's worth of short stories. I have a notion of working with my partner, who's also an artist, to create a children's picture book.

Rutledge: Derek Walcott obviously means much to you as an author. Have you met him personally? What is it about his stories that led you to adopt one of his characters for your own?

Hopkinson: I didn't adopt any of his characters. I did refer to three of them by giving three of my characters feminized versions of their names. Daddy worked with Derek at the Trinidad Theater Workshop that Derek founded. Daddy was one of the actors, and eventually was part of a pretty spectacular disagreement with Derek and a subsequent splintering off of people from the TTW. I was a child at the time. Before the break between the two men, my mother would drop me at Derek's house in the mornings, and his then wife, Margaret, would drive me and her daughter Anna to our schools (I think my parents had to be at work earlier than school opened). I saw Derek's plays rehearsed and performed. I don't remember if I ever saw *Ti-Jean and His Brothers*, but I've certainly read it. I did see *Dream on Monkey Mountain*. My father had a role in one production of it. I saw a production of *Joker of Seville*, with Albert Laveau in the lead.

The name Ti-Jean is the French equivalent of "Everyman." Early on in the writing of *Brown Girl in the Ring*, I realized it was a novel about three generations of women battling an evil in their lives, and I thought of the parallel with *Ti-Jean and His Brothers*, an early play of Derek's in which three brothers battle the devil. I wanted to acknowledge that connection to Derek's work, so I named the three women Ti-Jeanne, Mi-Jeanne, and Gros-Jeanne—the feminine equivalents of the brothers Ti-Jean, Mi-Jean, and Gros-Jean. I liked the idea of Ti-Jeanne as everywoman. I had to call Derek to ask his permission to quote from the play, and my heart was in my mouth, because I had childhood memories of him and my father shouting in fury at each other. But he was very gracious. I know too that, when Daddy died, Derek gave a eulogy at the University of the West Indies, which was a very respectful tribute to Daddy's contribution to Caribbean literature. I like the magic that operates in many of Derek's plays, the lushness and the exquisite wordcraft of them, and the fact that he uses Creole and music.

Rutledge: You include two passages in your novel that are not in English, French, Spanish, Creole, English, Pidgin, or Krio. What language is this, and what are the meanings of these passages?

Hopkinson: What's Krio? A type of Creole? The woman who speaks the passages to which you refer is Romni Jenny. She's Rom (some would say gypsy, but I gather that can be a term of contempt). The phrases mean something like, "Oh God, what an awful thing to happen," and a curse: "May cancer eat his throat!" I got them from the autobiography of a Rom man from Quebec. Last I heard, Toronto was one of the most culturally diverse cities in the world. I tried to reflect some of what that's like to experience. Did you think that I used the Rom words because I speak Rom? It was all part of the research I had to do to write the novel, like the research on heart transplant operations, and details of the Toronto landmarks which I describe.

Rutledge: The ability to speak a native tongue and English reflects Du Bois's double-consciousness. Are there other elements of your novel in which a character is split between European and non-European culture?

Hopkinson: Other elements than Romni Jenny, you mean? I guess the Russian couple that you meet in the beginning, Paula and Pavel, and the priest in the church in that scene. He's got at least a three-way split going, being a Euro francophone Catholic Quebecois living in anglophone Toronto, where I'm told that long ago it wasn't unusual for businesses to post "Help Wanted" signs which read, "Catholics Need Not Apply." But you don't see enough of the priest to know all that; it's in my head. A Canadian would probably pick up on some of it from the brief description of him.

All the Caribbean characters inhabit hybridized worlds. In the Caribbean, class divisions are clearly marked in language; an attuned ear can hear the points of demarcation. Caribbean people who emigrate (or who operate

26 CONVERSATIONS WITH NALO HOPKINSON

within more than one class level) learn to code-switch, to jump back and forth between various language usages as needed. Mami Gros-Jeanne does it when she deals with the street kids. She switches to a more Canadian English. Children of immigrants do a peculiar-sounding (to my ears, though I do it myself nowadays) thing where their accent and word choices sound neither completely of the old country nor completely of the new. That's how Tony speaks, and it was a bitch to write. For people from diasporic cultures there's more than a doubled consciousness. It's occupying multiple overlapping identities simultaneously. Throw in identities formed around politics, gender, class, sexual preference, etc., and you have quite the stew. There is no solid ground beneath us; we shift constantly to stay in one place.

Because Toronto is so culturally diverse, I see that multiple consciousness reflected in the work of many local artists who are my peers, whatever their media. We are the people who have more than one place or identity or culture that's home, and we're struggling to find modes of expression that convey how we've had to become polyglot, not only in multiple lexicons but also in multiple identities. The classical forms of artistic expression give us a base from which to work, but from there we have to break the codified forms and create new voices for ourselves. When I can make a pun that resonates multilingually across any number of four languages and three Creoles, who's going to understand it? When a character in one of my stories is bubbling (a Jamaican dance style) to a reggae song one minute and babbling about cockatrices the next, what is the reader to make of her? When I say I'm "predominantly" Black, does it convey any of the callaloo that is the Caribbean, that gives me a clan tartan, one Jewish great grandmother, and one Maroon, as well as Aboriginal, West African, and South Asian ancestry? Or do you think you hear someone who's trying to distance herself from her African origins?

For me, language is a particularly thorny matter. I've talked about code-switching between and among dialects and sociolects, and the increased complexity that happens when you throw in two or more languages. If I'm talking to another Jamaican, I'll probably use a fairly standard, though accented, English; that's base norm for a middle-class Jamaican. If I've been trying to tell my friend something that she's not been grasping and she finally gets it, I might switch into the vernacular to counter with, "Chuh man, after is that me a-tell you!" Using a Creole that we share is an ironic way of saying, without having to speak the actual words, "So we've finally found a base of understanding." It's a pretty complex set of codes. A lot of Caribbean identity is bound up in language. We have used it as a tool of resistance and politicization (Rastafarian "dread talk" being a clear example). We have hybridized the different languages that were in operation in the Caribbean into Creoles. Each Caribbean country has its own; a Creole speaker from (for instance) Jamaica will not necessarily understand one from Barbados. And each Creole has its sociolects that signal a speaker's class, level of education, sometimes even caste and race. On top of all that, we've gone through years of our educators trying to shame this textured, complex, rich "bad language" out of us and make us speak only "the Queen's English," whatever that means to anyone who isn't actually the Queen of England. The vernaculars were seen as debased, and in many places are still so seen. But when as a wordsmith I have the choice between saying "just before dawn" and "fore-day morning," which do you think will seem more evocative to me?

Some artists in the Caribbean have deliberately reclaimed their vernaculars by creating work in them. The first time that Miss Lou (Jamaican poet Louise Bennett) performed a poem written in Jamaican Creole, someone in the audience shouted out, "Is that you mother send you a-school for?"—criticizing her vernacular in the vernacular. It's important to me to try to reflect the place that language has in Caribbean identity. In *Brown Girl in the Ring*, I made the Caribbean characters mostly Trinidadian and some Jamaican, and I wrote their dialogue in the way they would speak it. Narrative I wrote in standard English. I've gotten a mixed reaction from readers. Some take to it pretty easily; some find it tough going for a few pages until they get the hang of the sentence construction; and some seem almost offended that I didn't write the dialogue in standard English. They see it as a naïve artistic choice. It may be, but to me it would be disjunctive and weird to make a working-class Jamaican man speak like a middle-class North American one. But I do understand why those readers are so disconcerted; it's something I'm struggling with too.

I think that quite a few things are going on here. One is that Creoles are oral forms. There is no standard spelling and it's difficult to capture them on the page. I wouldn't expect even a Caribbean reader to find the reading smooth going at first. (Though if they are from the country whose speech I'm representing, they have a bit of an advantage, particularly if they read the dialogue out loud.) I do use conventional spellings where possible—*you* instead of *yuh*, for instance. I'm trying to represent the vocabulary and sentence structure, not the accent. Another is that there's still an uneasiness around vernacular speech, especially Black vernacular speech. In this part of the world it can be seen as disrespectful to represent it. Memories of

Uncle Tom's Cabin and the Step'n Fetchit films make people uncomfortable. Some readers feel that I'm creating caricatures of Black people, that I'm representing us as uneducated and ignorant. People who read my use of Creole this way are dismayed at what they read as internalized racism on my part, when, in fact, I'm representing a different but no less complex version of English. I'm getting better at conveying the Creoles I use as the linguistic constructs they are, with their own rules for sentence structure and grammar. They aren't just accents or ignorance.

A third thing that's going on is that some people make the judgment that I've violated one of the conventions of "excellence," which is that "good" writing is with a few exceptions written in "clear" English. But it's not an inviolable literary convention in any artistic tradition; it's perfectly usual, for instance, for an excellent Caribbean artist to use Creoles to whatever effect he/she sees fit. *Excellence* means different things in different contexts. I'm asking readers to do something difficult, to take on something unfamiliar, mastery of which lies at the heart of their ability to comprehend the dialogue. I have to expect that some may bristle. I'm going to keep working at it, devise other methods for making it easier to read. Chip told me that a little dialect goes a long way; using a word or two suggests the vernacular without having to represent huge chunks of it. I think he's correct. The first draft of my second novel *Midnight Robber* was written completely in a hybrid Trinidadian/Jamaican Creole of my own invention, but I've since changed the language construction so that it's more like the first novel (standard English narrative but Creole in the dialogue). But how then do I represent the mindset of a people that is so tied up with the words they use *and how they use them*, if I don't represent those words themselves? I don't yet have a satisfying strategy. Amos Tutuola's magic realist stories in Yoruba English were well-received, so maybe there's a way. When I read the Trinidadian Creole of the opening passages of Dionne Brand's novel *In Another Place, Not Here*, I know I'm in the presence of a master poet. I have found that, if people who are unfamiliar with the dialect can hear me read a section of my work, reading it for themselves comes easier to them. Warner tells me that they plan to post a soundbite of me reading *Midnight Robber* on their website. I think that will help.

Another writer once said to me that since the ability to code-switch is practically a given in postcolonial diasporic cultures, it makes sense that writers from those cultures will use it in their writings. I agree with her. Creoles carry their own nuances and textures of meaning. They are a tool for communication that we have. Writing without them can feel like cooking a meal without the spices. It's still edible, even nutritious, but the cook knows how much more interesting it could be with a little piece of thyme and some garlic. This may sound as though I'm putting down unadorned English, but I don't believe there is any such thing, except perhaps in memos, and rarely even there. Every nook of every region of the English-speaking world tailors English to suit itself. That's one of the strengths of the language—its flexibility. How do I communicate to a diverse bunch of readers if I'm using Creoles? I'm still ironing that out, still asking for feedback.

Interview: Nalo Hopkinson

Mary Anne Mohanraj / 2000

From *Strange Horizons*, September 1, 2000, http://strangehorizons.com/non-fiction /articles/interview-nalo-hopkinson/. Reprinted by permission of Mary Anne Mohanraj.

Mary Anne Mohanraj: Nalo, how did you begin writing? Did you intend to become an author, or did you have a specific reason or reasons for writing each book?

Nalo Hopkinson: Each book, story, essay comes out of notions or images with which I want to play. My father was a writer, and I was always an avid reader who barely dared dream of becoming a writer. In 1993, I started taking writing workshops and became part of a writers' circle. I began to get short stories published. Then, in 1995, I attended the Clarion Science Fiction and Fantasy Writers' Workshop. My first professional short story sale was "Riding the Red" (in *Black Swan, White Raven*, eds. Ellen Datlow and Terri Windling); that was a story written while at Clarion. After Clarion, I set about trying to complete a novel, and the business of writing has progressed from there. It's been great to discover that I can link words and images together to form a story. For years I didn't think I had anything to say.

MM: I was a Clarionite too, and it had a tremendous effect on my writing; was the experience generally positive for you? Would you recommend it to aspiring writers?

NH: Clarion was equal parts difficult and exhilarating. If I had been a person with less life experience, someone who had never had my work critiqued by others, or had felt misunderstood by or isolated from the group in huge ways, the difficult would probably have outweighed the exhilarating. But for me, it was a great thing to do. At Clarion you get to spend six blessed weeks in an environment that's there to do one thing: support you in your efforts to write and to learn to understand writing better. Some of the friendships I formed there feel like they'll be around a very long time. I met some of my heroes there too, and had the benefit of some amazing instruction from them. I would definitely recommend it to aspiring writers, but would also tell them to consider long and hard that they will be spending an extended amount of time getting their egos bruised in the company of seventeen to nineteen people they didn't choose, and with most of whom they likely won't be compatible.

Clarion is also not a ticket to getting published. Only a portion of the people who attend Clarion go on to become published writers, and for many of them, it still takes years. What I found that Clarion did for me was to teach me some of the things I needed to know about the craft and the field in a hyper-accelerated time span. I could have picked much of it up on my own, but it would have taken years instead of weeks. The speed and the intensity of it seem to have bruised my brain, though. By the end of the six weeks of sleep deprivation and high-speed learning, I was exhausted. I had a day or two where I was prone to mini-hallucinations (lightning bolts out of nowhere, tiny mumbling heads in my computer screen). Too, it was about a year before I regained enough focus to be able to read a novel through. I went into Clarion a near-perfect speller, but now I make idiosyncratic mistakes all the time. Worth it? For me, absolutely.

MM: Let's talk a little about your background. I believe your ethnic heritage is Afro-Caribbean, but you currently live in Canada (*Brown Girl in the Ring* is set in a future Toronto). How has your sense of place affected your writing?

NH: I'm predominantly of African ancestry, with chunks of Scottish, Jewish, English, Arawak, and continental Indian in the mix. I was born in Jamaica, lived in Jamaica, Trinidad, Guyana, and the US, then moved to Canada in 1977 when I was sixteen. I've been here ever since. So really I was raised mostly in the Caribbean; I was practically an adult when I came to Canada. I guess I have a sense of many places, not of one. It's given me a sense that all places are unique, so when I write, I try to convey a strong sense of the location in which my story is set.

MM: I think you succeed—the worlds of Toussaint and New Half Way Tree are certainly unique and memorable. Both *Brown Girl in the Ring* and *Midnight Robber* draw heavily on Afro-Caribbean cultural traditions. Can you tell us a little about how that material worked into the novels? Did you start with the culture and derive a story from it? Vice versa? Some other method?

NH: No method, just madness. I think I tend to start with an idea for the main character and a bit of what she's like or what her problems are. The culture and folklore (and I also draw on the traditional Euro-Celtic folktales I was taught as a child—I'm not sure that's the correct way to identify them) become ways of illuminating the story, or referring to and playing with archetypes.

MM: I grew up with those Euro-Celtic tales too, as I imagine many of us have. The fantasy genre especially leans in that direction, which is why it's so refreshing seeing material from other cultures in the mix. But I have to wonder, given that science fiction does not have a long tradition of Afro-Caribbean writers—or even of Black writers, for that matter, aside from a few stellar exceptions—was that a concern, when you started writing science fiction? What drew you to the field?

NH: I was drawn to the field because I've always read in it. As simple as that. Editor Sheree R. Thomas has just put out *Dark Matter*, an anthology of 100 years of speculative fiction by Black writers. The stories in it date back to 1887. There are many writers of color—not just Black writers—who've published works of fantastical fiction, just few who are acknowledged as part of the genre. I would like to see those works enter the dialogue in the science fiction community, but I didn't worry too much about it when I started to write. I figured I'd write what moved me, then see if anyone was willing to publish it. That's been a successful strategy.

I do find myself longing for critical response from more people who share some of my cultural identities as well as a love and knowledge of science fiction and fantasy. That's been slow in coming. I was thrilled when Leo Dillon, coillustrator with his wife Diane of the cover of *Midnight Robber*, sent me a message to tell me that he's Trinidadian. I hadn't known that. It meant that when the Dillons read my novel before creating the cover art, Leo Dillon knew the culture from which I was extrapolating. I love that.

MM: So we know whom you'd like to have reading your work—what authors do you like to read? What book or books have had a strong influence on you or your writing?

NH: I will always have a deep awe and respect for the writing of Samuel R. Delany (and for the man too, come to think of it). Reviewers tend to read my work in relation to Octavia E. Butler's wonderful writing, but it's Delany who's had the first, strongest influence on me. I like that his work is transgressive, that it talks frankly about things such as sex and queerness and fetish behavior, and that he makes his readers look at taboos. I also like that he's such an amazing stylist, and that he insists on complexity of thought when you approach his work.

MM: Yes, a work like *Dhalgren* certainly pushes style to interact with his themes. Some readers find that too challenging—or perhaps even intrusive;

for them, it gets in the way of the story. You've clearly worked with style as well; how do you think that affects your writing? Do style and content blend seamlessly together? Do they play off each other? Does style ever interfere with story?

NH: The style/content dichotomy seems to cause at least as many arguments in SF&F as the science fiction/fantasy dichotomy. The extreme poles seem to be 1) those who believe that a story is just a story, the point of which is to entertain interesting ideas without getting emotionally engaged, and 2) those who recognize that the stories we tell ourselves are *about* ourselves, and have resonance in the real world that may be utterly, vitally important to readers.

I guess you can tell from the way I described both poles which one I tend to lean towards. No neutrality there. But even while I'm passionate about content, even while the fiction that engages me is the fiction that dares to be about something, I love inventive, masterful style. Combine the two, and you've got me. I think content and style are inseparable; different facets of the same jewel. Can they blend seamlessly? They can. They don't have to. Sometimes the getting there—the style—is half the fun, and as a reader one needs to go with it, enjoy it, and be less plot-driven than would be necessary with a differently told type of story. That will drive some readers crazy. Luckily, there are all kinds of writers.

MM: To return to other writers you enjoy. . . .

NH: I'm enjoying working my way through Ishmael Reed's novel *Mumbo Jumbo*. The depth and the breadth with which he references diasporic African history and culture jazzes me entirely, as does his sense of humor. That's one novel where the style *is* a huge part of the content. Jeanette Winterson's *GUT Symmetries* is another novel that blew me away, as did *Black Wine* by Candas Jane Dorsey, and *Cereus Blooms at Night* by Shani Mootoo, and *The Pagoda* by Patricia Powell. I recently enjoyed marina ama omowale maxwell's novel *Chopstix in Mauby*, which, like my first novel, also uses Afro-Caribbean spirituality as the belief system underpinning the story.

I appreciate the way in which Octavia Butler faces down harsh realities. In her "Xenogenesis" series, human reproductive behavior and sexuality has to change in order for us to survive. That's a tall order and Butler deals with it unflinchingly. Storm Constantine's novels have been favorites, as have Tanith Lee's. The "fairy tale" anthologies and novels (anthologies edited by Terri Windling and Ellen Datlow, novels by Terri Windling); Jane Yolen's work.

Pretty much the whole canon of feminist SF writers: people such as Ursula Le Guin, Maureen McHugh, Elisabeth Vonarburg, Suzy McKee Charnas,

34 CONVERSATIONS WITH NALO HOPKINSON

Jennifer Stevenson, Ellen Klages, L. Timmel Duchamp, Pat Murphy, Pamela Sargeant, Elisabeth Lynn, Kate Wilhelm, Kelly Link, Alice Sheldon, Joanna Russ, Karen Joy Fowler . . . the list is long and growing. I've only mentioned a very few of them.

MM: Since you mention feminist writers, can you talk a little about women in your writing, and in science fiction? What do you think of the way they've been represented? Are they generally portrayed accurately? Misrepresented? Underrepresented?

NH: Because of the work that many people did before me to bring women's voices to the field, I'm able to inhabit a science fiction community of my choice, where women are well represented in the writing, amongst the writers and in the discourse. But it's still perfectly possible to be an SF aficionado and never encounter that side of the genre. It's still perfectly possible to be told that women don't write good SF, that we're better at fantasy. Which is a crock. One thing I learned from working for years as a grants officer for an arts council is that if you have one set of traditional markers for assessing excellence in a particular art form, you will likely not recognize excellence from a tradition that uses another set of markers. Writing by women speaks to a different—though overlapping—set of realities than writing by men. Fully appreciating it takes learning to understand those realities.

MM: That's interesting; I'm not sure I've thought of it that way before. Before we go on, are there any other authors you'd like to mention?

NH: Certain of Kim Stanley Robinson's works, and William Gibson's and Ian MacDonald's. Pretty much anything by Gene Wolfe. *The Man Who Fell in Love With the Moon* by Tom Spanbauer. *Green Grass, Running Water* by Thomas King. *The Bone People* by Keri Hulme. In nonfiction, some of the works that are important to me are Robert Farris Thompson's *Flash of the Spirit: African and Afro-American Art & Philosophy*; writing on sexuality and society by Carol Queen, Susie Bright, Dossie Easton, Catherine A. Liszt. Caribbean folktales and myths collected by Philip Sherlock and Clinton V. Black.

MM: A long list of wonderful writers—thank you! What about the new work that is emerging? What challenges do you see facing speculative fiction writers today? What areas most concern you?

NH: The genre reinvents itself constantly, so I'm hopeful it'll keep finding its own challenges to take on. The biggest challenge right now is a professional one: the extreme state of flux of the publishing industry, which has been concentrating the sources of production, marketing, and distribution into fewer and fewer (and bigger and bigger) companies, and which has turned the individual creator into a "content provider" whose literary career can be scuttled the first time her or his sales dip. High numbers are what the publishing industry wants; solid writers with a small, loyal following have a hard time making a go of it. Individual editors still seem to care passionately about the work of writers they discover, but they're usually fairly small players in a huge industry. And now that technology is making electronic production and distribution easy and cheap enough that it begins to be able to bypass the publishing corporations, everything is up in the air. The way that the industry functions is going to change rapidly over the next few years.

The other challenge I see is that of the diversity of expression in speculative fiction. The readers seem to come from all over the place, but the writing that gets published (or that gets marketed as SF) still comes from a fairly narrow range of experience. The imaginative worlds that we're creating still draw heavily on Greek and Roman mythology and on Euro-Celtic folktales, and the futures we imagine still feel pretty Western middle class. And that's fair enough, because it's the primary cultural context in which many of the writers are situated. Some excellent writing has come and is coming out of those experiences. However, I also want to see more writing from the vast range of cultural contexts which makes up the world.

It's one of the reasons I love Jane Yolen's work, such as her short story "Granny Rumple" and her novel *Briar Rose*; she takes those Euro-Celtic folktales and interprets them through Jewish experience and history, and all of a sudden I have another understanding of tales that are already multifaceted and rich. It's masterful. I've had budding writers tell me that they love SF/F, but never felt they could write it because they don't feel a cultural affinity for pixies and unicorns. Or that they fear they won't find an understanding of the paradigms out of which they want to write, because they (the paradigms) don't come from the dominant culture. I think we need to expand our notion of what SF/F is.

MM: Nalo, to go back for a minute to the publishing problem, can you talk a little about what challenges you've faced trying to make a living as a writer?

NH: I'm still learning to handle the vagaries of a freelance income. My biggest problem is probably cash flow. It feels as though one is forever waiting for a check, and in the meantime, bills are piling up. It really burns me when people assume that the success of one novel means that I'm now financially solvent. The horns of the dilemma are that either one takes a job with a steady paycheck that leaves one no time or creative energy for writing, or one tries to retain creative energy under the constant stress of money worries. I'm trying to steer a workable course between the two. And I must add, really enjoying those stretches when I have the freedom to write. Lots of incentive to keep trying to find ways to make a go of it.

MM: Finally, what advice would you give the aspiring young writer? What are the important things they should keep in the forefront of their mind?

NH: I'd say learn to do the heart-rending thing of turning a critical eye upon your developing work. When you have managed to get a chunk of words on paper, those are clay, not art. You then have to sculpt them into a final draft. Be prepared to alter, delete, and rewrite until it's as good as you can make it at that point in your artistic development. Then do the scary thing of showing your work to the world; workshop your writing, submit your stories to editors.

MM: Painful, but necessary, I agree. Nalo, thank you so much for your time and thoughtful responses. It's been a pleasure having you with us, and I look forward eagerly both to the Caribbean fabulist anthology, and your own next novel!

NH: Thank you very much, Mary Anne.

An Interview with Nalo Hopkinson

Christian Wolff / 2001

From Christian Wolff, "An Interview with Nalo Hopkinson," *MaComère: Journal of the Association of Caribbean Women Writers and Scholars* 4 (2001): 26–36. Reprinted by permission.

Christian Wolff: What made you want to be a writer, and what was the particular appeal of the science fiction genre for you? Have you always worked in this field?

Nalo Hopkinson: I'm a writer in the fantastical genres of science fiction and fantasy, and I will always be, so long as I'm writing fiction. As to why I wanted to become a writer, it's the artistic tradition I was surrounded with growing up. My father was a poet, playwright, and English teacher. My mother worked in libraries. Science fiction and fantasy appeal to me because of the subversive possibilities of them. I can, for instance, create a world in which fat women are seen as luscious and desirable, or I can exaggerate and thereby call into question political conditions that are currently in this world.

CW: Most people probably regard Caribbean folktales and science fiction as two completely unconnected worlds. Do you see any convergences, stylistically and/or thematically, between the two?

NH: Science fiction and fantasy tend to look respectively at the future and the past, and they both examine the results of humanity's efforts to understand, explain and manipulate our environments, whether through devising tools, machines, methods of inquiry, or ritual codes of behavior. Folklore is one such system. Folktales encode mores and archetypes in story so that they are easily taught and passed on by word of mouth. So yes, wherever the folklore might originate, I do see lots of possible convergences between folklore and science fiction and fantasy, and so have many writers. In fact there's a whole subgenre of fantasy that consists of contemporary revisitings of ancient folktales. What's different is my using *Caribbean*

38 CONVERSATIONS WITH NALO HOPKINSON

folklore in science fiction and fantasy. There are only a handful of Caribbean writers in the genre, so a Caribbean worldview is not one that the genre experiences often.

CW: Do you write with a specific audience in mind, and how has *Midnight Robber* been received by the science fiction community and/or a Caribbean audience?

NH: I don't write with a specific audience in mind. I try instead to write the kind of fiction I would like to read. I don't know how successful that project is, but it is quite deliberate that I'm trying to insert a sensibility like mine (and here I'm referring not only to my racial and cultural background, but to any of the other experiences and points of view written in my body and my history) into this literature that I've read since I was a girl, that is so open to new ideas in many other arenas but that seems to have a limited analysis around racial politics. The prevailing attitude seems to be that, if we all just ignored racial differences, racial prejudice would disappear. I suspect that's left little room for people to have a voice who want to talk about and read about power and access as they impinge on race. It is very possible to do it, though, and there are some writers who do.

It's too soon to know how *Midnight Robber* is going to be received by different audiences. So far the reviews have been positive. Science fiction reviewers have tended to tell readers that they might find my use of Creole disconcerting at first. I'm not used to that. It never occurred to me that it would be considered unusual because I'm so used to literature written in the English dialects of one place or another. I've also had commentary where the reviewers took pains to opine that the novel could be viewed as fantasy rather than science fiction. I'm not certain where they get that reading because the novel is set in a technologically advanced society and there is no hint of supernatural beings or phenomena. I'm interested in why that's being said, though, because I'd like to know where the comment comes from. One thing I cherish is that what my work is doing is giving me a sense of where the Caribbean readers of science fiction and fantasy are. Some of them take pains to contact me when they like what I'm doing. It's always a pleasant surprise because the assumption is that science fiction and fantasy are literatures enjoyed only by European people.

CW: Do you see *Midnight Robber* as a utopian novel, or would you agree with Samuel Delany that science fiction cannot be utopian but has to reflect social dynamism in order to avoid being tyrannical?

NH: I'd have to read more of what Delany said to know if I agree with him. I do know that few utopian novels have worked for me; in fact, the only one I can think of at the moment is Kim Stanley Robinson's *Pacific Edge*, and I think it works because it does reflect dynamism and dissent in communities. I don't really see *Midnight Robber* as a utopian novel. The world of Toussaint has been set up to be as civilized as its designer could think to make it, in that the wealth of a fraction of the world no longer rests on the labor of most of its inhabitants, but it's not perfect.

CW: The introduction calls New Half-Way Tree the Adub version of Toussaint, the characters' home planet. What themes and characteristics of dub poetry do you see reflected in your depiction of that planet?

NH: I was thinking more of dub music. When I moved to Jamaica as a young teen, I was introduced to the concept of the dub side of a record, which contained more or less the melody, but with no words, and lots of bass. Listening to the dub side, you can hear complexities that have gone into creating the skeleton of the music that my untrained ear couldn't hear in the A side. New Half Way Tree is Toussaint without the layering on of humanity and human systems.

CW: The Midnight Robber is traditionally a very male figure in Trinidadian Old Mas' Carnival. What are the implications of making him the ideal Tan-Tan [the novel's *female* protagonist] aspires to from the very beginning of her involvement in carnival? How does her impersonation of the character as "Robber Queen" replicate and differ from traditional Midnight Robber qualities?

NH: You'd have to tell me what implications you see. If I wrote fiction as political premise first, my writing process would be very different. I came to the image out of glee. One day I was reading an ancient issue of *Caribbean Quarterly*; one devoted entirely to the historical practices of carnival. One article described the Midnight Robber mas' and in passing made mention of Belle Starr, the only woman the author knew to have played Midnight Robber. And, of course, the woman in me perked up at the notion of a female Midnight Robber, and of perhaps an invisible history of female Midnight Robbers. I started first from the empowering notion of how cool and butch it would be as a woman to play/be this physically imposing and arresting character who has at gunpoint reclaimed ownership of her body and her right to tell her story. Of course, Midnight Robbers never hurt anyone with their guns; words are both their weapons and their defense, much like those of calypsonians. They don't need external weapons; their tongues are powerful enough. The notion of giving a woman a similar type of physical power and agency to that of a man continues to be a compelling one in this time. In Tan-Tan's time, though, that's no big deal. Noone sees her fascination with being a Midnight Robber as a gender-bending choice. It allows me to draw readers into a world where both women and men have more choices for how to express their personalities; it's not so bound up in social constructions of masculinity and femininity. As Robber *Queen*, Tan-Tan willy nilly brings a woman's body and a woman's concerns to the roles. She tries at first to hide certain aspects of her femaleness, but eventually they reveal themselves and she has to deal with them.

CW: In her final speech, Tan-Tan not only confesses to the killing of her father but justifies her action in a way that seems to affirm agency for women in the face of patriarchal oppression in general. However, her adversary in that speech is a woman, her stepmother. What do you see as the ramifications of that final stand-off?

NH: I don't entirely agree with you. Tan-Tan justifies her actions by pointing out that she had used the tool she was given in the desperate circumstances in which she found herself. And she was given that tool with no explanation by someone who was being otherwise complicit in her abuse. Tan-Tan was pushed to the limit of her tolerance in an atmosphere of secrecy and torture, and she reacted. I do believe that agency for women is vital, but I wouldn't say that that speech speaks to my entire political position on the complex issue of societally condoned oppression of women. And yes, it's quite possible for women to be adversarial to other people, including to other women. For me, the ramification of that final stand-off is that the other woman acknowledges and ceases her part in the abuse that Tan-Tan has endured.

CW: Tan-Tan constantly has to leave "home" in the course of the novel, being exiled first from Toussaint, and later moving between different communities on New Half-Way Tree. How does this diasporic experience affect her? Would you say that, because of her position as a woman, exile has a different, perhaps more ambivalent, meaning for her than, say, for her father? Along the same line, *Midnight Robber* reads like a classic bildungsroman in some respects. However, unlike in familiar rites-of-passage-narratives which necessitate the separation, living on the margins, and reintegration of the hero/ine into her/his community, Tan-Tan does not return to her home planet at the end. What is the meaning of her remaining on new Half-Way Tree?

NH: She can't go back to Toussaint. You can't go home again. Even her home wasn't home. A few weeks ago I heard scholar Mary Hanna say that the notion of exile in Caribbean literature has become a positive thing rather than a negative one. The comment struck me because, like many of my peers living outside the Caribbean, my experience has been a diasporic one. As a result, home for me is a temporary zone (though, Pace Hakim Bey, not always an autonomous one). Home is where I've chosen to accumulate my stuff, and my ideal is to have a few such zones. Home is when I feel surrounded by chosen community, and that's always short-lived and partial. So I've come to a notion that home is fluid, changeable, and accretes around the resident rather than being a concrete, stationery place to which the resident goes. I doubt that I'm alone in that. So Tan-Tan doesn't go back home; she begins to learn to gather comfort and community around herself. She attracts home to her. After all, how does someone reintegrate into a community with which she is at odds? Tan-Tan's values have changed, and her needs. Even could she return to Toussaint, she'd have to learn how to create home for herself there, too.

CW: A victim of continued sexual abuse by her father, Tan-Tan has an abortion in her early teens and is pregnant again throughout the latter part of the novel. She finally decides to give birth to this second child. Why?

NH: I think she's around thirteen during the first pregnancy. She doesn't decide to give birth to the second child. She would happily have aborted it, but circumstances kept the means to do so from her, and by the time she got to a settlement that could likely have helped her, the fetus was practically at ten; it was too late. What she does do is come to a sense of determination that, having carried the child to term while enduring peril to herself, she was damned well going to retain the autonomy to care for it. Tan-Tan is thrown into circumstances where she doesn't have many choices around pregnancy and childbirth. She exercises what choice she does have, which is the choice to decide to be a caring parent. Partly my decision to write it that way comes from being aware that, despite the existence of effective birth control methods, most women in the world still have very limited choices around parenthood. Science fiction isn't so much about projecting into the future; it's about turning a lens onto the present.

CW: What are your reasons for using patois in your writing? How does the specific narrative perspective affect your choice of language in different parts of the novel? In your writing in general?

NH: I use it partly because it feels beautiful and natural to my ears. Realize that I live away and have for more than two decades; I no longer hear Creoles very often. Writing the ones I know temporarily invokes a space I no longer inhabit much anymore. In *Midnight Robber*, though, I was specifically talking about language and about how peoples, who as part of being colonized, have had a language forced on them can turn around and remold that same language in a conscious or unconscious resistance. Hence "Stolen

42 CONVERSATIONS WITH NALO HOPKINSON

Song," the poem at the beginning of the novel, which David Findlay graciously allowed me to quote.

CW: Could you comment on your use of names in the novel? What traditions/histories did you draw on and why?

NH: The people in the novel are multiracial, as the Caribbean is. I wanted to signal that. Ione Brasil, Antonio Habib, Doctor Kong, Quashee Cumberbatch, Maka, all reflect a number of Caribbean histories. They have (or I hope they have) echoes of West African, continental Indian and Asian, Spanish, Portuguese, and Maroon participation in the Caribbean. One of the embedded "folktales" in the novel is based on a story from the indigenous peoples.

CW: Contemporary theory has fluctuated between regarding carnival as either a celebratory inversion of dominant social structures or as a reaffirmation of those very structures in the process of channeling and containing popular discontent. Where would you position *Midnight Robber*'s depiction of carnival in this debate? Is there a difference in the significance of carnival as practiced on Toussaint and New Half-Way Tree, respectively?

NH: I wouldn't position the depiction of carnival in *Midnight Robber* in that debate at all because it wasn't one of which I've been cognizant, not as an existing dynamic of opposing arguments, anyway. Why can't carnival be both and more besides? Carnival on Toussaint has been institutionalized. It is a weird dichotomy, an institutionalized period of license. That's always been the dilemma of carnival. Carnival on New Half Way Tree is a romanticized memory. They're trying to recreate a feeling from a land to which they'll never return. And they may eventually succeed in rebuilding the systems and institutions which remake New Half Way Tree into an image of Toussaint.

CW: Granny Nanny is the system that spies on and provides for the inhabitants of Toussaint. Which aspects of Jamaica's national heroine, Nanny, did you incorporate into this construct? What do you see as the implications of the adoption of folktales for political ends?

NH: I set it up that the artificial intelligence nicknamed "Granny Nanny" (Grande Nanotech Sentient Interface) was not initially named after Granny Nanny. It's a nickname that humans jokingly gave her sometime after her creation, so there isn't necessarily a neat correlation between her characteristics and those of the freedom fighter Nanny of the Maroons. Granny Nancy's web (I also deliberately conflated the name with Brer Anansi) does not spy on the populace in the sense that her surveillance is not covert; it's known and has been contracted for. It's also known that she's programmed for privacy unless she judges that someone is suffering harm and that that might be changed by her intervening. Yes, it's a nuisance and an intrusion. It's accepted as a trade-off for greater protection for those who need it and for quality of life. Those who created and inhabited the planet saw it so and went to live on Toussaint knowingly under those terms. Some people would rather not have Granny Nanny's surveillance, and those can to some extent opt-out. But there are qualities of the legendary Nanny (the story behind the history, as opposed to the real woman behind that story) which the artificial intelligence is seen to share: she feels a bond of duty to the humans in her care, and she functions as an advocate for their well-being. As Anansi she teaches through story and song, and she can be capricious (certainly the house eshus that are her eyes and hands can) because she is a sentient entity who grows and changes. As to the adoption of folktales for political ends, it happens. Folktales feel like sort of cultural artifacts—or more like cultural sourdough starter, perhaps—that people take and retell to suit their own purposes. All storytelling has political ends and sometimes those ends are unfortunately more about enforcing conformity than about encouraging self-awareness.

CW: Toussaint's parliament is referred to as "Palaver House." This seems to resonate with Midnight Robbers' attacks on contemporary politics in Trinidadian carnival. What are your criticisms of the political process, and what made you want to explore the themes that you take on in *Midnight Robber*? Could you name certain topics that pervade your writing in general, and have there been social or political developments that have impacted your choice of those topics?

NH: I was going to simply pass on these questions, but I realized that I do have opinions about politics, so I decided to think about why I didn't want to answer them. And it's because if I wanted to lay out all my opinions chapter and verse, I'd be writing essays, not fiction. I want to tell stories. Most of my politicization has come through reading fiction for the enjoyment of it, and along with the stories being slipped ideas that made me think, question, sometimes made me disagree vehemently with the text. Partly I don't want to answer the questions because I've answered so many from other people, and sometimes I prefer for people to read my fiction and take away what they will from it, rather than asking me to dissect it and analyze it for them. That's a process of deconstruction, whereas I come to writing fiction from a process of synthesis, of trying to make stories that are informed by the ideas I've absorbed over the years. I don't want to reverse that process by disassembling my own work into its component parts; it sort of feels like being asked to destroy it. So I'm being resistant.

CW: Could you see *Midnight Robber* being turned into a film? Who would you cast for the role of Tan-Tan?

NH: I can certainly imagine someone optioning my work for film (I'm sure I could find uses for the money!), but I think that, of the novels I have written, *Brown Girl in the Ring* is the better bet: fewer special effects and settings, simpler story. Some of my short stories might also work better. Novels are generally just too long to squelch effectively into a ninety-minute format. I actually don't enjoy the notion of seeing my work interpreted into film. I'm surprised that this is the question that people always seem to ask me, as though it's the ultimately desirable culmination of my efforts. Whenever I imagine my work as film, I remember Whoopi Goldberg's attempting and failing utterly at a Jamaican accent in *Clara's Heart*. It was agonizing to listen to. But that's the mainstream film industry's notion of Caribbean culture, much as I love Whoopi Goldberg. Science fiction and fantasy with all their toys, gadgets, nonexistent beings, and impossible settings are so much more vividly imagined in the mind than on film; I'd still rather have text. The only science fiction and fantasy film I've seen that I found convincing and visually compelling was *Something Wicked This Way Comes*, which is an adaptation of a Ray Bradbury novel. It *looked* the way I had imagined it, and it seemed to stick fairly closely to the writer's original vision. Bradbury lucked out on that one.

I don't know who would play the role of Tan-Tan; I don't watch enough film to have an opinion. Depending on how the novel was adapted, it would need four actresses because Tan-Tan is seen at ages seven, nine, thirteen, and sixteen. Would be pretty demanding on them, too, what with the stuff she has happen to her. I'm more interested in who would be the director, and I'd fervently hope it would be someone Caribbean who reads science fiction and fantasy, which narrows the field considerably. My agent is trying to interest people in my novels as film properties, and, if that ever happens, I'm aware that the project then becomes the director's; it'd no longer be my vision, but hers, except that it would have the same title as my work, some of the same characters, and some similarities in plot structure.

CW: What are you working on right now? What are some of the things you would like to address in your writing in the future? Do you think you've made conscious efforts to change your style, and, if so, how would you describe that change?

NH: I have finished work on an anthology of Caribbean fabulist fiction. I'm currently working on *Griffonne*, my third novel. It will use a fantastical device to link the lives of three or four Black historical characters from different countries and time periods. Overarching themes will probably end up being sexuality, race, and power. But I'm always surprised at what metaphors end up being worked through in my stories, so really I'm talking through my hat at this point. In the future, I think I might like to address the tyranny of work, the way that the well-being of a few has always been built on the backs of a desperately unfortunate many, and how that "many" gets constructed and then Othered. Or I may just think about it a lot and never end up writing it. I will see what develops.

I think I'm developing a better sense of the "bumps" in my writing. In other words, I'm learning to pay attention to when a word or phrase pokes out, and to think about why that might be, whether it's a good thing or not, and to fiddle with it if I decide it's not. I hope in the long run it'll mean that my writing veers towards showing instead of telling. I have been trying to tackle a new aspect of my writing with each new piece. I wanted to portray male characters in more complexity, and think that in *Midnight Robber* I've begun that. I'll work it out more in short stories. I've wanted to portray sexuality more, particularly non-good-girl sexuality. It was fun, too, to write the small bits of *Midnight Robber* that showed a society where coupledom was not the necessary default. I dealt with female body image stuff in an earlier short story ("A Habit of Waste"), and I'd like to get back to that, but likely my take on it will be different. I'm hesitant to spell things like this out because putting it into words that will get published will feel kind of like writing a contract; I might feel compelled to do what I said I wanted to, and I don't want to lock myself in like that. The quick answer is yes, I'm consciously trying to change, if not my style, then the ways in which I tackle things. And I may make stylistic changes too.

Interview with Nalo Hopkinson

James Schellenberg and David M. Switzer / 2001

From *Challenging Destiny*, no. 12 (April 10, 2001), https://www.challengingdestiny.com
/interviews/hopkinson.htm. Reprinted with permission of James Schellenberg and
David M. Switzer.

Challenging Destiny: *Brown Girl in the Ring* was your first novel. How did you approach the writing process, not having written a novel before?

Nalo Hopkinson: Terror and deadlines. I had the first three chapters, and that took me about two years to write. And I'd actually written another novel in the interim—I was three-quarters of the way through it—that I was shopping around but hadn't had any interest in, so I put it aside. I heard about the Warner Aspect First Novel Contest and decided I wanted to enter that. So I had the first three chapters, which was what they wanted. I sent them that. I sent it to them early, figuring I would have time if they wanted to see the rest to write it. I figured it'd be a rejection anyway, because in general one gets more rejections than acceptances. Then, in two weeks, I get a letter back saying, "We'd like to short-list this. We want to send it on to the final round. Send us the whole novel. No drafts please." So I wrote the rest in three months. I didn't tell them that till after I got the contract. It's not a process I'd recommend to anybody. What happened was I was plotting as I went. I didn't know where the novel was going. I ended up with a main character strapped to a gurney surrounded by the bad guys and thought, "Well, OK. She can't die. What am I going to do next?" I finished that scene two days before the final deadline. There were no drafts, because who had time? It has that feeling of breathlessness when you read through it, because that's how I was writing it. When I got to the end I didn't know I had—I got to a point and thought, "OK, I don't know what to write now." And I realized that was because I had pretty much tied everything up. That's how I knew it was done.

CD: With more experience now, how do you regard *Brown Girl*?

NH: There are things I would go back and develop more—I would develop the character of Rudy more. I might try to develop the politicians more, but politicians are fair game. There are ideas I would probably work through more subtly. It is pretty much a book that leaps out at you. I think one will always think that—you go back and look at anything you've worked on, and you realize in that time span your process has changed, or you've grown, or you've changed as an artist. I try not to worry about it too much. The trick is to save that knowledge and put it in the next thing. That way, with each piece that you publish, you have a map of your development as a writer.

CD: Why did you set *Brown Girl* in a run-down Toronto of the future?

NH: It wasn't that much different from the Toronto of the present. That was one thing—I didn't have to do much research that way. They say, "Write what you know." So I started with the familiar location. It also had to do with what was happening in Toronto at the time, and still is happening: government funding being pulled from absolutely everything. I had gone through Detroit a year earlier to go to Clarion—I am a graduate of Clarion—and so I'd gone through Detroit to get to East Lansing. Detroit is a ghost town. There are people there, but at night it's dead. The streets are full of potholes. Everything feels run-down. And it's because of exactly that same kind of process—support leaving the city core, and so jobs leave the city core, and then people with anything to lose move after it. What you have left are the people who have limited choices. And I found out that economists have a name for it, because it's a documented phenomenon that can happen to cities if city planners and city government don't know what they're doing. It's called the "hole in the doughnut" syndrome. Because you end up with a city core that's just destroyed and everybody fleeing to the suburbs as fast as they can. It was clear to me that a lot of what the Ontario government was doing—it's like they're using Detroit as a manual. So that's part of what I was reacting against. I also just wanted to set something in a place I lived. And Toronto's a really interesting place. It allowed me to use Ryerson, and use the CN Tower, and use Riverdale Farm. For research you get to hang around Riverdale Farm and ask them where the turtles go in the winter. It was a cool thing to do.

CD: With *Midnight Robber*, there's a backbone of hard SF and then the culture and myth that you brought to it. How do you balance those two things?

NH: That was the novel I had three-quarters written, that wasn't quite working yet. And that after I sold *Brown Girl* sold it and then had to rewrite. And I already had some idea of how to rewrite it. Partly it was from talking to a professor named Uppinder Mehan who used to lecture at the University of Toronto and who is originally from Ontario. He was talking about writers from continental India writing SF. The problem being that to an audience from here, because we may not know their cultures, we can't tell when the writers have done science fictional extrapolation from those cultures. Another thing he pointed out was that if Indian culture had developed without the colonizing influence of the West, the words that they use for technology would be different words, because they would have developed their own technologies and their own metaphors for speaking about technology. In the West, we use words that are based in Greek and Roman myth to describe our technologies and sciences. We call a space ship *Apollo* or a psychological phenomenon "Oedipus." So I got to thinking: what metaphors for technology would a future Caribbean culture use? That meant I was picking things out of Caribbean mythology the same way that we do here for Western technology. So I think that's how it started, with that seed idea. I call the operating system for the house an "eshu," and that's based in West African religious beliefs; Eshu is the deity who has the power to go everywhere and see everything. Once you start doing that, it kind of snowballs. It's very easy to start to blend the technology with the mythology, because we do it all the time. In SF, we like to think of science fiction as one thing and fantasy as another, but they bleed into each other.

CD: Genre seems to be about boundaries and definitions, but you seem to be having success with creating a hybrid. How do you feel about the way genre is defined?

NH: I didn't know that the differences between SF and fantasy were so contentious until five years ago. I was reading pretty widely. I was reading mostly fantastical literature, but that could be anything from Isaac Asimov to *Gulliver's Travels*. I didn't put names on things; I didn't check the spine to see what it was supposed to be first. If it had something that couldn't exist in the real world, I was interested. Partly I'm able to hybridize genres out of ignorance. But there are more and more writers doing that, refusing to accept the boundaries. I think the boundaries, though sometimes helpful, are artificial; they're there to help the booksellers sell books. They're there to help the people who like to read that kind of stuff find it. But essentially I think both SF and fantasy talk about the ways in which humans manipulate their worlds. That could be technology, it could be religion, it could be customs, or it could be a new way to make a clay pot. Both literatures—if you accept that they are two separate literatures, and I don't— are doing that. Talking about what happens to us and our societies because we are tool users, because we change our environments and our realities to suit ourselves.

CD: *Midnight Robber* seems to be a story of disenfranchisement. The character loses utopia at the very beginning, and gradually strips more and more away until all she has left is the power of the story of Midnight Robber.

NH: She has her two feet and an imagination.

CD: Is the power of story a metaphor for the writer? How do you think about the role of the storyteller, and the power of that, because that seems to be her triumph at the end?

NH: Clearly the thing is based in the whole power of storytelling. And that's partly because I grew up with so many folktales; read them in the library, occasionally heard them on television from local performers. And had a father who was an actor and poet. He used to give one-man performances of his poetry. I saw lots of plays performed, too; Daddy was one of the actors in the Trinidad Theatre Workshop, and some of his colleagues such as performance artists Dem Two took their own small shows on the road. So the art of verbal storytelling is very much part of what I grew up with. Coming out of Caribbean literature—which also draws on storytelling quite heavily—it seemed like a natural fit for me.

Tan-Tan's victory is a victory won through words—I guess that is a very powerful metaphor for a writer. The whole image of the Midnight Robber, which is a real masquerade that people play at carnival, tells a story about disenfranchisement. The Midnight Robber's speech is about being the son of an African king and kidnapped into slavery, escaping, and becoming a bandit in order to survive. But it doesn't tell the story plainly. The people who become Midnight Robbers have to write their own speeches, and they do so by combining the most sonorous words they can find—the words have to be beautiful in themselves, it's not so much about meaning. They'll take words from the Bible, words from westerns, and combine them into this speech. When you read it, it could almost be nonsensical. It makes sense if you listen to it sideways. The triumph of the Midnight Robber is when he can hold your attention, and get you to be so amazed by the beauty of these words, that you give him money. So I did think it was a really powerful metaphor for this little girl to take on—that's all she has. Violence is not going to work, and she doesn't have a home anymore. The whole idea of being exiled from home is very much a legacy of 500 years of African slavery. People have said the book is a metaphor for slavery. It's not; not that plainly, anyway. It is an analogy for that sense of exile when you've been moved from your home at least twice. For people from that legacy who are now in the African diaspora, Africa is not our home; for most of us, if we went there we'd be just as lost as anybody else. But there is a sense that that's where our ancestors started from. That sense of not being able to go home again is very much something I'm playing with.

CD: When did you know that you wanted to be a writer?

NH: I let myself know in 1993, when Judy Merril was going to be teaching a course in SF writing through Ryerson and to get into the course you had to submit two pieces of writing. And I had none. I'd been writing articles on fitness—I was a fitness instructor—for a couple of Toronto papers, and that was it. So I wrote something for Judy's class, which turned out to be the beginning of *Brown Girl in the Ring.* I had no idea where it was going—knew nothing about plot. Looked at it and thought, "That's six pages and this thing needs to be longer. Oh my God, what do I do now?" I got into the course, which then never ran because there wasn't enough registration. But Judy being Judy, she called up the six of us who'd been accepted and she said, "Come meet with me. You don't need to pay anybody to do this. I'm going to show you how to run your own workshop." And she met with us once, and I remember Brent Hayward saying, "So do we come back next week?" And she essentially said, "No, I don't want to meet with you again. You go off and do it. I don't need to do this with you." That's how the writing group started. So it wasn't until '93 that I begin to think about fiction writing—bear in mind I had a writer for a father and so in my mind, that was what daddies did, not daughters. It took a while to let myself know that that's what I wanted to do.

CD: So then it was after *Brown Girl* that you started writing short stories?

NH: No, they were happening simultaneously. I was workshopping short stories in the group. Brent had already written a novel and he was working on his second. Bob Boyczuk had been to Clarion, had written short stories. I was way behind. So I was writing short stories to catch up—even just to their output, never mind their grasp of craft.

CD: How do you like writing short stories versus novels?

NH: At this point, I prefer short stories. You can keep them in your head better. A novel feels like wrestling a mattress—your arms are always too short. With a short story, you can take two or three themes and work them through and have a refrain and echo and a nice, satisfying ending. With a novel you're always going to forget something and have to remind yourself to pick that thread up again. Or I do. Novels do pay better—and it's nice to have that book on the shelf with your name on it. Your mother really likes that. But I think I'm finding short stories, when I can write them, more satisfying.

CD: You recently had an anthology come out, *Whispers From the Cotton Tree Root: Caribbean Fabulist Fiction.* How did that project get started?

NH: I was at ICFA, the International Conference on the Fantastic in the Arts, a couple of years ago. I gave a reading. Afterwards two men approached me and told me that they were editors of a new publishing house and asked if I'd ever considered doing an anthology of Caribbean fabulist fiction. And I said, I wanted to edit but let's talk about it once I get back. And we did, and that's how it started. I had them talk to my agent and we figured out we could do it.

Then I had to go about inviting people, which was an interesting process in itself. As I said, I grew up in the Caribbean literary community so a lot of the people who I invited were people I knew as my father's peers. So I would send out this very formal submission letter—sometimes I didn't know them, I just knew their names—saying, "Dear Mr. or Mrs. So-and-so. Here's who I am. I'm working on this anthology. Here is the call for submissions. I'd be honored if you had a story for me to consider." And I'd get back an email that said, "Child, I used to change your diapers. How is your mother? Sure, I'm sending you a story." And then I'd think, "Damn. Suppose I don't like it, after all that?"

It's been really intriguing being in the editor's shoes. Because usually you're the writer, and you're the one complaining about the editor. Now I get to see that those cryptic letters about "does not suit our needs at this time" are often nothing but the truth.

CD: Did you enjoy the editing, and would you like to do it again?

NH: I did enjoy it. I hated the administrative part. Keeping track of when was this story published, how much money do I owe this person—that's a nightmare. But the editorial process was a lot of fun. What I did was get all the stories in, and began to get a sense of which I felt were strong. When you cluster them together they begin to develop a shape of their own, so then you're looking for more work that fits it. Often literally if I rejected a story it was because it didn't fit, or I had something else that did something similar that I thought was stronger. That's pretty difficult to communicate. With a couple of people, particularly younger writers, I'd say, "This isn't working for me. The story is promising. Do you think you could work on it?" Some people did, and some didn't.

Towards the end of the process—I was just about wrapping up—I got an email from someone who said he'd just graduated from Clarion, he was also from the West Indies, and he just wanted to say hi. And I said, "I'm working on this anthology. I only have one SF piece. Do you have anything?" And he said, "Yeah, I do, but I've got to finish it up. I'll send it to you tomorrow." Which he did. I liked it—I thought it needed some changes, I asked him to do those, he did them, and I bought the story. Which was when he told me that he hadn't had a story. He'd pulled a Nalo on me: he did exactly what I'd done to Warner. He didn't have a story; he'd written it that same night I asked for it. Nothing like incentive. That's Tobias Buckell.

I contacted Kamau Brathwaite, who's an old, old friend of my father's and one of the most respected writers in the Caribbean. And as far as I knew he was a poet. I wasn't asking him for work, but I was asking if he could put me in touch with a list of writers for whom I was searching. He emailed me back a bunch of emails and phone numbers, and said, "Here's this piece I've been working on." And there it was. It isn't quite a poem, and it isn't quite a story—it's sort of a hybrid. And it was gorgeous. And it was brand new—I had a brand-new Kamau Brathwaite story sitting in my in box. So I had this range of work—Lillian Allen, writer/activist in Toronto, gave me her first fiction piece. Pamela Mordecai, a children's writer, poet, and editor who's also Torontonian, wrote her first SF story for me. Roger McTair, who started out as a writer but nowadays mostly is a documentary filmmaker, pulled a story out of his trunk and worked on it and sent it to me. Camille Hernandez-Ramdwar from Toronto sent me a terrifying, sad story that I loved immediately. Claude-Michel Prévost, SF writer living in Vancouver, sent me an excerpt from a script on which he's working. H. Nigel Thomas from Québec also sent me a story I liked very much. Then I got pieces from people in the Caribbean, from Caribbean people in the US and UK—Wilson Harris, an absolute genius (his work in some ways puts me in mind of Samuel Delany's) and one of the doyens of Caribbean fiction, sent me a powerful, complex piece. It was just wonderful—as they began to come together there was a shape happening.

CD: In the introduction you talk about there being a gap between your own sensibilities as more of a SF writer versus some of the stories. What did you mean by that, and how do you think that happened?

NH: SF is a North American literature. Sometimes a British literature, sometimes a Slavic literature. But it's nowhere else in the world—the whole ideology behind it comes out of this surrounding, this culture of making machines to change the world. Samuel Delany once said it's the literature of the people who create technologies. North America creates technology and sells it to the rest of the world. A sense of ownership of technology isn't there for a lot of other nations. Thinking about the effects of technology happens in different ways. There's lots of fantastical and fabulist writing, but the iconography of SF where I can say "ansible" and you know what I mean—I can't do that in the Caribbean. I'd have to explain it. Whereas if I said "duppy" here, you don't know what I mean, but they sure as hell do. I had to try and force a hybrid. I would say, "I'm writing fantastical fiction," and the writers I'd contacted would say, "I don't know what that is. But here's a story. It has a ghost in it. Will it do?" And sometimes it would, and sometimes it wouldn't.

There's one piece in there that I love, Ian McDonald's "Pot o' Rice Horowitz's House of Solace," which is a hilarious piece but not at all fantastical. The things that happen in that story could absolutely happen, but what made me decide to take it is the metaphors he uses are metaphors for the fantastic. He uses people going to westerns and karate shows at the drive-in as the iconography by which they understand their world. He talks about the grocer who has these wonderful products—he sells marshmallows and peacock's tongues, and to the people in the little backwater town where he's opened his shop, both are equally magical. That's the kind of thing which made me decide that the story would fit. The anthology is right on the edge of slipstream for a genre reader. The rest of the world probably won't care that much.

CD: Is being a SF writer what you thought it would be like?

NH: Yes and no. The yes comes from going to Clarion, where you had at least six professional writers and you could ask them what it was like. And they were only too happy to tell you. So we were warned about some of what to expect as professional writers: contracts, agents, that kind of thing. So that part has been not unexpected. The unexpected part has been that anybody cares that I write what I do. Occasionally having people walk up to me in the street and say, "You're that writer." When I'm doing something embarrassing, like buying toilet paper or something. That's kind of creepy. Nice, but creepy to think that a stranger can look at your face and know who you are. Know who part of you is, anyway. It pretty much has been what I thought. There have been unexpected things, like being asked what I think of the illustrations on book covers. I don't know that the publisher actually much cares what I think, but she's always done me the courtesy of at least asking. We were told at Clarion that you'd find out what your book cover was when you got the book.

What's also surprising is that people think because you have a couple of books out that you're making money. I've had professional organizations ask me to travel at my own expense to other countries to work for them for free, expecting that I'd be pleased at the exposure. Fine if they can't afford

54 CONVERSATIONS WITH NALO HOPKINSON

to pay, but to expect me to spend what is the equivalent of a month's living in order to work for them—I don't ask my grocer to do that, I don't ask my plumber to do that. A convention is a little bit different. I go to those by my own choice, and I sometimes get to give a reading and talk about my writing. It's a way to meet readers and meet my colleagues. I consider cons to be professional development, and I come up with the money for those when I can. And when I've been a guest of honor at them, the con has paid my airfare and hotel bill. There's a recognition there that I'm working for them and so they need to at least enable me to be there.

CD: On the back cover of the anthology it says you're working on something called *Griffone*. Can you tell us about that?

NH: It's my third novel. I don't like talking too much about the plot of something while I'm still trying to figure it out. This time I had to write a plot beforehand, because I had to sell it to my publisher. So now I have an outline of sorts. It is going to be magic realism—it's time travel. In my head I'm calling it my African women's sex magic novel, which usually makes people perk right up when I say it. It might not turn out to be that. But it's something to aim for. I am a few chapters into it. It's going to take a lot of research. With every new novel, I discover something that you should never do as a novel writer. For instance, never create an action-adventure hero who's breastfeeding; that would be *Brown Girl in the Ring*. Never write a whole novel in Creole; that would be *Midnight Robber*. With this one it's: never write a novel that exists in three time periods and three different countries simultaneously—unless you know those three very, very well. Which I don't. Eighteenth-century Haiti, nineteenth-century Paris, and fourth-century Alexandria. That was very silly of me, and I'll never do it again. The next novel after this is going to be a great fat fantasy—I'll make it all up.

CD: What's your project with the way that you've used language in your novels and stories?

NH: I had a specific project with the second one that's probably summed up best by "Stolen," the poem at the beginning of it written by David Findlay. The first line of the poem is, "I stole the torturer's tongue." In many ways, that's what Caribbean Creoles did. I wanted to see what a language might look like that was shaped by its own history. I think part of what was happening was when I would write stories and workshop them, and I would write people speaking the way I know people speak, and if they were speaking Creole I would get comments like, "She can't use a word like this because she's obviously not educated enough." Educated has nothing to do with your accent, or the way you choose to speak when you're using the vernacular (and every language has its vernaculars). So it was partly my thinking about how to get it across that someone might choose not to sound North American but might nevertheless speak in vernacular. And I have other colleagues who are North American—I have a friend who's an African American woman who, when she writes her Black characters in a futuristic context, has been told in her workshops, "No one's going to speak like this in the future." Apparently we're all going to sound American—white, middle-class American. So it was interrogating that a little bit. That kind of hegemony of language. And then trying to figure out: how would you write something futuristic and still keep a sense of the language and a sense of the history of the people in the story?

I've blended three English Creoles—Jamaican, Trinidadian, and there's the occasional Guyanese reference. Which are the places in the Caribbean where I've lived. All of which meant more research into language. I swear, that'll be my first criterion now when I write: no research. I blended the languages to see what would happen. It isn't so much an ongoing project—it was a project for that novel. I will always have characters from the places I call home, and I'll always try to make them speak the way they might. That's really difficult to put down, because often we're talking about an oral form. If you tried to directly transcribe the language you use when you're sitting talking with your buddies it would not work in writing. So trying to get a sense of Creoles on paper, and still have it be readable and understandable—and sustain it for 400 pages—was work. And I'm still trying to work it through with the new novel a little bit—I'm not doing it as heavily. I'm trying to get a sense across of how the characters think about language. The main characters you meet at first are in Saint-Domingue—Haiti before the Haitian revolution. They are speaking French Creole. Of course, I have to write that in English, but I want to get a sense of how they think about language. Because the language they're speaking is a combination of many African languages and French and probably Spanish.

As to why it's so important, Creoles in particular are often subversive languages. They come out of having to take on a language of the colonizer and then change it to meet your own needs. I wanted to get across a strong sense of subversion and even playfulness that can happen when a language grows that way.

Much of this stuff is plain intuitive—I don't sit down and think, "OK, I'm going to interrogate the hegemony of . . ." You're halfway through before you think you know what you're doing. But I don't really know until somebody critiques it and tells me what they see. So really, I'm making up the answer to your question as I go along!

CD: You've received some awards and been on juries. How do feel about that process? Do you find it helpful?

NH: I come out of having spent nine years facilitating juries for the Toronto Arts Council. I was a grants officer for art projects in literature, visual arts, media and digital arts, dance, and music. So I was running upwards of eight juries a year in all those disciplines. What that's meant is that getting rejection letters is a lot easier for me. Because I've been through the kind of process by which people get accepted or rejected, I know some of the pressures. It's easier for me not to take it personally.

That was very different than actually being on juries, which I've done for the Tiptree Award, the William Crawford Award, the Ontario Arts Council Writers Works-in-Progress Grant, the Short Prose Competition for Developing Writers from the Writers' Union of Canada (we probably got some submissions that were shorter than that title). Being a juror is yet another side of the arts funding table. There's being the artist, the administrator, the funder, the producer, the juror; it's a many-sided table. With an award, you're usually looking at work that someone's worked very hard to get across and that's already been published. That's different than a grant, which is meant to help support the artist while they're creating the work, with no pressure about whether it's publishable or not. A grant is to allow you the freedom to explore, to push the envelope. I find that when I'm a juror, being a writer myself, you're very aware of the work that's gone into this thing so you're rooting for the person at some level, no matter whether you think their work succeeds or not. It makes it sometimes heartbreaking to make those decisions about yes or no. There's not as much at stake with an award because at least the work has already been published—it's gone through that process of recognition, and is out there in the world with a chance of its own to garner praise. With a grant jury, though, where the works aren't created yet or aren't finished yet, and the person might need this money in order to do so, the stakes are really high. Being a juror is a thankless task. What I like about it is that you get to see a wide range of what's going through your peers' minds. Writing is sort of a response to other people's writing, so you get a sense of what people are working on, what's exciting people right then. Those things you give the grant to that year are going to be next year's new books. So will some of the projects that you don't give a grant to, because the writers will somehow find a way. So that's really exciting. I like doing all of it. I think I'm going to be on the Nebula jury this year, as a volunteer. I like getting to see the work, and the free books are nice too.

CD: What are some of your favorite books that you've read lately?

NH: Elisabeth Vonarburg's *The Maerlande Chronicles*, an epic exploration of gender, society, and language which blew me away. I'm doing so much reading. I'm reading something now that I don't know yet if I'm going to like when I get done it—I'm halfway through. It's a new one by Jonathan Carroll and it's called *The Wooden Sea*. I got to reread Suzette Haden Elgin's *Native Tongue* recently, which is just a romp. It spoofs everything about sexism in the most unkind ways—it's big fun, and I really like it. Candas Jane Dorsey's *Black Wine*. I just read *Ten Monkeys, Ten Minutes*, a collection of short stories by Peter Watts, which impressed me. I'm really liking the way he complicates his characters' lives, even when I disagree with what some of his premises seem to be. And the way he writes women characters. I love anything Samuel Delany puts out. No, I won't start on the nonfiction, because I won't stop.

CD: What do you do these days when you're not writing?

NH: Not writing? What means this? I worry about not writing when I'm not writing. It's become a job now. That's what I'm primarily doing to keep my head above water. Sometimes I don't quite manage. When I'm not writing I'm doing all the administrative stuff that supports writing. I do a couple of hours of writing a day, and the rest is answering letters, filling out forms, putting things in my calendar, planning for courses I'm going to teach. I've noticed that a lot of professional writers, if you ask them what their hobbies are, they look at you and go, "Well, I used to . . ." It's like that for me. I used to be a fitness instructor. I used to take silversmithing courses. I used to make crafts and sew my own clothing. I used to be able to have a conversation that didn't include a literary critique anywhere in it. I still try to get out to arts events in Toronto a lot because I have that connection with the arts community and I'm interested. I love to go dancing, but that doesn't happen much. I think about writing, I talk about writing, I hang out with people who are thinking and talking about writing. It's very insular.

CD: When you're talking about teaching, you're talking about teaching writing?

NH: I'm going to be teaching a course in utopian fiction at University of Toronto, and then I'll be teaching one on SF and one on SF writing.

CD: On your website, you have a section about SF writers of color. Could you tell us about that?

NH: I put that there because people ask. Because it's one of the things that clearly makes me unique in SF. I'm one of maybe six Black novelists

58 CONVERSATIONS WITH NALO HOPKINSON

in the field. When I wrote it, I was still thinking about Uppinder's article on writers from the continent of India writing SF there and the difficulties in communicating what they were trying to get across. I had been in touch with a man named Gary Bowen who is a First Nations horror writer, who had put together a project called the Decolores Project, which seems to have gone to a dead link on the web—but he had created a bibliography of all the SF, fantasy, and horror writers of color and Jewish writers that he could find. And we'd been talking as he went through that process. Almost every convention I go to, somebody wants to put me on a panel about why there are so few writers of color in the field. And I got kind of tired of doing Diversity 101. So I put it on my website and just don't go to any more of those panels. But it is a thing that you wrestle with. Gloria Naylor, who wrote *Women of Brewster Place*, her novel, *Mama Day*, is fantasy, and she's got a collection of short stories that are all fantastical. Why can't I find stuff like that when I go into a SF bookstore? Why can't I find Larissa Lai's *When Fox is a Thousand* and Thomas King's *Green Grass, Running Water* and Ashok Mathur's *Once upon an Elephant*? Lai, King, and Mathur are in Can Lit, but they could easily be in fantasy too. And yet people are saying there are no writers of color in the field. Because their books don't have "SF" and "fantasy" on the spines, a lot of SF readers don't know about them. In fact, some writers of color would be insulted if you were to identify their work as SF or fantasy. There are complicated reasons for the notion that people of color don't write SF and no one person or industry is to blame. I'm still thinking through that stuff, because people don't stop asking, and I don't stop wondering.

CD: So you think it's also genre boundaries that are happening or genre identity?

NH: It's genre identity, particularly with SF that came out of the pulp era. It was essentially in its beginnings a literature of white boys and big toys going to places where people didn't look like them and conquering them. Most of us (people of color) are living through the effects of that history and to us it's not an exciting adventure story. It wouldn't occur to a lot of non-readers of SF and fantasy that the genres have progressed—have in many cases taken on that history. If all that non SF/F readers see reflected in the media is the kind of "Galaxy Wars" big budget film which so often replicates and glorifies the notion of militaristic conquering, it wouldn't occur to them to pick up a novel by Spider Robinson or Jim Morrow. So that's part of it. Part of it is we think differently about what's fantastical and what isn't. So books like Toni Morrison's *Beloved*—Toni Morrison is not going to think of that as a fantasy novel. She knows she's telling truths in it, so she's not going to think of it as something unreal. It's just a different paradigm for thinking about fiction. The work's out there. You don't tend to find as much science fiction as fantasy by writers of color, but they're both out there, and the numbers are growing. Partly because I have that page on my website, I hear from younger writers of color who are SF and fantasy writers. Who are saying, "Thank God. I won't get laughed at anymore. People won't tell me I can't do this, or people like us don't write this kind of fiction." So I've been able to be a little cheering team.

Nalo Hopkinson: Winging It

Charles Brown / 2001

From *Locus Magazine*, October 2001. © *Locus Magazine*. Reprinted with permission.

"It's wonderful, just amazing to get short-listed for the Nebula and then the Hugo a few weeks later, but it feels a little fast! I know people who have whole successful careers and never get short-listed for those awards. Recently I was at a science fiction symposium at a university in North Carolina. The writer guests were me, Mary Doria Russell, and Octavia E. Butler. I'm sitting on a panel with Octavia Butler and remembering being twenty-two and discovering that there were Black science fiction writers, and finding all her work and reading it in about a month. I just devoured it. As a twenty-two-year-old, I hadn't even thought I could become a writer—and now I'm sitting on a panel with this woman whose work meant so much to me, talking about *our* writing! I mean, what do *I* have to say? Then I get home, and there's an email from a woman who says she's just read *Midnight Robber* and really liked it, and she's thanking me for it, saying she was on tour and it was wonderful to have this book to read when she wasn't performing. And she says, 'My name is Janis Ian.' I look up the name (which seems familiar), and she's the woman who wrote 'At Seventeen'—the song that got me through being seventeen! So it's been scary. It sort of feels like a set-up for *hubris*. I'll have to wing it, as I have been doing, figuring out what I'm doing as I go along. I also have a short story collection coming out in December. And in between all this, I'm taking an MA in writing fiction, just trying to put some academic credentials behind what I'm already doing so that I can perhaps have a bit of teaching income.

"I quit my job in 1998, and now I am officially a starving artist. But I won't go back to working full-time, if I can possibly avoid it. Being able to choose not only my own time but the work I do in that time has been very precious, so I'm hanging on to that as long as I can. I have become my own chief cook and bottle washer, even more than I ever was. So I' m not only having to find the time to write, I have to find the time do all the administrative stuff that comes along with that—dealing with people, deciding if I'm going to go to events or not. People are asking me to come to universities and talk to them, so I have to write presentations, that sort of thing. That's a whole new world, and totally different from the science fiction scene. I wear more hats now—that's what happened! And I'm beginning to discover why people who have successful creative careers sort of disappear from their friends' lives. I've come to the point where, if I want to pick up the phone to call a friend, I'm weighing the amount of time that's going to take from things I need to be doing in order to eat.

"I'm struggling to get the third novel written. Again, it's a conceptual leap for me. With my first novel, I got short-listed for the Warner Aspect First Novel Contest, and then had to write the thing. The second one is actually a novel I wrote first and had been shopping around unsuccessfully until I realized there was an essential problem with it that I would have to tackle before it was publishable. I always think I've given myself lots of time—'I'll take my time on this one.' Then, two months before the deadline, I'm still tearing my hair out. With the second novel, I found myself rushing again, trying to get the concepts into my head and turn them into the story I'd been working on. The day before the deadline for that one, I got a phone call from my mother's partner saying she was in Emergency with chest pains. I rush up to the hospital with my laptop. She's doing OK. So I'm sitting there beside my mother's bed typing away at the computer, making the nurses nervous because they're not supposed to let any electronic devices into the room. Once my mother was home and everything was fine, I emailed my editor saying, 'I'm going to be just a little late. My mother was ill and I had to be with her in Emergency, but it's OK, I took my laptop and kept working, and now I just need a few more hours.' I got back an email: 'You took your laptop to *Emergency*?!' Which is when perspective returned and I thought, 'Yes, that was probably a bit much.' But my mother, having been married to a writer, took it in stride.

"When I'm confined in an airplane for a few hours with nothing to do— that's when I have the time to do the research and get ideas for my stories. I don't fly very well—my inner ear *knows* there's nothing below me, so I have to take what Americans call Dramamine (and alcohol helps). What it means is, I'm essentially flying stoned and reading sociology and critical theory, and I get these wonderful ideas. Sometimes that's a very good thing.

"But with this third novel, it may have been a little too much of a good thing. What happened was, I had just won the Campbell, and my agent Don

Maass called to congratulate me. He said, 'Now's the time to write a new novel proposal.' I'd gotten this beautiful idea while I was flying, so I wrote it down and sent it to him. Betsy Mitchell at Warner Books said, 'Yes, we'll buy that.' Which, of course, now means I have to write the thing! It's going to be an historical fantasy. Three different time periods, three different countries—none of which I know anything about. I sold it in March of 2000, and Betsy said she'd like it in September. I said I didn't think I could do that, so now I have until next February to basically absorb a topic that I flunked out of in school. (I'm not a history person.) The title will be *Griffonne*—it's a grade of mulatto, and I am using these problematic words deliberately, because that's how Black people were thought of during slavery, the plantocracy 'graded' us racially according to how much white blood we had.

"The word *griffonne* has a feminine ending, so it's a clue that I'm talking about a woman. Women who were called *griffonnes* were very light-skinned and were supposed to be sexual temptresses for wealthy white men. I'm writing about the life of that type of woman, and about how gods come to be, and I'm using a couple of historical characters—Jeanne Duval (one of Baudelaire's mistresses) and a figure that the Catholic Church sometimes has been sure exists and sometimes says is just a myth: Gypsy Mary, Saint Mary of Egypt, the "dusky saint" who started her life as a prostitute in Alexandria. I'll try to get to France later this year. Haiti would be perfect, but I don't know if I'm going to get there. And I'm really finding out what a job it is to try to accurately represent someone else's culture. Before this, all my books had been written (to some extent, anyway) from the inside. I was never a working-class single mother like the protagonist of my first novel, but I knew the culture she came from and shared it. This time I am learning it as I go along, and just hoping that I represent it accurately—all three of them!

"Becoming an editor was something I had wanted to do for a long time. I have been a literary grants officer, a grants juror, a writer, a reader, so I've been on many sides of this multi-sided literary table, and I wanted to see what editing would be like. I hadn't really thought about it seriously though, because my hands had been full. Then I went to ICFA for the first time. I gave a reading, and afterwards was approached by the two men who had just started up Invisible Cities, a new press to publish essentially slipstream fiction. They asked me if I'd ever thought of doing an anthology, and I said, 'Yes, but I haven't figured out what on.' They said, 'Caribbean fabulist fiction.' I said, 'Sure. What's fabulist?' When I began collecting stories for that anthology, I was coming out of this very genre-based perspective of science fiction and fantasy, but now I was looking for Caribbean writers where there is not really a tradition of speculative writing. There's definitely a tradition of magical realism and fantastical writing, but not in the codified ways we're used to that let us know we're reading a science fiction or fantasy story. So I was looking for some sort of unholy marriage.

"I put out a call for submissions, and because I didn't have a lot of time, instead of making it an open call, I targeted people. I come from a literary background—my dad was an actor, poet, and playwright—so I made a list of people who I thought would be good based on what I knew of their work and sent them the call for submissions. Immediately I ran up against one of the problems of being an editor. I'd send out this wonderfully respectful letter to people who had been distant icons in my life for years. 'Dear Sir, Dear Madam, Would you care to consider submitting a story,' and I'd get an email back: 'Child, how is your mother? I used to change your diapers. Of course I'm sending you a story.' I'd read that, knowing I would not put every story I got into this anthology, and I would have to reject some of them. That was the first problem, having to say no to people who had been perfecting their writing since God was a boy. I thought of Ellen Datlow, and I was strong. How do you tell a famous writer that a story needs more work? You take a long walk around the block, you have a good stiff drink, you write the email seventeen times, and then you send it! I did that with one person, and he sent me another story which I *did* like, but it was a scary moment.

"There were some wonderful discoveries. I got a brand-new story from Kamau Braithwaite, one of the preeminent poets in the Caribbean today. I hadn't even asked him for a story because I didn't think he wrote fiction. I'd asked for contact information for somebody else. But Kamau sent me a piece I loved. It was the very first piece I got, and he set the tone for the whole thing, because it wasn't quite fiction and it wasn't quite a poem and it wasn't quite fantastical—in fact, it was a dream, which is a total no-no in science fiction and fantasy but which worked for what I was trying to do. An old friend of the family, who's again a poet, Pamela Mordecai, wrote her first science fiction story for the anthology, 'Once on the Shores of the Stream Senegambia,' and it got shortlisted for the Tiptree.

"A young man emailed me. I don't think he knew I was doing the anthology. He had just graduated from Clarion, and he was also from the Caribbean, and he just wanted to touch base. I asked him if he had a story, and he said yes he did but it needed cleaning up and he was in the middle of exams—I should have recognized this line since I've used it myself!—and he would send me a story the next day, which he did. I eventually bought it; of course, he'd had no story—he'd written it that night after speaking to me. That was

64 CONVERSATIONS WITH NALO HOPKINSON

Tobias Buckell's 'Spurn Babylon.' I got a story from Wilson Harris, who is our Delany in some ways, very complex and layered thinking processes. This story was incredible. He would build a metaphor out of a totally unexpected conjunction of ideas and take that metaphor and build on it, build narrative, so there was this architecture of story that you had to pay attention to, word by word by word. It asks a lot of the reader, and there's a big payoff when you pay attention.

"So eventually I had an anthology with wonderful pieces from a wide range of Caribbean writers. It got good reviews from *PW, Locus, Black Planet, SF Site, Library Journal,* and a few others. Not a lot of reviews, but all of them were quite positive. Three of the stories got short-listed for the Tiptree. One of them was mine, and I know the Tiptree Awards, so I knew what that signified. The other two short-listed writers I had to contact and start from the beginning: 'There was this woman, her name was Alice Sheldon . . . ,' and explain to them the wonderful thing that had just happened to them! And now the anthology has been short-listed for the World Fantasy Award.

"The editing experience must have changed my own writing, but I'm not sure how yet. The book just came out last November. One of the things it did for me was reconfirm the ways I've been using language, because in the science fiction community, what I'm doing with language is seen as new. In Caribbean literature, it's not new at all, so it was kind of like coming back home to have other writers who also work with Creoles and vernaculars.

"Looking at my own short fiction, I still need outside eyes. My collection *Skin Folk,* coming out in December, was a journey that dates back to the stories I was writing at Clarion and before. To go back into that place, only now you're doing it from a bit of distance, you can see more. I can start to see what my obsessions are, and some of them surprise me. Who would have thought I would have so many pregnant ladies? (Pregnancy's not an experience I've had or even particularly envisioned myself having.) And I can see how my work has changed, how things have gotten more sophisticated or have gotten more condensed to a technique. So it gives me a better sense of where I might want to start to push at my craft again to open it up, where I might be getting a little sketchy with the way I deal with my pet concepts, or where there are ideas I haven't tackled yet. So it is heartening. I wrote five new stories for the collection too. One of the stories I had in *Dark Matter* has been picked up for Suzy Bright's *Best American Erotica*—'Ganger (Ball Lightning)'—though I didn't think of the story as erotica. The few times it got reviewed, people either called it 'very sexy' or 'spine-tingling horror'!

The first piece of mine that I consider to be erotica is going to be in my collection. So I was creating new work for the collection at the same time as I was editing. No wonder it was so difficult!

"As far as I can tell, my readership includes science fiction and fantasy readers, Black readers, Caribbean readers, women readers, and kind of an intersection of any of those, *and* anybody else who just happened to pick the thing up because it looked interesting. People who like the Dillons' cover. . . . I was so happy to get that Leo and Diane Dillon cover! I had not known that Leo was from Trinidad. He'd read the novel before they did the painting and had sent word to let me know that he'd enjoyed the Carnival references. That meant a lot to have someone who knows the culture I'm talking about *and* knows science fiction. I've been buying books with Dillons' artwork for a long time.

"Things are moving so fast, it's a little like tumbling downhill, but I haven't bucked up against a rock yet. Still, it's not always easy. For instance, you have academics wanting to interview you, and they don't mean, 'Let's sit and chat,' they mean, 'I want to unpack your head.' When I'm working on a new story, I don't like to talk too much about it, but often that's what people really want to know—what's the new book about? And often the academic interview means they pose you questions they've thought about for a week or two, and you spend the next month answering! The plus to that process is that out of it you can get someone's critical analysis of your work, someone who's gone through it and looked for elements that either you were putting in there deliberately and hoped someone would recognize, or that you put in there unconsciously and didn't recognize yourself. That kind of critical analysis tells you a little bit more about your own writing.

"But going to an academic environment to speak to a bunch of people whose job it is to think critically about things, when I have no academic training, is daunting. I do not speak po-mo. My grasp of postcolonial is shaky. So people pose questions and I ask them to translate. So far, they've responded very well, for which I think I have to thank postmodernism. Yeah, I guess I have picked up a little of it along the way after all. Because of that notion that everything is text, that you could read the back of a cornflakes box and find something interesting you could say about it. I think I could get up there and sing 'The Good Ship Lollipop,' and academics would find something analytical to say about it! Well, come to think of it, so would I.

"The science fiction community is more familiar to me. I know the faces. I kind of know what the values are, while I don't quite get it yet for the academic field. I don't know how much of this happens to other science

66 CONVERSATIONS WITH NALO HOPKINSON

fiction writers. Because my upbringing has been so hybrid, people who understand one aspect of what I'm talking about miss the connections in the others. If you're writing a story, you can build those connections in: make up a world and inform readers about it as you go along. With interviews though, sometimes the mishearings are very instructive. One interviewer sent me a transcript afterwards so I could make corrections, and sometimes I said one word and she had heard another word entirely. The sentence that most sticks in my mind was where she had me saying, 'Judy Merril was a lesbian in those days.' I stared and stared at this sentence that I knew had not come out of my mouth. The only thing I could come up with that I might have said is a word I don't normally use: 'leftist.' To this day, I don't know what I actually said about Judy to that interviewer. But I'm glad that I caught her mistake.

"I've been finding the divisions between the science fiction community and the 'Other' (mainstream literature). We in SF entrench ourselves. Sometimes that's good. It's wonderful to be in a group of people where we share language and culture, but sometimes it limits us. There are more people out there reading science fiction than is apparent from attending cons, and it's a much more diverse community than I thought. What I find frustrating when I'm reading the work of a lot of beginning writers is what feels like a failure of imagination—not in the level of invention, which is often high, but in the scope people don't seem to think they can step outside the boundaries of the genre tropes, so much work by new writers is fairly awash in brave starship captains, sullen vampires, and raffish elves. The genre has room to be pretty damned big, and it changes, so pushing outside the tropes a little bit could mean the genre has to grow to encompass your vision, rather than you being constrained by the genre. We still have a certain conservatism, not just ideas but where you can go with those ideas. I find work that is horribly derivative of stuff that was original the first ten times it was done but has now degenerated into a blurry, comical shadow of its former self. We're taking the work of our classical writers and using what was *their* invention as the 'used furniture' of the genre, instead of thinking beyond that and inventing our own metaphors and our own ways of looking at the world.

"I used to hear more experienced writers and editors say, 'God, if I see one more story of the lost prince seeking to regain his throne, I'm gonna hurl,' and I'd think I hadn't seen that many. Well, now I have! I've developed a veritable allergy to orcs and blasters. We seem to have about five subjects on which we dote: the pseudomilitary federation, the animals who bond lovingly with humans, the predatory alien race, the magical alien race, and so on. But there's so much more out there in terms of the imaginative and fantastical world, and in terms of what we experience in our actual worlds and might want to explore in our fiction. And when writers are using the same settings over and over, they often don't feel very well imagined. People are doing things that people in those actual situations don't do. It just wouldn't work. I suspect the scholars are looking for a little more than the same old furniture—I think 'used furniture' is a Bruce Sterling term, and it's great. So maybe that's why more science fiction writers don't get a response from the scholarly community. I wish we would push our own boundaries a little bit more. There are some people who are already combining ideas in ways you don't usually see on the genre shelf. There always have been. I want more."

An Interview with Nalo Hopkinson

Diane D. Glave / 2001

From Diane D. Glave, "A Conversation with Nalo Hopkinson." *Callaloo* 26, no. 1 (2003): 146–59. © 2003 Johns Hopkins University Press. Reprinted with permission of Johns Hopkins University Press.

Diane D. Glave: How has your family, the environment/landscape, immigration, and the publishing industry influenced your work?

Nalo Hopkinson: My father was a writer, actor, and an English and Latin teacher. My mother worked in libraries most of my life, and still does. So basically my parents have influenced me by surrounding me with words and story. My brother Keïta does the same. Visual art is his medium; he paints his stories. So he brings a painterly analysis to my work that I find really helpful, because it's such a different mode of "seeing" than a text-based one. Being surrounded with text and story and people who make text and story was like an informal apprenticeship. I could have learned how to string sentences together without school; I only needed to pull a book down off the bookshelves at home or attend a performance by my father or his peers.

I suppose one writes about one's surroundings. Anywhere I've lived, either in the tropics or in North America, it's been primarily in urban settings. I write about urban environments a lot, but what I find is that North American understanding of my work sometimes focuses on the "tropical" part of my experience to the exclusion of the "urban" part. Though when I write, I don't think, "I'm going to reveal some significance about this urban setting." I just put the story in a cool place; for example, *Brown Girl in the Ring* (1998) literally begins on the corner of a street near where I used to live. I was walking home one night, passed a junkie in a doorway, and he mumbled at me, "We have to get to know one another better, you know." That is one of the first lines in *Brown Girl.*

Sometimes I'm asked how emigrating from the Caribbean to Canada has affected my writing. I should point out that I lived in the United States when

I was a kid, and returned to North America—Canada—in my mid-teens. Still, in some ways, winter feels like going into space. It's varying degrees of cold in Toronto for almost eight months of the year; you need a space suit for survival when going outside. It's like suiting up to go jaunt on the moon. No wonder I'm a science fiction writer. What really gets my goat, though, is the people who think it's totally acceptable when I say that it's cold to tell me that I really should go back to the Caribbean because people from hot countries aren't made for cold climates. That kind of rhetoric was at one point used by Canadian immigration to refuse entry to Canada of people who came from warm climates, on the grounds that they wouldn't be suited to work here. Conveniently enough, the warm country people also tended to be the dark-skinned people.

Because of my dad being a writer, he had a lot of colleagues who were also writers. Many of them moved here [Toronto], so when I began to think about writing too, I had quite a few literary "aunties" and "uncles" to mentor me. It's been wonderful. People have been very generous as mentors, both from within the Caribbean community and in the greater literary community. I think of writers like the late Libby Scheier, who was teaching creative writing in order to bring in some much-needed income but who, when I was just starting to learn, let me take her course and pay for it bit by bit. Money is time is bread to an artist, so I recognize the huge generosity of writers, artists, and scholars such as Roger McTair, Lillian Allen, Marlene Ziobrowski, Pamela Mordecai, Kelly Link, David Findlay, Jennifer Stevenson, Dora Knez, Peter Halasz, Debbie Donofrio, and Delia Sherman (I haven't named even half of them!), who take the time to read and critique my work, and of the critique group I belonged to here in Toronto: Bob Boyczuk, Brent Hayward, Laurie Channer, and Peter Watts. Writing to me feels like a conversation where one aspect of it is that writers respond to other writers. So when a writer's work either astounds or irritates me, it can impel me to create work that responds through my own personal vision. It's like I'm talking to that writer: agreeing, disagreeing, or just adding in my own two cents' worth. I like to quote other writers a lot, because so many of them have said things that have stuck with me. Bits of Kamau Brathwaite's poetry, for instance. Or I read the quirky, elegant stylings of a Kelly Link, so next time I write a story, I'm paying particular attention to my own stylings, or I read Patricia Powell's *The Pagoda* (1998) or Shani Mootoo's *Cereus Blooms at Night* (1996), and I learn something about how we gender bodies, and how that might operate from a Caribbean context and sensibility, so perhaps I write a story that also talks about gendering bodies.

In other aspects of the literary world I also lucked into Betsy Mitchell, the then-editor-in-chief at Warner Aspect, who wants to see more work by people of color in the genres of science fiction and fantasy. She didn't know when I won the Warner Aspect First Novel Contest that I was Black—I won it based on the strength of my manuscript—but when she found out, she was delighted. And as the editor-in-chief of Warner Aspect, she was in a good position to make that increased diversity start to happen. Generally I've found people to be enthusiastic and supportive.

Glave: Did Ursula Le Guin influence you in terms of feminist speculative fiction?

Hopkinson: Yes, Le Guin certainly did influence me. At different points in my life, she's come out with something that has affected my thinking profoundly. She's like Chip [Samuel R. Delany] in that. I like her wry sense of humor and her ability to reinvent herself, to look at her previous work and point out where she thinks her vision was lacking. Takes quite the personality to point out one's own flaws. My favorite novel of hers is *Always Coming Home* (1985). Its storytelling sensibility is non-narrative. Matter of fact, that sensibility is contrasted with that of the neighboring nation in the novel, who are belligerent conquerors who think of everything in terms of hierarchies: good, better; stronger, strongest. Le Guin doesn't demonize the people from that nation, though. A woman from the former society falls in love with a man from the latter, while their two nations are clashing. Beautifully done. And it has poetry and songs, and drawings. Feels more like non-Western approaches to art, which tend to combine the different artistic disciplines and media. She's like Chip in that.

Glave: How has Samuel R. Delany influenced you?

Hopkinson: Chip values language. He chooses every single word carefully in his pieces. And he valorizes people who we are taught to think of as beneath our concern. And he talks frankly about non-normative sexuality. He's such a relief to read because he talks about things that we aren't supposed to name, and says, this is no more aberrant than any other human behavior, and it's way more common than we like to pretend it is.

Glave: How do you identify, if at all, with the following literary genres: traditional speculative fiction primarily by and about white men, the African diaspora, feminist speculative fiction, Caribbean literature, and Caribbean fabulist literature?

Hopkinson: When you say "primarily by and about white men," I think of the 1950s pulp era of science fiction, which was largely a North American movement, and which in many ways was adventure stories for white boys with high tech toys. So often the women in those stories were June Cleaver from *Leave It to Beaver* or Mary-Ann from *Gilligan's Island*. Not by any means always, but often. Many stories of the type I'm describing seemed to be about traveling to strange and exotic new worlds and colonizing the natives. A good example of that kind of thing is the old *Tom Swift* novels.

When those people of color who are not interested in science fiction try to explain to me why that is, that science fiction trope of colonizing foreign races is the reason I hear most often. The good news is that science fiction and fantasy writers have a solid tradition of interrogating that very trope. So if Black readers are willing to take it on, I can point them to works such as Delany's *Neverÿona* series (1983), or Maureen McHugh's *China Mountain Zhang* (1992), or *Mission Child* (1998), or Octavia Butler's *Kindred* (1979), or Thomas King's *Green Grass, Running Water* (1993).

How do I identify with the works of African diaspora writers? Of course, I am part of that African diaspora that you just named. Well, since I'm primarily interested in works of the fantastic, my community there would be writers such as Charles Saunders, Nisi Shawl, Steve Barnes, Eric James Fullilove, Octavia E. Butler, Tananarive Due, Samuel R. Delany, Ama Patterson, Sheree Thomas, Ishmael Reed, Linda Addison, etc. Coming from the Caribbean, I bring a different experience to my writing but I see commonalities in the work of the North American writers I just named with the fantastical work of, for instance, Black Caribbean writers such as marina ama omowale maxwell, Kwadwo Agymah Kamau, Opal Palmer Adisa, Marcia Douglas, Glenville Lovell, and so on.

I always enjoy talking to the other Black writers who are navigating that hybrid space of genre-identified science fiction, fantasy, and horror, as well as being part of Black literary creation. But they are not my only touchstones. My bookshelves are filled with fantastical and speculative fiction by writers of all kinds of backgrounds, from all kinds of places.

What does my work have in common with the work of Black North American speculative fiction writers? For one thing, most of us seem to recognize the subversion of the dominant language that is code-switching. I think it was code-switching. Sometimes I code-switch, sometimes I don't. It depends on what the story needs. I don't remember if I said that in Caribbean literature and in other postcolonial (is that a bad word too?) literatures, use of Creoles has been part of the literary traditions for a while. I think I only cause raised eyebrows because I'm doing it to write science fiction and fantasy.

For example, even though the vernaculars into which we switch may differ from each other somewhat, we also share an understanding of the

72 CONVERSATIONS WITH NALO HOPKINSON

difficulties and the opportunities in science fiction. Speculative fiction is a great place to warp the mirror, and thus impel the reader to view differently things that they've taken for granted. It can also allow us in a way to accelerate or intensify the status quo, or follow it along a course of logical progression, and to look at what some of the results might be. An early example is Czech writer Karel Capek's story "*R.U.R.* (Rossum's Universal Robots)" (1920). Karel's brother Josef coined the term *robot* first used in that story, creating it from the root of the verb *to work*. At that point, robots didn't exist, but Capek's story envisioned how the increasing industrialization of factories might affect workers. Much science fiction does that kind of visioning. Employ that science fictional strategy from a Black perspective, and that act of visioning, of groping for a new perspective on the world and the people in it, takes on a very personal character. Samuel R. Delany has said, "We need visions of the future, and our people need them more than most."

Glave: Tell me more about how you subvert the dominant language in your novels by code-switching.

Hopkinson: I've only set out to do so in one novel, *Midnight Robber* (2000). It is in part *about* language, hence "Stolen," the poem by David Findlay, which starts it off: "I stole the torturer's tongue." I come out of a tradition of Caribbean writing where some of the writers have been deliberately claiming and valorizing Creole, so it's nothing new to me to write in Caribbean English(es). Part of what I was trying to do was to imagine how Caribbean culture might metonymize technological progress if it was in our hands: in other words, what stories we'd tell ourselves about our technology—what our paradigms for it might be.

The current metaphors for technology and social behaviors and systems are largely from Graeco-Roman mythology. We call our spaceships *Apollo* and our complexes "Oedipus." We talk about cyberspace. So I wondered what metaphors we [Caribbean people] would create for technologies that we had made, how we would think about those technologies. So in my novel *Midnight Robber*, the communication system which they use—a future equivalent of a telephone which includes sight and sound—I called a "four-eye," which is one Caribbean word for a seer, the being who can see into all dimensions and communicate with the beings there. The operating system, which governs a building, is called an eshu, who is a West African deity who can go everywhere, see everything

And I found that as I wrestled with the language usage in the novel (I had combined Trinidadian and Jamaican), I ended up with three modes of address: a more or less standard English for the narrative; one type of vernacular that was the mode of "pay attention"; and another that signaled opposition. So in the more standard English narrative I might say, "She went to the store," but in dialogue someone might announce, "Is to the store I going?" (getting your attention while they announce what they're going to do and emphasize where they're going); and if there was a problem with them going to the store and they were being defiant about it, they might say, "Me gwine a-store, seen?" There was also a notion in my mind about Rastafarian "dread talk," about the ways in which it uses language to reveal the rotten roots of some of our ideas: words such as "shitstem" for "system," for example, or "downpress" for "oppress." That kind of subversion and reinvention of the language causes the listener to pay attention, to examine the thing which the word identifies and to think about what that thing really signifies. It's a strategy very familiar to a science fiction writer! The runners in the novel (an oppositional underclass that the reader first encounters as rickshaw operators) are the community where I located some of that habit of verbal resistance.

Glave: Samuel Delany describes one of his experiences with racism in his essay "Racism and Science Fiction" in Sheree Thomas's edited volume, *Dark Matter: A Century of Speculative Fiction from the African Diaspora* (2000). To paraphrase, at a Readercon conference the planners seated you and Delany, the only two writers of African descent, at the same book-signing table with over eighty participants in attendance. He describes this incident as socio-visual racism. What did you think of this incident?

Hopkinson: At first, the incident felt only a little odd to me, but I didn't think much about it. I had just gotten off a plane, was high on the Dramamine I need to take to combat disorientation when I fly, and I was stoked to be sitting beside my idol at a table signing books. It was a first for me. But afterwards, I began to think more about it. As Chip says, the concom (convention organizing committee)—and I have to say that they are very diligent, hard-working, and accommodating folks whose convention I've always enjoyed—simply programmed us according to available time slot. It didn't occur to them that by putting me and Chip to sign together, they were unwittingly sending a message that the remarkable thing about us was our race, not our writing. It turned us into a curiosity. (Even amongst the con attendees who weren't writers, I only saw perhaps four other people who were visibly Black, and another scant handful of non-white folks.) Understand that the received wisdom in the science fiction community is that "race doesn't matter." In other words, they try very hard not to treat anyone differently because of their race. So in science fiction, you have a group of

74 CONVERSATIONS WITH NALO HOPKINSON

generally pretty forward-thinking people trying to be color-blind in all that they do so that no one gets excluded. That's very important. It's a political strategy aimed at inclusivity in a community where too many of us were judged to be the freaks in the regular world, and we don't want to ostracize anyone that way. So one risks feeling quite churlish in the science fiction community if one points out that while color-blindness is a step in the right direction, it doesn't erase racism. It was Chip who I heard say to someone at that same con the year previous, in response to her comment that she "just didn't see race," that if she couldn't see something that threatened his life almost daily, then she couldn't be a very good ally for him. In fact, I think it was at that same con that someone said to me that I was clearly "a product of the Chip Delany/Octavia Butler cloning program." That kind of thinking puts a primacy on our race over our writing that is not in the least color-blind. I don't think that the concom understood that, and I fear that they still don't, not entirely. I fear that the "lesson" they learned was never to put me and Chip together in their programming, rather than to look at the relative lack of racial diversity at many science fiction conventions, and see what strategies they can come up with to battle it at their own event. But I think things will change. The following year, they allowed me to organize a panel on how to make SF more diverse. The majority of people on the panel were people of color: writers, editors, and publishers in the field. A couple of carloads of folks of color attended that day's programming specifically because they knew that panel was happening. And for my first time at a Readercon, I got to see what the con might look like with a more diverse attendance. It brought tears to my eyes. The auditorium where the panel was held was packed, too, everyone participating, asking questions, making comments, talking to each other. Clearly, I'm not the only one itching to see more diversity in the field. We went right to the end of our hour. Then someone from the concom came in and told us that since they could see that the discussion wasn't over, they'd found us another room where we could continue as long as we liked, which we did. As Chip himself took pains to point out, the people on the concom are good, smart folks doing their best in a world in which racism is so pervasive that sometimes it's difficult to know how to subvert it. I hope that more good things will come of this.

And by the way, the man who made the cloning comment meant it as the sincerest welcome. He, like many science fiction readers, is actually happy to see more writers of color in the field. However, the way that he thought to express it clued me in that for some, our value may be in being "exotic," i.e., rare. In fact, a few years later, I was on a panel about the anthology *Dark*

Matter: A Century of Speculative Fiction from the African Diaspora, and in response to the moderator's question about whether *Dark Matter* heralded an influx of Black writers into the field, someone in the audience said, "If there gets to be too many of you, you'll become too common." If our value is in our rarity, there ain't no wave gonna happen. We won't get published in any large degree, because editors will be assessing our race ("Oh, got enough of those"), not the quality of our writing.

Glave: Would you like to share any other examples?

Hopkinson: Oh, I have tons of others. The science fiction community is part of the greater world, after all. Racism happens in the world. But I also have many examples of some very savvy support from lots of people in the community. For instance, as a result of the essay by Delany that you just cited, I asked Wiscon (the annual gathering of the feminist SF community) if they would consider starting programming of interest to people of color. Jeanne Gomoll and Debbie Notkin of the programming committee not only championed my request, but they helped me put together a committee of savvy people of color in the community to work on it. Out of that has come the Carl Brandon Society, which exists to promote knowledge about works of science fiction, fantasy, horror and magical realism by people of color. And for the past two years, Notkin, Gomoll, and others on the Wiscon concom have given unstinting and invaluable support to our fledgling society. Makes sense to me that it's found a home in the feminist community.

Glave: Some reviewers describe the language in your novels as Black vernacular, particularly *Midnight Robber*. Do you consider the use of the term *vernacular* archaic, racist, or colonialist since the term *vernacular* is generally used by whites to identify the language of what they consider primitive cultures?

Hopkinson: It's a term I use myself, because I haven't been given any education in the matter. Sometimes I use "Creole," and sometimes I'll be specific about where it's used, by saying, for example, "Trinidadian English." I guess that also tells you that English-speaking people should more or less be able to follow it. I do point out that these are languages with their own grammars and vocabularies. Sometimes I say "Nation Languages," after Kamau Brathwaite. The language in *Midnight Robber* can be tricky to describe, because it's a blend of Trinidadian and Jamaican. I also point out to people who try to exoticize Caribbean Creole that their cultures have their own vernaculars too; wherever they come from. When people who are not Caribbean read *Midnight Robber* out loud, they tend to slip into whatever vernacular they're comfortable with, be it New Orleans or Northern Ontario.

Glave: Should novels like Charles Johnson's *Middle Passage* (1990), Gloria Naylor's *Mama Day* (1988), Toni Morrison's *Beloved* (1987), and Toni Cade Bambara's *The Salt Eaters* (1980) appear in African American and African literature, or speculative fiction in the bookstores?

Hopkinson: I think that if the bookstores can afford it, those books should appear wherever they're relevant; on the literature shelves, and the Black folks shelves, *and* on the science fiction shelves. If the bookstores can't do that, the libraries can. The genre designations are only useful, near as I can see, for two reasons; one is for readers who like a particular type of literature to find more of that type, and the other is for the publishers to be able to signal to them that this is something they might like. It doesn't make sense to me that although William Burroughs is in the science fiction canon, Ishmael Reed is not.

When I read Toni Morrison's *Beloved*, she blends African American women's and speculative fiction literature, while making a powerful statement concerning racism and slavery in the United States.

Glave: How are you making similar statements concerning colonialism and imperialism by whites and revolution and rebellion by people of African descent in your fiction?

Hopkinson: It's a good question. I wonder how it's possible not to make the statement. As soon as you start describing a people or peoples, you find yourself talking about their history and their experience in the world. So if I have Caribbean people and Asian people and European and mixed race and what have you in my novels, they didn't get to be how and where they are in a vacuum. That's where that "color-blind" thing feels to me like it has only limited use. Overdo it, and your characters end up reading like brownwashed, white, middle-class, Western people. Like those dolls that they give black hair and dark skin to, but don't change any of their features. The day some of those black-painted dolls start showing up with high, round butts, full lips, and kinky hair, I might actually buy one for some child I know.

In *Brown Girl in the Ring*, my main characters started to come alive for me when I began thinking about what their family and economic configurations might be. It's common in working-class and poor Black communities for the mother to leave her child with her mother while she goes to seek her fortune elsewhere, because the area they're in is too economically depressed for there to be much opportunity. That's not exactly what happened with Ti-Jeanne's mother in *Brown Girl in the Ring*, but it was the thinking behind the way I set up her family.

Glave: So do you consider this in direct correlation with racism, imperialism, and colonialism?

Hopkinson: Yes, I do consider it in direct correlation. It's pretty clear that for the past 500 years or so, the fortunes of the European nations were built on the backs of Black and other racialized bodies. That has repercussions into the present day, because the work hasn't been done to even the imbalance in any big way. Black communities and countries still tend to be economically depressed relative to whites'. The same is true of the poorest white communities. They underwent their own kind of oppression. The first indentured labor to be shipped to certain parts of the Caribbean were poor Irish and Scottish people who became servants rather than go to debtors' prison. This stuff is complicated. It's not binary. The boundary lines between haves and have-nots are blurry. And power relationships and their historical effects infuse all our societies. For that to change, something fundamental about the nature of humans or human understanding has to change. That's one of the places where science fiction and fantasy can be really exciting, where they can envision how that change might come about. Octavia Butler talks about this a lot in her work.

In *Midnight Robber*, the reasons that Caribbean peoples have banded together, all the races of them (remember that the characters are mixed race, as most Caribbean people are), have everything to do with the history of exploitation that has made the Caribbean what it was. Ben tells Tan-Tan that when she wears the ship hat on her head (which was an ancient Carnival tradition); this time it represents a ship in which people made the crossing to the new land as free people this time, and of their own will.

Glave: As opposed to the Middle Passage which was forced? Or labor for Europeans in Africa, which again was forced?

Hopkinson: Yes. They've done so deliberately in opposition to the history of forced labor that decimated the native peoples of the Caribbean and press-ganged millions from Africa, India, China, and poor people from Europe. Even centuries later, those people on the new planet, even if they've managed to create a more equitable set of societies, won't have forgotten all their histories. Some of it will remain in stories, in sayings, in the names for things. It will inform the way that they see the world. Change will happen, but it will be slow.

Glave: Describe your experiences with the writing process, publication, and recognition concerning your early short stories and your first novels.

Hopkinson: I come from a literary family. My father was a writer, actor, poet, English and Latin teacher, and my mother is a library cataloguer. So the idea of being a writer was a familiar one to me. I took it on as an apprenticeship and sought out people willing to teach me. That has worked quite well. For one thing, I already had a community of writers—my dad's peers—who were willing to be mentors at one level or another. And it may have meant that I was a tad bit less defensive (not so's you'd notice, my writing group would probably say) in the workshopping process. I didn't feel that my words were sacrosanct, and I was willing to try to learn how to craft and re-craft them until they worked better. I took writing workshops. I had to borrow the money to attend Clarion, and there Bob Boyczuk from my writing group was a big help. He thought it important that I go, and he had some cash he could lend for a finite period of time, and he took the chance that I would pay him back. Which I'm happy to report that I did. Then I entered the Warner Aspect First Novel Contest once I was finished with Clarion. I was already starting to publish short stories, and I had already been a runner-up for an award for one of them. My novel *Brown Girl in the Ring* made an impression on Warner Aspect and on judge C. J. Cherryh, and so I won the contest. As fortune would have it, Betsy Mitchell, the editor-in-chief of Warner Aspect, was thrilled to learn after I'd won the contest that I'm Black. I emphasize, "after I'd won the contest," because I've heard people muttering that I only won it because of my race. The slush pile readers and the contest judge did not know my race. But once Betsy found out that I am a person of color, and she and Warner Aspect have since made a point of publicizing my work not only in science fiction and women's venues but in Black venues as well.

In other words, I've had a lot of support. I need to also mention the arts councils of the various levels of government in Canada, from whom I've gotten grants from time to time, which allowed me to write. Those grants are mostly adjudicated by juries of writers. They are the ones who decide which projects are worthy of support. People have generally been quite wonderful to me. In return, I try to push my craft as much as I can; try to make it as good as I can understand how to. It does feel like a type of contract. Financially, I'm in the same battle that most artists have when they try to make a living from their art, but I think it's getting better. And the payoff has been that I get to work at something about which I'm really passionate. That's wonderful, and very precious.

Glave: Was there an alternative to freelance work?

Hopkinson: Working a regular job that would have me crying every morning when the alarm clock woke me up, anxious during the days that I mightn't perform up to scratch, exhausted most evenings, and spending much of my life depressed and feeling trapped. That's what my life was like.

Glave: Would you share some examples of African and Caribbean spiritualism and healing in *Brown Girl in the Ring* and *Midnight Robber*?

Hopkinson: In *Brown Girl*, Mami Gros-Jeanne is a healer in Afro-Caribbean traditions. She's also a trained nurse. So she has both conventional medical training and the spiritual/herbal lore of the tradition of Orisha worship, which she practices. In Orisha, the spiritual is allied with the corporeal. Herbs and good food heal the body, but the mind and soul need to be taken care of, too. So while Mami is quite capable of making up a poultice to treat a skin condition, she can also lead a religious ceremony to heal the spirit, and she can cook up a mean pot of soup to nourish the body. She's a cranky soul though. She knows life's tough, and she doesn't want to coddle the people in her charge. So she's not as tender as perhaps she'd like to be with her grandchild. But there's a scene where she and Ti-Jeanne are fighting, or they would be, if either one of them trusted themselves to speak, and Mami wants to make up, but she's too proud to say so. So she cooks. She makes Ti-Jeanne's favorite dumplings. I think I said something like, "Cooking in the love she couldn't speak." Mami's a very familiar type of matriarch. My mother was quite in love with Mami. I think she really recognized what the character was about. Before she read each new chapter, Mummy would phone me to find out if anything bad would happen to Mami in the chapter.

In *Midnight Robber*, I haven't given an overt form of religion to the world I created. But I did build in spiritual beliefs. The operating system, the artificial intelligence that oversees each building, is called a house eshu, after the West African deity who was given the gift by the Great God to be everywhere and see everything.

Glave: How are Ti-Jeanne in *Brown Girl in the Ring* and Tan Tan in *Midnight Robber* influenced by a blend of traditional Caribbean culture and postmodern/apocalyptic technology?

Hopkinson: They live in modern worlds, in both books, which means they are both influenced by their histories and have access to certain technologies. Just like you and me. That feels like one of the things that's a conclusion for you as a scholar to draw, not one for me as a fiction writer to explicate. But let me take a stab. I don't think the technology clashes with the traditions. Human beings are really plastic, and we manage to incorporate both. Not perfectly, but somehow. Especially since they both come from us: the technology and the traditions. And eventually, any successful technology becomes traditional. Nobody thinks twice now about putting a telephone in a "traditional" novel.

Glave: Do people of color, particularly those of African descent, receive enough screen time and character development in speculative film and television? Are various stereotypes of African Americans such as the Sapphire (bitch), Mammy (nurturer), and Sambo (male/simpleton) reinforced?

Hopkinson: We're getting on screen more in those films, but there's room for a *lot* more. I think that'll happen when there are more Black directors making the stuff. As to stereotypes, I find that you get two types of representations: either the color-blind (i.e., white painted over) one, or the unconscious stereotyping. We still get cast mostly as also-rans who sacrifice ourselves nobly so that the hero—who just happens to be white—can save the day. I find I tend to pick the films to go see where they have let me know that women and people of color have prominent roles. SF film still mostly sucks, though, so there's perhaps another job there that needs to be done: to first tell good stories, not more bad westerns in space. One thing I liked about *Supernova* (2000)—which blew chunks otherwise—was that it had three characters of color, and only two of them bought the farm. Of course, one of them was the obviously gay character, and that would be a topic for a whole 'nother lecture. Angela Bassett gets to kick some serious butt, though. And then they decide she's too old to play Storm in *The X-Men* (2000). Too *old* to play a goddess? (Storm to me directly references Oya. I wonder if her creators know that?) And don't get me started on the DJ character in *The Fifth Element* (1997), with Bruce Willis and the skinny chick in Band-Aids! That film where the "universal language" sounds suspiciously Latinate in base, and the "perfect human" is European, and the fat lady is de facto a figure of derision. Chris Tucker is very funny, and I like that he performs Blackness in ways that would make my grandmother's hair fall out, but he played right into the stereotype there with the news announcer character. Can we give the bisexual brothers and the drag queens a break, please? A sexually opportunistic clown. I went to see that film with a Black bi man, and I was so embarrassed. Though, to be fair, Tucker's role in that film is a tough call. His character is the only one who's succeeding. He's being what he wants to be, he's out about it, he's having fun, and he's getting rewarded for it; his career is clearly on the rise, he seems to be rich, and he's getting lots of sex. That role was clearly a lot of fun to play. I like to think that the Bruce Willis character only queer-bashed him out of pure envy of someone who'd found a way to live the life that suited him.

I like some of the sensibility that Hype Williams brings to his music videos. Very science fictional, but simultaneously very grounded in a Black aesthetic. I absolutely loved the "fat chick in space" video he did with Missy

Elliott! And Julie Dash's *Daughters of the Dust* (1992) gives me hope for Black magic realism/fantasy on film. Wish she'd make more film. Years ago, she was supposed to be working on a cyberpunk video game with a Black female protagonist, but I never heard what became of it. I hear that she read *Midnight Robber* and liked it. Then there was Will Smith in *Wild Wild West* (1999), a total piece of fluff as a movie, but the really wonderful thing about Smith is that as soon as you put him in a film, there goes your color-blindness. Even the way he moves brings an African sensibility to the work. *Independence Day* (1996) had tons of problems, but Smith played his character as a Black man. He did the same in *Men in Black* (1997). One thing, though, the locus of the foreign "other" just moves to where Hollywood thinks we might be less likely to complain about it. Angela Bassett's character in *Supernova* survives, but the queer Black engineer dies to save them all. Killed by his own computer, the love of his life. Everyone else on that ship gets some nookie but him. And the old man, I think. In *Independence Day*, there was the nice gay man who just wants to be with his mother when the end of the world comes. He bites it. And there's an alcoholic who "redeems" himself by flying knowingly to his own death. And the stripper who can only be a good woman if she quits her job. Sheesh. If a film has deaths in it, somebody's got to be the cannon fodder, but one wishes they could try to give the impression of some roundedness of character to those people. They don't have to be caricatures.

Glave: What about the *Star Trek* franchise in television and film?

Hopkinson: It has actually tried from the beginning to include actors of many races. It suffers from that color-blind disorder, but they are there, and they often have prominent roles. Still, "Star Trek" does some weird things. The Ferengi as the Shylocks of the galaxy, and the Klingons (what a yucky name) as the galaxy's hoodies. At least, it looked to me as though in the beginning of *Star Trek: The Next Generation*, many of the actors who played Klingons were Black. I think they wised up, though. That doesn't look to be true any longer.

Glave: So they get no credit for an attempt at multiculturalism?

Hopkinson: Sometimes they earn the Jar-Jar Binks Medal of Shame. I suspect that the *Star Trek* franchise is responsible for the phenomenon I see in many aspiring science fiction writers, in which whole races of people (alien races, lest we draw the parallel too easily with human ones) get characterized with a single quality. Klingons are violent. Ferengis are avaricious. Except the humans, of course, who are fully realized characters. Aliens who break the pattern of their race to become more fully realized,

82 CONVERSATIONS WITH NALO HOPKINSON

become more human thereby and often abandon their cultures to live with humans and try to act more human. Data just wants to be a real boy. It reifies internalized racism in a really weird way. What's doubly weird is that the original creator of *Star Trek*, Gene Roddenberry, was one of the first people, if not the first, to dare to put a Black woman in a prominent role on a television series. He and Nichelle Nichols (who played Lieutenant Uhura) got so much flack for that decision, but they stuck with it. And her role as a competent ship's officer was played as a woman of African descent, not color-blind at all. This stuff is complicated.

Glave: Describe one of your most recent endeavors, *Whispers From the Cotton Tree Root: Caribbean Fabulist Fiction* (2001). What motivated you to edit and contribute to this collection?

Hopkinson: I'd been vaguely thinking about editing an anthology, but hadn't come up with anything concrete. Then I attended ICFA (International Conference of the Fantastic in the Arts), and after my reading, I was approached by the editors of Invisible Cities Press, which is a new small press out of Vermont. They asked if I'd considered editing. I said yes, but that I hadn't come up with a project that grabbed me. They said, "Caribbean fabulist fiction," and we were off.

Because of my father's connections, there were lots of writers I could approach for stories. But as to putting my own story in the collection, I was torn. Sometimes it's not a good idea to do so; it can look as though you as editor only cooked up the project to provide a vehicle for your own work. But Invisible Cities thought it would be a good idea for me to put my own story in, and a number of people convinced me that since there are at the moment so few Caribbean writers doing genre science fiction and fantasy, it would leave a gap in the collection for me to leave my own work out. So I had another editor look at my story and give me suggestions.

Glave: Yes, you needed to add something of your own because of your prominence in Caribbean fabulist fiction.

Hopkinson: I'm really wary of attaching superlatives like that to myself. Jamaica Kincaid is better known than I am. So is Antonio Benítez-Rojo and Wilson Harris, and Maryse Condé with her novel *I, Tituba: Black Witch of Salem* (1994). Tons of Caribbean authors who have written fantastical work are much better known than I am.

Anyway, I ended up with a dream roster of writers, from the doyens such as Benitez-Rojo, Wilson Harris, and Kamau Brathwaite, through writers who'd never tackled the genre before, such as Pamela Mordecai, to brand new discoveries such as Tobias Buckell, who had just graduated from

Clarion. Not to mention all the old hands: Jamaica Kincaid, Opal Palmer Adisa . . . and the themes of history and family and humor and language and race were so powerful throughout. I was very happy.

For me, so long as things defined in the real world as being impossible are in the fiction, I lump it all in as the type of work I like to read. I didn't know how the anthology would be received, because it's a hybrid: not quite mainstream literature and not quite genre fiction. But it's gotten quite good reviews, and three of the stories have been short-listed for the Tiptree Award, and the whole anthology was short-listed for the World Fantasy Award.

Glave: Would you like to share anything concerning works-in-progress?

Hopkinson: My third novel, *Griffonne*, could be labeled as historical magical realism. I'm having to do a lot of research, and that's slowing the writing down, but it's coming along. It's essentially about how Black women's bodies and sexualities get conceived in white imagination through the lens of slavery. And it's about godhood.

Glave: When will it be published? What period in United States or Caribbean slavery will you focus upon in the novel?

Hopkinson: For the purposes of this novel, I'm not making a difference among United States and Caribbean slavery. Same phenomenon played out different ways in different places. I may end up talking a little too about how slavery worked in ancient Africa. It's due at the publisher in summer of 2002, which means it'll come out in summer of 2003, if I turn it in on time. If I tell you the periods and places covered, it'll reveal too much about the novel, so I'll leave your curiosity piqued.

Glave: We don't often talk about African slavery. Africans enslaving Africans was a more benign process than European enslavement of Africans to some.

Hopkinson: No, we don't talk about it much. I don't know what'll happen when I hit that section of the novel. The character there isn't technically a slave, but a bondservant. Steve Barnes just released an epic novel, *Lion's Blood* (2002), which is an alternate history that's based in slavery in Africa. I think this is the type of work that Steve has been dying to write for ages. He says that when he first began writing SF, he didn't believe he could get anything like that published. I suspect he's correct.

A Conversation with Nalo Hopkinson

Jené Watson-Aifah / 2001

From Jené Watson-Aifah, "A Conversation with Nalo Hopkinson," *Callaloo* 26, no. 1 (2003): 160–69. © 2003 Johns Hopkins University Press. Reprinted with permission of Johns Hopkins University Press.

Jené Watson-Aifah: What made your parents choose to leave the Caribbean to move to Canada?

Nalo Hopkinson: My father had chronic kidney failure, and he was on dialysis. Daddy was working for the Guyanese government at the time, and they recognized that the kidney failure was killing him. Whenever he got ill, they would have to airlift him to Trinidad for treatment, and a couple of times he nearly didn't make it. What happened was that the Guyanese government made my father a diplomat and sent him here, because Canada has excellent treatment for this condition. I'm very aware of what a privilege that was for him, and so was he. He came to their attention because of the work he had done as an actor, poet, and playwright on an international stage. Other people in Guyana with his condition were dying of it, because there was no treatment available there.

Watson-Aifah: What lessons did your father teach you about craft?

Hopkinson: He taught me to keep working at it. I still haven't learned that lesson completely. On his deathbed he was working on a poem, so he taught me obsession, I would think. He would do things like take the family to a city in Ontario called Stratford, named after the Stratford in the UK. It is a place that runs plays all through the year. It specializes in Shakespearean plays, but it produces others as well. My father would take us up to Stratford in the summer, and as we were driving he'd have his copy of whatever Shakespearean production we were going to see. He'd reread the lines in the car on the way up while my mother drove. He already knew many of them by heart, because he'd acted in them, but he would still crib when we were on the way to the performances.

He taught me to have reverence for words and story, how the two flow together. And both my parents gave me a love of books. Between my father, the playwright, poet, and actor, and my mother, who still works in libraries, we had a house full of books and more entering all the time. Neither of them censored what I read. I could take anything off the shelves.

Watson-Aifah: Is your mother a librarian?

Hopkinson: She's a semiretired library technician. She catalogues books. I'm very careful about the distinction, since a lot of my friends are librarians, and they tend to be touchy about the difference. Librarians have master's degrees, while library technicians don't have to.

Watson-Aifah: What dreams did you have for yourself and the course of your life when you were growing up?

Hopkinson: I didn't know what I wanted to do. I loved reading, but writing was something daddies did [*laughs*]. The professions that the world was presenting all sounded really boring. If I'd had a sense of how many interesting careers there were out there, I'd probably have ended up doing something with my hands, ironsmithing and silversmithing, likely.

I actually didn't start writing until after my father died in 1993. I didn't think I could write and didn't dare think about it. It wasn't until Judy Merril was offering a science fiction writing workshop here in Toronto that I thought about trying it. Judy Merril was originally from the US, from New York. She was one of the most influential science fiction editors of her day and a writer herself, part of the feminist wave of science fiction. She was someone I greatly admired, and when I saw that she was offering a course I thought, "Well, I've always had this secret desire to write. Let me try." I had to write something to get into the workshop. Up until then, I had written some nonfiction and was publishing articles on health and fitness in a local Black newspaper, but no fiction. For Merril's class, I wrote a vignette that I had no idea what to do with. It was six pages long, and I hadn't a clue of how to finish it. I handed it in as it was and got accepted into the workshop, which never ran because there weren't enough people signed up. But Judy called the six of us who had gotten accepted and said, "Look, you really don't need to pay anybody to do this. You're all bright people. I'll show you how to workshop for yourselves." And she met with us once and showed us how. Then she said, "Go away now." And that's what we did, and a core group of us kept workshopping together for about six years. Those six pages became the opening for *Brown Girl in the Ring.*

Before that, I did what paid the rent. Except for hobby courses I took in jewelry-making and metalsmithing—two things I'd still love to be able to do if I had the time—I didn't feel any great calling to any particular career. I'd kind of fall from one thing to the other. I actually became a fitness instructor so that I could get paid to exercise. That really was the only way you could get me in a gym regularly. So, I didn't have any particular ambition to do any one thing. I might have tried to become a dancer, but when I was learning dance as a teenager, I was horribly shy, and people kept telling me that I was too fat. I believed them, too, and spent years dieting and hating myself. But now I look at pictures of myself then and realize that I was actually lean and muscular. Too robust for the aesthetic ideals of the forms of dance I was studying, but by no means fat. Now I am fat, and it gives me great glee to know that the first dance performance I ever did was a few years ago in "Indigo," a solo dance work created for me by a local choreographer specifically because he liked my grace and my curves.

Watson-Aifah: What part did or does formal study play in the development of your writing style?

Hopkinson: I didn't follow a course of formal study. I attended workshops, and while I don't think they had much to do with my style, they had a whole lot to do with my craft. I have recently completed an MA in writing popular fiction, but that's because I can't make a living at writing, and I need to be able to teach in order to supplement my income. Because I'm a published author who's working on my third novel, it was a little odd. I kept telling them they should just have given me the degree; I've done the work [*laughs*].

I don't think it's necessary for writers to take courses. But I think it can help to speed up the process of improving craft. And it can teach you that when you put words on paper they aren't anything yet. What you've done is gathered clay. You have to then be prepared to sculpt them and nip bits out here and tuck bits in there until you have something that's going to hold together. I find what happens with more inexperienced writers is that they fall into the trap of thinking that the very act of putting words on paper is complete, that everything is done once they've made that effort—and it *is* a huge effort, no mistake about that. But they sometimes convince themselves that their words are sacrosanct and shouldn't be altered in any way in the belief that they're somehow more true if they let the words remain the way that they come out. The words might be more true, but they're usually not good craft. I think it's a kind of terror that leads people to act that way. If they admit to themselves that their piece isn't holding together and needs a lot of work, then they might have to do that work. Speaking for myself, while I'm writing a piece, I'm almost always certain that my imagination isn't up to the task I've set for it. It can be scary.

Watson-Aifah: Outside of the realm of literature, who are some people—artists and others—who guide you along your path? What do you draw from them?

Hopkinson: My brother, Keïta, who is a painter. He knew he was going to be an artist when he was four. Work is life to him. When my brother critiques my work, he does it in terms of form, color, light, and texture. This gives me a whole new insight into whatever I happen to be working on. Keïta is one of my best cheerleaders. He's very enthusiastic about what I've done and what I've accomplished. He's always trying to get the word out about me. I remember him phoning me once from his gym, which is fairly close to where I live, to tell me that he'd been working out and bumped into Gregory Hines. Keïta went up to Mr. Hines and spoke to him, but instead of bringing up his own work, he pulled out pages from my website that he carries around in a knapsack. And that's what he gave to Gregory Hines. Keïta is six feet tall, can lift a truck with one hand, and loves me dearly, as I do him. So, he's one person.

And I've mentioned my writing group. We haven't met for about a year and a half now, but from 1993 on, we motivated each other. When I was writing *Brown Girl in the Ring*, trying to finish it in two months, they were workshopping it for me every two weeks. When I thought I couldn't do it, it was Brent Hayward from the group whose confidence kept me going. Samuel Delany has always, whether he knew it or not, been a mentor of mine. He was one of my teachers at Clarion. Having a Black, gay man who is courageous enough to incorporate his life, his philosophy, and his thinking into his writing, and to make that writing science fiction, was very affirming. He continues to be very supportive. Actually, all of the six writers who were at Clarion when I was—Karen Joy Fowler, Joe Haldeman and his wife Gay, Pat Murphy, Nancy Kress, Tim Powers—continue to nudge me along in their own ways. People ask what's the value of doing something like Clarion. Among other things, you get sort of ready-made mentors. They keep an eye out for you. Clarion was a place where I was introduced to a community of writers.

A lot of my father's peers are here in Toronto, friends of his who are writers or other types of artists. They're like artistic aunts and uncles. They read my work and offer suggestions and encouragement. They invited me to participate in conferences and workshops before I even dared to think of doing so. I could spend hours naming them. Fine writers like Pamela Mordecai, Olive Senior, Lillian Allen, and Roger McTair have been amazingly supportive.

Watson-Aifah: What process do you go through in delivering your projects from idea to finished product? Does it still feel like you're "wrestling a mattress" when you're in the throes of piecing it all together?

Hopkinson: [*Laughs.*] Yes, I do. Particularly with novels, because it's so hard to see clear to the other end. You have so many threads that you're trying to weave together, and it's so easy to drop one—or twelve—and forget to pick them back up. I thought it would get easier. Suzy McKee Charnas tells me that it never gets any easier. With each one I think I'm pushing myself a little bit more. I'm now on my third novel, *Griffonne*, and it's hell. I'm having to do a whole lot of historical research. I failed history in school. I was basically interested in English and French class. Everything else I kind of stumbled through. Now I'm having to get serious.

Watson-Aifah: Does your mother help you do your research?

Hopkinson: Certainly. She looks out for information and so does my brother. I also have my good friend Laurel Taylor who is a librarian and a science fiction reader. I have actually been helping my mother lift the books that she's cataloguing at home now. I come across really neat stuff that way.

Watson-Aifah: Describe your typical day of work.

Hopkinson: I wake up very early, mostly because I don't sleep very well. If I could sleep longer I would. I'm usually up between seven and nine; I sit at the computer, but I'm not writing. I could happily spend a day browsing the internet and answering email. At some point during that day, I will try to force myself to write, and a couple of days out of every week it actually happens. This is further complicated by the fact that I am now surviving as a freelancer, so there are always a million things I could be doing to immediately put food on my table and keep a roof over my head.

Part of the reason, too, that I took the MA was so that I had university deadlines to meet every month. So even though I didn't have to hand the novel in to the publisher until six months after my graduation, I had to hand in a certain number of pages to my mentor and the people in my academic critique group. That kept me producing regularly. When I have deadlines, I put myself on a schedule and manage about half the time to stick to it. Then I'll write about a page or two per day. People who can churn out four or five pages a day, who are happiest when they're writing, make me very envious. Octavia Butler talks about writing every day. She's in her fifties, so maybe in about ten years when I'm that age, I'll be that disciplined. Right now, it's always a battle trying to get myself to open the file and write. I've tried a number of tricks, like telling myself that I can't open email until I've written the other things. My brain fools me, and I find myself in the email program downloading new messages before I'm even aware that I've clicked the mouse button. I continue to be amazed that I get anything written at all. My process is to just keep returning to the computer until writing happens.

If I do a paragraph and that's all that's coming, I consider myself to have had a productive day. Enough of those paragraphs adds up to a story eventually.

Watson-Aifah: Are there ever times when your attempts to integrate your academic training with traditional storytelling techniques collide?

Hopkinson: It might if I ever had a lot of academic training, but I don't. None of the workshops I took were degreed. Again, the MA I recently received is called Writing Popular Fiction and is deliberately non-academic in approach. They're not teaching an intellectual approach to it; we learn through writing. So, no it's not been a problem. In fact, I find that when my work is being analyzed by scholars and they ask me about the postmodern, postcolonial this, that or the other, I have no idea what they're talking about [*laughs*]. I have them explain in simpler terms; otherwise, we sit there and blink at each other. I was interviewed by a woman scholar last week and the whole interview was very difficult. She kept asking me things like, "Place yourself in the historical context of feminist science fiction and history and give me some examples." That's an essay question! I don't set out to place myself in any context when I write, when I'm trying to tell a story. Critics and scholars get to do that. I don't get to be that presumptuous. Besides, I don't know those words [*laughs*]. Actually, now I'm learning them because I have to. I had no idea what postcolonial was supposed to mean up until a year or two ago. And I still don't really know what *postmodern* means. I throw these words around, but I don't really know what I'm talking about.

Watson-Aifah: Many women suppress the impulse to write for a living because they think that they have nothing to say. I read on one of the pages of your website that you felt the same way. How did you move past this?

Hopkinson: That's a hard question. I think simply by wanting to and by putting myself into situations where I had to produce. For example, entering a contest so that I would have a deadline or enrolling in an MA program put me in a position where I had to write and people helped me do it. During the first three years of being in the writing workshop initiated by Merril, our group met diligently every two weeks. Every two weeks I had to have something in, had to have something on paper. I actually couldn't do that now because my schedule has become insane.

Then I went to Clarion. I didn't really have the money to do it, but Bob Boyczuk from my writing group had a bit of cash that he was willing to lend me. He said, "Look, I need you to repay this, but I think it's important that you go." I wasn't sure that I'd be able to repay him. I wasn't even sure how I was going to eat while I was there. All I knew was that I owed this friend of mine a couple thousand dollars, I wasn't working for six weeks, I couldn't write, and I was terrified. During the first week of Clarion, Joe Haldeman and his wife Gay were teaching. Joe would ask the class what we wanted him to talk about, and one day someone said, "Writer's block," and he gave a lecture on it. I don't really believe in writer's block, but I knew I wasn't writing. He said, "Probably the worst way to deal with writer's block—and I don't recommend it to anyone, though many people do this—is with drinking." I said, "Ha! I can't do any of those other high-flown things, but I can do that!" [*Laughs.*] I had a couple of beers—I can't even drink very well, I had like two or three beers—had a nap, woke up, and wrote the most terrifying story I've ever written in my life. It scared me. But finally I was writing. Then about halfway through Clarion, I learned that a grant for which I'd applied had come through. That helped me make up for the cost of the program.

I've continued to be productive by giving myself deadlines. Or rather, when a publisher agrees to buy a novel, I realize a few months before the due date that I have to produce a manuscript and had better get on with it. Bit by bit, I'm getting better at writing. At least now, I feel more comfortable with the notion that I have things I want to communicate. That's no longer a problem. The struggle remains in figuring out how to do it.

Watson-Aifah: How do family responsibilities or personal life coexist in your life?

Hopkinson: I date artists. They understand. That makes it easier. As for my family, my mother lived with a writer and my brother is an artist. I have neither chick nor child, by which I mean that I don't have children. I don't even have a cat. The plants—bless them—mostly manage for days on end without my attention. Every few days, I look up and one is wilting and I water it. They keep growing somehow. I have a have a sweetie who waters them when I'm away. Other than that, many of the people in my life are also creative people or freelancers. They understand the vagaries of income, energy, and crazy obsessions that one lives with. I remember one day Bob Boyczuk phoned me and said, "What are you doing?" I said, "Washing dishes." He said, "You must have a deadline, then." And I said, "Shit, how did you know?'" [*Laughs.*] I live in an appallingly untidy apartment. I step over bits of paper and discarded clothing until I can't stand it anymore. I don't have people I have to be responsible for in such a way that would require me to establish a routine or do the dishes regularly. I have every admiration for people who do, but I'm not rushing to it myself. This lifestyle is what I would choose regardless. I have a very strong community around me, and the way I conduct my daily life is pretty much up to me.

Watson-Aifah: I think that books like Claudia Tate's *Black Women Writers at Work* are important but there aren't many like it on the market. And why do you think that relatively few women writers of color write memoirs or works about their creative processes? Do you plan to?

Hopkinson: I might, but at this point in my career it's too early for anyone to really care. I know there are individuals out there who would care, but I really don't have a substantial enough body of work or a name recognizable enough to make a publisher care. And I'm at a stage now where I really have to think about that kind of thing. Can I take up a project that will require two years of my life, but will not feed me? It's probably a problem for a lot of writers, but I think this is true in different ways for Black women writers, many of whom do not have their lives arranged the way I do. Many of us are supporting families and have to keep doing what will make the money flow. I know that Black women writers are starting to publish memoirs and how-to books. Jewell Parker Rhodes has a wonderful novel called *Voodoo Dreams*, about the life of Marie Laveau. She recently came out with a manual for Black writers called *Free Within Ourselves*. This might be what we, people who fear that we shouldn't dare be writers because it's not a "serious" profession, need. I can't think of anything else out there, so perhaps you're right. One can find individual essays. Ursula Le Guin has compiled collections of her essays, and I find them inspirational. I had never thought about it. There are enough people writing about the process of writing, and there are enough Black women writers out there teaching writing, because again, that will pay the rent.

We can get the guidance if we look for it. For example, when I started taking workshops, often I couldn't afford it. Often they were being taught by people like me who were poor. I remember Libby Sheier—a Jewish woman, not a Black woman—who was a poet in Toronto who taught writing workshops to make ends meet. Rest her soul; she died last year. I wanted so badly to take her course, but I couldn't afford it. She asked, "Well, look, can you pay me in installments?" And she let me pay her fifty dollars a week. I knew she couldn't afford to wait for that money, but she did. But, if I had just said nothing, if I hadn't asked Libby for what I wanted, then I would not have gotten to take a workshop with her. I wouldn't be at the stage that I am today.

Also, Lillian Allen was one of the first Black women writers to encourage me in not just the craft, but also the practicalities of writing. She was the one who said, "How come you've never applied for a grant?" Or, "You've gotta charge what you're worth, girl."

Watson-Aifah: In your essays, you write about subverting the genre of science fiction/fantasy. Tell me how your perspective differs because of your specific type of hybridity. And in what ways do you see the imagery and themes of your work as being the same as what is being produced by other writers of color, specifically within the African diaspora?

Hopkinson: The similarities start with a love of language and a love of story. The kind of signifying that I do as a Caribbean person is very different from what a Black American person would do, but I recognize that it has the same historical roots. I recognize it when it comes from them and they recognize it when it comes from me, even if we don't have a language or immediate culture in common. We recognize the roots that it comes from. There is a similar aesthetic. You can really see this when you read works like *Dark Matter: A Century of Speculative Fiction from the African Diaspora.* There are Black writers from the US, from the UK, from the Caribbean, [and] there are connections between our work. Part of the issue with being a Black person writing in a genre that still has few Black people writing in it is that there are genre conventions which have been established by a writership that largely does not share your cultural references. Whether it's romance, mystery, fiction, or literary fiction, one has to learn how to read the conventions and protocols in each genre to spot some of these similarities. For instance, in science fiction, if I say, "She flew across the room," I may mean it quite literally, while in literary fiction you know that this is a metaphor. And as a Black, Caribbean person, I have my own cultural references for the magical or the futuristic. I share some of those with other Black and/or Caribbean writers, even if they don't write science fiction and fantasy. When I put out the call for entries for the anthology of Caribbean fabulist fiction that I just edited, and I used the term *science fiction*, the writers I was approaching didn't necessarily understand what I was looking for. Then I translated the term, and explained that stories about duppies, rolling calves, and such could be considered fantasy/science fiction/magic realism. After that, potential contributors would say, "Oh, OK? I've got a ton of those. You want to talk about the Orishas? Yeah, I can do that."

Watson-Aifah: An image that I see frequently in Black women's fiction, including yours, is that of the root-working grandmother. Her presence suggests a lot about ritual tradition and family. What does this figure mean to you?

Hopkinson: It surprises the shit out of me to find that I have written so many stories with grandmothers in them! I only have one grandmother, and I didn't meet her until I was thirteen or fourteen. I only see her once a year now. But there are these grandmothers front and center in my short stories "Riding the Red" and "Greedy Choke Puppy." And you're right, there is this notion in Black women's fiction that people don't tend to operate singly. Our families are important. My work does not reinforce that whole notion of the science fiction hero who goes off by himself and saves the world. My work is woman-centered because that's what I know, and that's what I grew up with. My protagonists tend to have to build community around them before they can do anything. Also, I think that both young and old people tend to be somewhat outside the loop. Most of them are not holding down jobs or raising children, and they tend to be sidelined by the rest of society. So, it feels natural to me that children and elders might be in cahoots in going out and having adventures together while everyone else is busy with the dailiness of life. I think that's the real reason why I've written so many stories with grandparents and young people in them.

Watson-Aifah: And particularly in the case of *Midnight Robber*, there is this strong element of spirituality, this sense of there always being a world beyond the one that we can see.

Hopkinson: Yes, I did that a little in *Midnight Robber*, more metaphorically than in the actual world of the story. But it is there. I find that I can't separate a spiritual life from a technological life. When *Brown Girl in the Ring* came out, a lot of people who are used to conventional science fiction asked me why I was mixing science fiction with fantasy. My answer has always been that that's what you do in everyday life. You might be a heart surgeon and deal with impressive technology and biology, but you might say a prayer before you cut into somebody. You don't leave out that hope that there is something bigger than you that can help you along. I think that much of the Western world is sort of embarrassed, reluctant to talk about the unseen.

Watson-Aifah: Why and for whom do you write? What responsibility do you feel to your audience?

Hopkinson: I'm still trying to figure out who my audience is. I'm meeting them one person at a time. When I first began to workshop and present these really weird stories to my writing group—all of whom were white, middle-class Canadian men—Bob asked me, "Who are you writing this stuff for?" My first response was, "Me!" I was trying to incorporate the things that I had been longing for and hadn't been able to find. I loved fantasy, and I was reading ones that used folklore from everywhere around the world except where I was from. I loved science fiction and these fantastic worlds it creates and the ways in which it speculates on our world and social systems. But, the characters' lives bore little resemblance to mine, their bodies looked nothing like mine. So I began writing as an act of faith, hoping that if I once wanted to find this kind of writing, there were other people out there who would find what I did interesting. Maybe it would fill a gap for them in some way or another.

There are a lot of things I try to do. One is to represent bodies that aren't conventionally beautiful. I try to have lots of good-looking, thick women and men in my writing [*laughs*]. I have one story about a man and a woman who are lovers. They're both chunky, they're both big and Black and strong. The main character enjoys that about herself and her lover. I try to represent how we Black women deal in the world, how we often try to save the world with babies on our hips and family at home that we have to look after. I try to make sure that I don't have to default to straight, white, middle-class values as the only good way to be. I try to throw in surprises. I think there are many types of Black lives that don't get talked about. We are as complex as any culture on this earth. We're trying so hard to get the rest of the world—not even so much the rest of the world, but the white world—to recognize that we are respectable, deserving human beings. As a result, we only show a tiny part of ourselves. One of the many things I've learned from Samuel Delany is that we must have the courage to show more than that.

"Making the Impossible Possible":
An Interview with Nalo Hopkinson

Alondra Nelson / 2002

From Alondra Nelson, "An Interview with Nalo Hopkinson, in *Social Text* 20, no. 2: 7–113.
Copyright, 2002 Duke University Press. All rights reserved. Republished by
permission of the copyright holder, Duke University Press. www.dukeupress.edu.

Alondra Nelson: I've heard you describe your writing as speculative
fiction. Why do you prefer this description of your work to having it defined
as science fiction, for example? How do you define speculative fiction and
how did you come to write it?

Nalo Hopkinson: I don't know that I prefer speculative fiction (spec-
fic) as a description. If I've said that, it would depend on who asked me the
question and why. To those who insist that my writing isn't science fiction, I
say, yes, it is. To those who insist that it isn't literature, I say, yes, it is. When
I'm simply asked what I write, I use whatever definition I think the audience
will either understand or be curious about. As to my definition of spec-fic,
I describe it as a set of literatures that examine the effects on humans and
human societies of the fact that we are toolmakers. We are always trying to
control or improve our environments. Those tools may be tangible (such as
machines) or intangible (such as laws, mores, belief systems). Spec-fic tells
us stories about our lives with our creations.

I write science fiction and fantasy (and some would say, horror) because
that's what I read. Most of the fiction on my shelves is speculative or
fantastical in some way, and always has been. As a young reader, mimetic
fiction (fiction that mimics reality) left me feeling unsatisfied. The general
message that I got from it was: "Life sucks, sometimes it's not too bad,
but mostly people are mean to each other, then they die." But, rightly or
wrongly, I felt as though I'd already figured that out. I felt that I didn't need
to read fiction in order to experience it. But folktales and fables and the

old epic tales (Homer's *Iliad*, for instance) felt as though they lived in a different dimension. It wasn't until later that I would learn words such as "archetype" and "metaphor" and begin to figure out what attracted me to Anansi stories and fantastical tales. As a child, I just vaguely knew that I wanted stories that transcended the quotidian "life sucks and then you die." Call it escapism, because at some level it is, but I think that goes back to human beings being tool-users. We imagine what we want from the world; then we try to find a way to make it happen. Escapism can be the first step to creating a new reality, whether it's a personal change in one's existence or a larger change in the world. For me, spec-fic is a contemporary literature that is performing that act of the imagination—as opposed to the old traditional folk, fairy, and epic allegorical tales, which I think of as historical literature of the imagination. And here I need to qualify, because all fiction is imaginative and much of it transcends the quotidian. I'm just trying to identify science fiction/fantasy/horror/magical realism as fiction that starts from the principle of making the impossible possible.

AN: Speculative fiction is an apt umbrella description of your work because it is a genre that, as you say, comprises other genres, including sci-fi, fantasy, fable, magic realism, and horror. Your writing seamlessly interweaves the conventions of many of these subgenres. *Midnight Robber* contains elements of sci-fi (the omniscient neural network or internet that you call Granny Nanny), fantasy (Tan Tan takes up residence in a magical world of tree-dwellers), and horror (there is a sinister or melancholy tone to the story as well); while *Whispers from the Cotton Tree Root* is divided into themes that range from "Crick Crack" to "Science" and "Dreams." Is this alchemy of conventions common among other writers of genre fiction? Do you think that the anxiety to classify your work stems from this blending of themes and styles?

NH: Well, first I want to say that when people have said that there are elements of fantasy to *Midnight Robber*, I've had to wrack my brains to think what those might be. I finally decided that it was the three "folk" tales that form the triple spine of the book. I wouldn't have said the beings in the tree; I tried to make them as scientifically plausible as I know how, which admittedly isn't much!

For all that I've been reading science fiction and other fantastical fiction since I was a child, I didn't grow up in a SF community. No such thing in the Caribbean. I began attending cons [science fiction conventions or community gatherings] regularly in 1996. I didn't know that there was an ideological debate between science fiction and fantasy until I was preparing to attend the Clarion Science Fiction and Fantasy Writers' Workshop at Michigan State University in 1995. That was when I figured out, from things my fellow students were saying, that there is and has been a bitter pitched battle between the two for decades.

I guess that fusion of the genres is characteristic of my writing if only because I'm not very good at remembering to tell the genres apart. But too, when my work is coming from a Caribbean context, fusion fits very well; that's how we survived. We can't worship Shango on pain of death? Well, whaddya know; he just became conflated with a Catholic saint. Got at least four languages operating on this one tiny island? Well, we'll just combine the four and call it Papiamento. Can't grow apples in the tropics for that apple pie? There's this vegetable called *chocho*, and it's approximately the right color and texture and pretty tasteless; add enough cinnamon, brown sugar, and nutmeg, and no one will know the difference. It's a sensibility that I'm quite familiar with and enamored of (and it's great for writing postapocalyptic cities). Other writers do it, though; take Ian McDonald's *Terminal Café*, for instance. And people are still arguing over whether Karen Joy Fowler's *Sarah Canary* is a historical piece or a first contact story.

I do get wary of getting typecast. The Caribbean still has this allure in this part of the world of being an "exotic" tropical paradise, so the setting and the language in some of my stories seem to overshadow everything else in some reviewers' eyes, and that's mostly what they talk about. One reviewer stated that *Midnight Robber* was light beachside reading, and I really wished I could ask him about what it was that he saw when he read the book. Not that I minded the review, which was positive in its own way, but I'm still struck sometimes by the difference between what I think I've written and what readers get from the text, and sometimes I'd like to know more. Every writer has to struggle with that. At a con a few months ago, a woman had all kinds of questions for me about things she hadn't quite followed in the book, although she'd enjoyed it. It was as much a learning experience for me as it was for her; I got a glimpse for a moment into how she had interpreted elements of the novel that I had meant to be understood quite differently.

In December 2001, my publisher released a collection of my short stories. When they showed me the cover that they wanted to use, I was very pleased, because it's gorgeous work. It shows a young Black woman dressed in a loose white dress and head wrap that hints that she's going to some kind of Orisha ceremony. She's standing at night among the tall canes of a tropical sugar cane field. She's carrying a lit candle, and beside her at head height is a snake twined around one of the canes. After a few days of exulting over the cover, though, it struck me; most of the stories in the collection are set

98 CONVERSATIONS WITH NALO HOPKINSON

in Toronto! I had hoped it would have a cover that was sort of Michael Ray Charles meets cyberpunk. I pointed the Toronto settings out to my editor, and she said she realized that, but that my readers were used to the kind of cover image she had chosen and to the occasional dissonance between it and my content. It's odd. That kind of cover worked very well for *Midnight Robber* (and it was a chance to have a cover painted by the dynamic duo of Leo and Diane Dillon). We'll see what it does for *Skin Folk*.

AN: What type of extrapolation do the conventions of speculative fiction allow that is not allowed the realist or social realist fiction writer?

NH: If I were to write mimetic fiction, I'd be to some extent limited by what is known of the world. If my realist character were a young, straight, fat, middle-class woman living in North America, we can all pretty much guess at the types of struggles she might have around body image and developing as a sexual person. We could also probably come up with a similar list of ways in which she could try to resolve those problems. What would make the story unique are the particular events and texture of the life that I would imagine for that character.

However, in fantastical fiction, I can directly manipulate the metaphorical structure of the story. I can create a science fictional world in which relative fatness or slimness has about the same significance as eye color, but only persons under five feet, five inches are considered beautiful. I can show people desperately trying not to grow taller and taking pills intended to cure them of the "disease" of tallness, which is considered to be epidemic in their society. I can show people who develop emotional disorders related to being tall. Another thing I might do is to create a fantastical world in which my fat protagonist magically becomes thinner in order that she can convince people to ignore her, so at the moment when she finally would be considered beautiful, she disappears. (Hey, maybe I should write that. No, too late now.)

In other words, one of the things I can do is to intervene in the readers' assumptions by creating a world in which standards are different. I can blatantly show what values the characters in the story are trying to live out by making them actual, by exaggerating them into the realm of the fantastical, so that the consequences conversely become so real that they are tangible.

AN: Writers of speculative fiction may create new metaphors, but the genre is nonetheless filled with characters who are thinly veiled metaphors for racial others—monsters and aliens, for example. How did you reconcile your affinity for the genre with its tacit racial politics?

NH: In part by writing from within the realities of racialized others. We will inhabit the future, but what will that future mean to us who have a history of being racialized? And we certainly inhabit a metaphorical landscape, but how do our histories and our experiences in the world lead us to paint that landscape? A friend recently took me to a landmark, a little stone pillar sunk into the ground at the waterfront of an American city. She said, "This marks the spot where this land was discovered." A little taken aback, I said, "You mean, it marks when the white people first came here?" She blinked and replied, "I guess, but we call them pioneers." Well, OK, but they aren't the discoverers of that land. They aren't its first pioneers by a long shot. It had already been discovered and inhabited centuries before. What would the story of that second discovery be if told from the eyes of the previous Native inhabitants? For that matter, never mind the white landing, what would the story of the first discovery be—the centuries when Native peoples were taking up residency on Turtle Island? That's an epic in itself, with its own tales of loves and hatreds and battles and treaties. So another strategy I have is to sometimes refuse to write yet another plea to the dominant culture for justice, and instead to simply set the story of the "Othered" people front and center and talk about their (our) lives and their concerns.

I look at the publishing industry, and for a while it seemed that the way to get published and recognized as an important Black author was to write about the horrible things that happen to Black people living in a system that despises us for our skin color. And I think it's vitally important to write about that. We need to continue writing about it; in fact that's one of the things that the novel that I'm currently writing is about. But if that's all that's getting published, I think I'm justified in suspecting that the industry was and is eroticizing Black people as victims, as though that is our value to the world. However, now I'm also starting to see more "Black" novels that write about the full lives of Black people, everyday racism included.

AN: *Midnight Robber* begins with the poem "Stolen" by David Findlay, which repeats the phrase, "I stole the torturers tongue." How was this poem intended to reflect on the novel?

NH: I kind of hate telling people that I planned for them to think anything in particular in response to something I've written. For one thing, it's not nearly so calculated a process for me, because by writing, I'm often trying to work out what *I* think. For another, there will be a number of different interpretations to any piece of fiction, and that's part of the fun. Anyway, David wrote that song after he and I had been discussing *Midnight Robber* while it was in progress: what I was trying to do with it, particularly with language. I hoped that the song would give the reader a notion of some of the sensibility behind many Creoles. But I may have been too subtle. It's

100 CONVERSATIONS WITH NALO HOPKINSON

incredible to me, but I'm slowly realizing that a lot of people don't know that Africans sold into the European slave trade were forced with extreme prejudice to take European names and to stop speaking their own languages, so those readers won't know that the resulting Creoles are part enforced compliance, part defiance, and a whole lot of creativity. But I think that people will get *something* out of David's song, so I don't worry too much about it.

AN: One of the distinctive elements of your fiction—particularly in the context of spec-fic—is your use of Creolized language. Earlier you mentioned Papiamento, the language derived from Spanish, Dutch, Portuguese, and African influences, that is primarily spoken in Aruba and Curaçao. Do you use this in your fiction? What other dialects do you use in your writing?

NH: No. I've only used Creoles that an English speaker would understand. I mentioned Papiamento once in *Midnight Robber*; I made it one of the languages that people from my twin planets speak, because I didn't want to give them *Star Trek* syndrome, where alien worlds have only one culture and language. I've only heard Papiamento spoken once in my life, and it's a language I'd like to learn sometime. I also majored in Russian and French, and studied German for a year, so language is something with which I love to play.

The dialect I use most in my writing is Trinidadian, because that's what I speak the most handily. I can do a smattering of Jamaican, especially if I consult with my mother and grandmother, and I can throw in a word or two of Guyanese. *Midnight Robber* blends all three.

AN: How has your use of Caribbean-inflected language been received?

NH: Well, you know, to me it's not a new thing to write this way. Reclaiming oral speech patterns has been a growing practice among Caribbean writers for years, and also for writers from any country that is aware that it has a vernacular or two (and they all do, never mind the white Torontonian who once said to me, "I don't have an accent; *you* have an accent! I speak, like, normal, eh?"). So I was a little surprised to get so much surprise. But mostly it's been received quite well. Caribbean readers seem to like the blend of Creoles that I did in *Midnight Robber*. Science fiction readers are generally up for a challenge, so most of them have waded into the language with a will and many have told me that they've had fun there. I recently received a fan letter from Japan, and that impressed the hell out of me because the gentleman had read *Midnight Robber* in the original. It hasn't been translated. My agent has warned me not to expect too many offers to translate it into other languages because of the hybrid Creole in which it's written. I have a friend who thinks it would do well in Yiddish, and from what little I know of that language, I think he has an interesting notion there. The language I use in *Midnight Robber* is as much a sensibility thing as it is specific words, and Yiddish, near as I can tell, carries the historical sense of being the language of a people whose diasporic spread has at times been forced upon them, and it also, I think, has the sense of being a language "of the people."

AN: You distinguish your work from that of "traditional folk, fairy, and epic allegorical tales," which you describe as "historical literature of the imagination." And yet, though your novels and short stories are set in the time of the possible, your writing is filled with historical references, especially to Caribbean culture, and it is apparent that significant historical research goes into your fiction. How do you use history? How would you characterize the historical work of your novels? Are you using a different sense of history or the past than what is used in a fairy tale?

NH: How do I use history? I'm still figuring that out. Much of sci-fi draws on European history and folklore, to the extent that simply to mention a name—Oedipus, for instance—calls up a wealth of associations without the author needing to say another word. It's like the Black actor Paul Winfield playing an alien in "Darmok" (an episode from the fifth season of *Star Trek: The Next Generation*). He declaims, "Darmok and Jalad at Tanagra," and everyone from his culture knows the tale he's referring to and the parallels he wants to draw to his current situation. The humans, however, are just baffled. They don't know the lore of that culture. If I wrote, "Nanny with her cheeks clenched," only a few people would have any clue who or what I was talking about. So I find myself having to first describe the Caribbean history or the folktale, then create my metaphors once I've done my info-dumping.

It's difficult to do that in a short story. I'm still devising ways. I can only have so many history teachers, graduate students specializing in folklore, librarians or folktale-spouting grandads conveniently show up to tell the audience what they need to know. I have a story that's stalled right now, and I think that's partly why. In a novel it's a little easier, because you can put in a tiny bit of info-dump at a time over the course of the whole novel, and your readers will slowly piece together what you're trying to tell them.

AN: Critics have hailed you as the heir apparent to a Black science fiction tradition most often associated with the work of Octavia Butler, Samuel Delany, and Jewelle Gomez. Recently, two important works have been published that extend the timeline of Black speculative writing, expand its lineage, and enlarge its geographic scope. Sheree Renee Thomas's edited collection *Dark Matter: A Century of Speculative Fiction from the African Diaspora,* in which your work is featured, includes the early-twentieth-century work of W. E. B. Du Bois and George Schuyler, thinkers who have rarely been characterized as writers of speculative fiction and whose work is understood as far afield as that of, say, Delany or Butler. Your edited collection, *Whispers from the Cotton Tree Root: Caribbean Fabulist Fiction*, contains the writing of noted Caribbean novelists Kamau Brathwaite and Jamaica Kincaid, who are probably little known among avid readers of sci-fi or fantasy. How would you describe this moment in Black speculative writing? Is it the advent of a new wave of Black science fiction, simply the emergence of new categories for African diasporic fiction, or the extension of an extant tradition?

NH: Danged if I know. I'd like to think that it's all three. A wave comes from a source, and for it to exist, there's gotta be people to dub it a wave. I definitely want to see more spec-fic being published by Black writers, so whatever it is that's happening, I hope that it continues and strengthens. One of the many things I like about Sheree's anthology is that by printing new fiction alongside reprints of over a century ago, she's proving that we're here, and we've been here awhile. For myself, what I was trying to do with my anthology is to reveal that hybrid place where magical realism (an "Othering" term in itself, since it's so often used to refer to and exoticize fantastical fiction by hot country peoples), genre science fiction, and fantasy coexist. The book hasn't made as big a splash as *Dark Matter*, but so far, readers of both literary and speculative fiction seem to be quite happy to be plunged into that zone of shifting paradigms.

Having an anthology of writing by Caribbean people also allowed me to complicate an idea I encounter in the north: that "Caribbean" equals "Black." I hope to see more and more writing by people of color. An anthology or two written solely by people of color would be nice. I can think of all kinds of things that would be nice, but I'm very wary of ghettoizing us all over again, of putting us in a place where the mainstream can say, "we don't need to publish that work, because they have their own vehicles." Or, "well, we already have one story by a person of color so they're already represented and therefore we couldn't possibly publish a second." Someone recently said to a panel of Black sci-fi writers, "But if there get to be too many of you, you'll become too common." I don't want to be a talking dog act. I don't want our value to be in how uncommon we are. That's a good strategy for keeping us on the outside and our numbers limited. I'd like to see people of color represented in strength at all levels of the industry: more editors, more publishers, more design people, more marketing people, more graphic novelists, more comic book artists. I'd like it to become perfectly common-place that the instructors at spec-fic writing workshops are 30 to 50 percent people of color (and representation just as strong of working-class writers, queer writers, disabled writers, older writers, non-American writers; luckily, all these things overlap). The possibilities for imaginative fiction as a world literature are endless, but I think that the spec-fic industry is at this point limited in how it thinks about it.

Recently, a group of us have started to come up with ways to foster the development and the visibility of spec-fic by writers of color (www.carlbrandon.org). We are a tiny, scattered group of people at the moment, so we're only able to take baby steps as an organization, but perhaps it will grow. I hope so.

AN: Who is Carl Brandon? What type of activities does the Carl Brandon Society do? Are all of the members writers?

NH: Carl Brandon was the first Black fan to make a name for himself in the science fiction community. Carl Brandon didn't exist. He was the fictional creation of white writer Terry Carr, who was in part responding to someone's racist comment that Black people had no place in the science fiction community. Terry created Carl Brandon as a nom de plume, and Carl proceeded to become very active in the fan community, producing a fair bit of writing about events in the community. A lot of people came to think of Carl as a friend, and it was a bit of a traumatic event in science fiction fandom when the hoax was revealed.

Three years ago, a bunch of people, most of us people of color, met at Wiscon (the annual gathering of the feminist science fiction community) to begin to discuss how to raise the profile of people of color in the sci-fi community. The Carl Brandon Society was born out of that. We have no official membership criteria; anyone can volunteer. But we do have a steering committee that is and will continue to be comprised largely of people of color. That steering committee includes fans, writers, editors, and scholars. We chose the name Carl Brandon partly in tribute to Terry for raising the issue of race in sci-fi fandom. Partly it was a sense of irony, too, a wry awareness that the first acknowledged Black fan in the community was a true invisible man, more à la Ralph Ellison than H. G. Wells. Partly it's an homage to Wiscon and the feminist sci-fi community, which provided us a meeting place, making a point of continuing to program panels on issues of race, and which has funded the photocopying costs that allow us to distribute our annual bibliographies of writing by sci-fi authors of color every year to the hundreds of Wiscon attendees. It's an homage because of James R. Tiptree Jr.,

104 CONVERSATIONS WITH NALO HOPKINSON

another famous sci-fi hoax: a woman writer (Alice Sheldon) who masqueraded as a man for years in order to get her work published.

As to what types of activities we do, not very much yet. We are a handful of people, we're spread out all over the globe, and when we do manage to meet, it's only once a year at Wiscon for an hour or two. So far, we've managed to get a website under construction, and we've begun, as I've said, creating and distributing an annual list of sci-fi and related nonfiction published by writers of color in the previous year. Individual members have facilitated panels on issues of race at various sci-fi conventions in the United States. We have a free listserv going (called carlbrandon) at www.yahoogroups.com. We hope at some point to sponsor an award, but we have no funding and little infrastructure yet. It will take time. We have to build a groundswell of support and enthusiasm first.

AN: How would you describe a con to someone who has never attended one? How did you learn of the first con that you attended?

NH: The first one was in 1982, in my first year of university. It was a small con organized by the science fiction club that I used to attend in the Canadian high school from which I'd just graduated. I knew nothing of cons, and despite having attended the sci-fi club for a year (that's how long I attended high school in Canada), I knew and understood nothing of the sci-fi community. But I was a new immigrant to Canada, so the sci-fi community seemed no more strange than Canada and Canadians themselves did. Anyway, they organized this con in a Toronto hotel. I remember that the guests of honor were C. J. Cherryh (who, fifteen years later, would be the final judge for the first Warner Aspect First Novel Contest, which launched my career as a novelist when I won it). Of course, Cherryh didn't remember meeting me, and I myself didn't even make the connection until my novel had already been published. We had a brief and pleasant email chat about it a few years ago, and John Norman, who writes the infamous "Gor" novels (Old World sword-and-sorcery set on an alternate, magical, preindustrial Earth where women are the sexual slaves of men). What an odd combination of guests; I can understand that now that I know a little bit more about both authors. I wonder what their conversations with each other were like.

Back then, all I remember was that C. J. Cherryh had stunning blue eyes, beautifully contrasted by curly black hair (blue eyes are one of those novelties for me; in the Caribbean, they're in the minority) and that John Norman wore a dark-colored suit the whole weekend and was quiet, unassuming, and extraordinarily polite. I remember that the other members of the SF club encouraged me to wear a costume. I loved the notion, because I'd never played mas' [masquerade] at Carnival time in Trinidad; I'd jumped up in the streets as tens of thousands do, but I'd never been part of a costumed band. And I'd only ever had one opportunity to celebrate Halloween, and that was at six years old when we were living in Connecticut while my father was at Yale University on a graduate theater scholarship. (I guess I should clarify that Halloween is not celebrated in the Caribbean.) So I tried to figure out what costume to wear. This was before Arnold Schwarzenegger had made the first *Conan* movie with Grace Jones playing a barbarian. This was way before Tina Turner as Auntie Entitie in *Mad Max beyond Thunderdome*, and Grace Jones again in the campy vampire film *Vamp*. Not that it's changed at all nowadays, but I think my only models then for Black women masquerading the future or the fantastical were the Trinidadian mas' bands, which I didn't think would translate to this solo northern medium, and the amazing costumes of the 1970s funk group LaBelle, with Patti Labelle, and the divine Tina Turner as the Acid Queen in the film *Tommy*. Oh, and of course, Nichelle Nichols as Lt. Uhura in *Star Trek*, old school. And I sure as hell couldn't think of anyone Black in the literature who would be so recognizable that I could dress like her and people would know who I was masked as.

So began one of my first lessons on Blackness in sci-fi and fantasy. Who as a Black woman could I be who would be recognizable to people at the con? Too dark (I thought) to have the proper pallor for a vampire, too thick-thewed (I thought) to be a fairy, so even the generic tropes of the genre wouldn't serve me. I suspected they wouldn't recognize anyone from LaBelle or the Acid Queen (and I was probably too conservative then to have had the nerve to play the Acid Queen), so I chose Lt. Uhura. Watched a lot of *Star Trek* (which I always did anyway) and made myself a *Star Trek* uniform out of red polyester and gold braid. I couldn't quite figure out the insignia they wore, but while browsing at Bakka Books, Toronto's science fiction bookstore, I discovered to my amazement that there were whole manuals devoted to nothing but schematics of every aspect of *Star Trek*. From the layout of the *Enterprise* to the various officers' costumes. I didn't know whether I was appalled or relieved to discover that the too-brief-for-dignity dresses of the female officers came with matching red panties, so that even if you inadvertently flashed a glimpse of crotch while falling all over the ship as it lurched in the progress of a battle with the Romulans, at least what you were flashing would still be in uniform.

I couldn't afford a *Star Trek* manual (and didn't really want it; typically for me. I was more interested in the story aspect of *Star Trek*), so I memorized the insignia and used the embroidery function on my sewing machine to make myself a copy of it. I don't think I made the red panties. I think I made the skirt of my costume a little longer than regulation so that if I revealed my bottom, it would at least be by choice. Wore my costume to the con with my shiny black high-heeled boots and styled my (then) straightened hair into the famous Lt. Uhura bob. Years later, when I gave my partner a picture taken of me in that costume to put up on my website (www.sff.net/people.nalo/), he misread the bob as a flattened Afro, and Photoshopped it back up to what he thought its spherical glory had been. When I told him that in fact I'd had straightened hair, he was incredulous. It so doesn't jibe with his image of me that he couldn't bring himself to correct what he'd done. So the image of me as Lt. Uhura on my website shows me (and by extension, her) in full, Afrocentric, Angela Davis Black power mode. Which is the fantasy of the first water, I guess. The character of Lt. Uhura actually devolved politically from the full participating role that Gene Roddenberry had originally envisioned to that of intergalactic receptionist. I gather that there had been hate letters to *Star Trek* for even having a Black character in a permanent role, and the producers became nervous and made Roddenberry write smaller and smaller roles for her. Nichols herself only stayed with the show because none other than Martin Luther King asked her to, told her that she gave Black people in America a vision of themselves having a future.

How would I describe a con? Well, I generally don't attend the costume cons or the media cons unless I've been specifically invited to them. As always, I'm more interested in the book side of things. I think I'd have to describe what's common to them all, which is science fiction community. And frankly, though I can sometimes find some of the ways of the community vexing and strange, I'm still blown away by a literature that has a following so strong that the readership voluntarily organizes conventions where writers, readers, gamers, costumers, actors, critics, and the occasional scholar can meet, hang out, and play. I could probably attend a con every weekend of the year on this continent. This wouldn't happen if I were writing purely mimetic literary fiction.

It's a very strange and very specialized environment, but out of that comes a strong sense of community, and I value that. I also value that the community is made up of the folks like me who were the weirdos in school, who couldn't figure out why lipstick could only be some shade of red, or why a relationship was supposed to happen between only two people, or why men weren't supposed to wear lace miniskirts. There's probably no "alternative" lifestyle that's unfamiliar to sci-fi community, and that makes it one community (I have many communities, some of which often don't intersect much at all) in which I can feel at home in certain aspects of my outlook on life. One thing for which I long is many, many more Black and brown and yellow and red faces, and there are a few of us trying to make that happen.

Sci-fi community is very liberal (and there's a bit of an irony to a Canadian—and a Caribbean, for that matter—saying that about Americans, because we don't, have the American fear of socialism, so to us with our three-and-more party systems, "liberal" is middle-of-the-road, leaning to the right). Generally, the feeling in sci-fi community is that everyone should be welcome, and that racial differences shouldn't matter. It's an excellent beginning, but in practice what it tends to mean is that someone who brings up the issue of the inequities of race can make people uncomfortable and as a result can be seen to *be* the problem. It's a weird twist that can turn the people who are being racialized into the racist ones for daring to mention that there is not an even playing field. That kind of prejudice is not ubiquitous in the sci-fi community, but I'd say that it's pervasive enough that it can make sci-fi community a less welcoming place than it would like to be. I know that a lot of the people of color in the field notice it; we talk about it.

AN: One of your contributions to *Dark Matter* is a short story entitled "Ganger (Ball Lightning)" about a heterosexual couple experimenting with a high-tech body suit that heightens sexual pleasure. Did Samuel Delany's fiction writing—*Dhalgren* and the Neveryon tales, for example—influence your decision to write about sex and sexuality? Do you plan to continue creating fiction that blurs the line between the erotic and the fantastical?

NH: When I read Delany's novel *Dhalgren* at about twenty-two years old, it blew my brain apart and reassembled the bits. That man hacked my mind. When I later read his autobiographical work *The Motion of Light in Water*, and began to learn something about the experience that had gone into making the man, I sort of fell in love. It hadn't occurred to me that one could write science fiction and fantasy as metafiction about the process of creating a story. At the time, I didn't even have the words to explain or even understand what he was doing; all I could do was to be swept away. I didn't realize that you could use science fiction and fantasy to talk frankly and personally about the sexual and other lives of marginalized people. I suspect, though my memory may be faulty, that his work and James Baldwin's were the first fiction that I read that incorporated sexual acts between queer men, and I think that when I was reading the Baldwin, I was too young to know what a big deal that was—probably didn't even understand the sex scenes. If my memory is correct, then I'm blessed that that reading experience came to me from two *Black* men, because queer Black men's lives still feel like a mostly silenced topic in the world. A local Toronto paper just published an "exposé" in which they seem to be claiming that what gay Black men want is to be closeted, which, of course, ignores the input of all the outspoken brothers out there.

What was your question again? Oh, right; yes, I would say that Chip was one of the first people from whose work and life I drew courage when I began to write about sex and sexuality.

Writing by people such as Carol Queen and Susie Bright and Elizabeth Lynn also helped, and the collection *Pomosexuals: Challenging Assumptions about Gender and Sexuality*, edited by Carol Queen and Lawrence Schimel, and *Transgender Warriors* by Leslie Feinberg, and *Beneath the Skins: The New Spirit and Politics of the Kink Community* by Ivo Dominguez Jr., and the seriously rude, Black gay S&M comics of Belasco, and one of bell hooks's autobiographies, where she talks about trying to negotiate a polyamorous relationship with her partner, and postings by people such as Juba Kalamka and Ayizé Jama-Everett on your own AfroFuturism listserv, and the efforts of erotica publisher and sci-fi/fantasy writer Mary Anne Mohanraj, and of erotic sci-fi/fantasy publisher and writer Cecilia Tan, and writing by bisexual Black theologian Eliahou Farajaje-Jones.

In other words, I've been systematically gathering about myself the thoughts on sex and sexuality of a bunch of freaky women, transfolks, and people of color: the people who, like me, might think that green is a perfectly good color for lipstick, and that five people in a relationship can be a good idea, and that gender ambiguity can be hot. When I was a misfit girl living uncomfortably in a highly normalized world, science fiction and fantasy were the first literatures I read that wrestled head-on with normativity, a way of being in the world that works for me in some arenas and flat out makes me suicidal in others. Who knew that the fictions that sometimes gave me reason to remain alive were lived experience for many very real people?

Damn, I've strayed away from your question again. Yes, I probably will continue to write about sex, and I'll probably continue to try to write about it in a way that explores the edges. The man and woman in "Ganger (Ball Lightning)" are a heterosexual Black couple having "het" (and, I like to think, hot) sex, but they've nevertheless wandered into some gender play: something that neither one of them addresses directly in the story, and that isn't even really central to their dealings with each other, but that indirectly helps to force out some issues in their relationship that they haven't been dealing with very well. That story is about to be republished in *The Year's Best Erotica* by Susie Bright. I was unimaginably thrilled to be receiving communication from Susie Bright, asking if she might publish one of my stories. One of the utterly cool things about writing is that it has helped me meet some of the people who've been formative to me.

My short story collection, *Skin Folk*, contains a story that is the first one I've ever written deliberately as erotica. I do fret a lot about how those elements of my work will be received by the more conservative people in my communities, but the alternative would be to try to chop bits of myself off again in order to be acceptable. As I get older, I find it harder to keep doing that type of self-mutilation. I very much fear being attacked by people about whom I care who don't like what I'm doing, but the fear isn't silencing me very effectively anymore. It helps when I'm in the grip of the fear to know that there are people who've been walking this road ahead of me. It helps that there are Chip Delanys in this world.

AN: How did you learn about the Clarion Science Fiction and Fantasy Writers' Workshop?

NH: I think I was sixteen years old when I first heard about it. I was living in Georgetown, Guyana, at the time. I'd read all the science fiction and fantasy in the local public library and was jonesing for more. I complained about it to a friend of my aunt's, a Black man, and he lent me some of his precious collection of sci-fi novels on condition that I return them to him. One of them was a collection of Clarion stories that talked about the Clarion experience. I can't remember, but I fear that I may not have returned his books to him after all, because I still have that one, at least. In that self-absorbed way that young people can have, I knew his face and I knew that he was a family friend, but I wasn't too clear on his name, and I didn't know how to contact him. And, of course, it didn't occur to me to ask my aunt. Anyway, when I read the description of Clarion and what goes on there, I longed to attend myself. But I wasn't a writer. Didn't think I could be a writer. But the longing never went away.

I was a student at Clarion in 1995. Clarion is a six-week graduate level workshop for writing science fiction, fantasy, and horror. You're accepted on the basis of some samples of your writing. Every week there is a different writer in residence who leads the workshop sessions and lectures on some aspect of the field. It's an exhausting, all-consuming experience. I loved it.

AN: Having returned to Clarion as an instructor this summer, do you have a sense that the alternative perspectives and stylistic fusion that you and other writers have brought to speculative fiction have influenced younger writers? Did the schism between sci-fi and fantasy exist among students as it had when you were at Clarion in 1995?

NH: Yes, there's still an ideological battle between sci-fi and fantasy. That feels to me like one of those sibling battles that rages for years, perhaps lifetimes. It's a battle that gives us a perverse kind of pleasure, and it'll be around awhile. And writers have been effectively fusing science fiction and fantasy way before I tried it—and many of them, way better. In fact, I'd say that they only split when they became marketing categories. Case in point: as with my novel *Brown Girl in the Ring*, Emma Bull's excellent novel *Bone Dance* fuses Orisha beliefs with a science fictional future in a broken-down city, and hers was published years before mine. At Clarions East and West in 2001, there was a multitude of approaches to storytelling in the group, and a few people were quite upfront about working to create some kind of fusion between their cultural traditions of storytelling and the narratives of science fiction and fantasy. I suspect some of that is the influence of more senior writers, and some of it comes directly out of the interests, experiences, and sensibilities of those emerging writers themselves.

AN: Students of Clarion workshops are expected to forge the future direction of sci-fi and fantastical fiction. Reflecting on your experience as an instructor at a recent workshop, what does the future of speculative fiction hold?

NH: What does the future of speculative fiction hold? I have no clue. Despite the reputation that science fiction writers have, speculative fiction is really not about predicting the future. That strikes me as an oddly boring enterprise; the real future is always so much more absorbing and complex than anything we can imagine. What I would *hope* will begin to happen in SF/F/H is that, in the same way that women writers and readers are claiming a place in the fantastical genres, there will begin to be more diverse expressions of people's lived experiences of race, culture, class, sexuality, social structures, and gender, and that more of those expressions will begin to come from outside the United States.

Breakdown or Breakthrough: A Conversation with Nalo Hopkinson on Race and the Science Fiction Community

Isiah Lavender III / 2005

Unpublished interview conducted at the Twenty-sixth International Conference of the Fantastic in the Arts in Fort Lauderdale, Florida, Saturday March 19, 2005.

Isiah Lavender III: Lots of people seem to think that speculative fiction by people of color is about to explode. But it can't happen without a conversation about race. Race makes an otherwise progressive community too afraid, too upset, too angry, too uncomfortable, and perhaps too cowardly to jump into the deep end of this conversation that they seem to suggest that they want to have happen. By "they," I, of course, mean white people. So we avoid the talk. It can't be avoided if science fiction is to live up to some of its utopian potential. This conversation needs to take place. As I like to think of it, it is a breakdown as opposed to the breakthrough that I am looking for in this field that other people seem to be suggesting that they want.

Nalo, I consider you and your unique style to be the breakthrough that speculative fiction needs in ways different to those provided by the big two, Samuel R. Delany and Octavia E. Butler, in their monumental works. For example, your use of "Creole" languages and spiritual belief systems as well as your editorial work. These are truly valuable contributions to the field. Having said this, these are the kinds of issues that I would like to discuss with you today on this beautiful Florida afternoon. And I just invite you to ponder how would you like to start?

Nalo Hopkinson: Well, God, there's just so much to say. I mean, even if I just start with your comment that Delany and Butler have been able to make the breakthrough. Certainly, for readers of color and for people paying

112 CONVERSATIONS WITH NALO HOPKINSON

attention to those issues, the work of Delany and Butler has definitely been a breakthrough. And if you sit down and examine their work through a filter that recognizes race as an issue, a lot of what they're doing is revolutionary, and revolutionary still. So, I don't think it's so much their content. I think what happens is as with any form of oppression the people most concerned with or think about it the most deeply are the people most negatively affected by it.

IL: Sure, but isn't it strange how they've gone silent?

NH: Who?

IL: Delany and Butler.

NH: I don't find them silent. Octavia talks about it as much as she ever did. She's always been fairly outspoken but quiet. She's not out there waving placards, but put her on a panel and you'll know what her opinions are pretty damn quick [*laughter*]. And Delany always has spoken about it and speaks about it in his critical work. I think he's somebody who wouldn't say it, but he hasn't stopped talking about this stuff. I think part of the complication is when you are trying to talk about multiple identity sets. He's both Black and gay, for instance. I've heard him say it's difficult to make room to talk about both of them. And they affect each other. You can't sort of single one out.

IL: Sure.

NH: So, I think that's part of what happens. So I don't think they have gone silent. I think they've been out there producing work for a very long time, and they're still doing what they do at the speed that they do it. What happens in the field which I see elsewhere is a combination of respect and fear. So people who aren't affected by these issues, or people who are white essentially, very rightly want to make sure that the people of color speak first. But there is also a fear of speaking out at all, a fear of saying the wrong thing. But I don't think that only the people negatively affected by race should talk about it because everybody is affected by race.

IL: Oh, definitely.

NH: But, particularly in the US, there is this liberal, well-meaning—I don't want to step on anybody's toes, I don't want to make anybody angry—that shuts down conversation because they're so going to keep silent.

IL: That's not the only time. My paper presentation wasn't the only time that happened. I asked a question when we were discussing the second chapter from Justine Larbalestier's book, *The Battle of the Sexes in Science Fiction*, at the round-table discussion, and I put a race and gender question out there and just—HUSH—silence.

NH: Hmm . . . hmm.

IL: It was like the whole issue was elided and the group moved on to something else. The same thing happened this morning. I think it had more to do with me being a Black person asking about the way other European science fictions have been written in their own original languages and have managed to cross back over the ocean to the United States, which is the imperialistic force that it is today in science fiction. I mentioned the Strugatsky Brothers, Stanislaw Lem, Karel Capek, and people of that stature, but it went quiet. The only think I can attribute that to is as you know being a Black person.

NH: It's terrifying.

IL: They are terrified of me! Me! I mean, look at me: I'm harmless. [*laughter.*] Right? But I don't understand. I don't know if I was reading that situation correctly.

NH: You may very well have been, and it is perturbed. It contributes to a silence and it is not very healthy. Last year at ICFA, Andy Duncan, who was in my anthology *Mojo*, contacted me beforehand and said he wanted to do a panel on *Mojo*, which I hadn't even thought of, so he was the one who did it. And, of course, *Mojo* being what it is, we ended up talking about race and people not from a particular race writing from that perspective. And it was a wonderful session; a lot of people came. I was on the panel, Andy was on the panel, and Ellen Klages was on the panel. She had a story that I craved to put in *Mojo* and could not get the space. And it made room for me to talk about why I had constructed *Mojo* the way I did, where I deliberately invited white writers, and I would have invited, I think I did invite some First Nations writers, but no other race. Black predominantly, white, and First Nations, and that's it because the whole idea of *Mojo*, the whole idea of this West African Diasporic magic influence comes out of this history of Columbus and slavery. And therefore, these are the three main groups of people who have a place in that conversation and so I acted as a curator; I wore a number of hats. I acted as a curator in thinking about how I wanted to do it, and then when I did my call for submissions, I first invited Black writers who I felt could write well to the topic, and then I invited everybody else that I thought could write well to the topic. Then I took off that hat, and when the work came in, I no longer paid attention to what race people were; I just was editing the best stories I got. And I could not have contrasted that to other anthologies, where in the interest of being fair to everybody the editors don't do that. They don't try to be proactive about increasing the diversity. And I've seen anthologies based in other cultures, cultures of color, that have not a single writer from that culture in it. And there are good reasons for that happening a few years ago, but now not so much. But in the US, in this culture, to do something like that is considered affirmative action, which is considered a bad thing for some bizarre reason, perhaps because affirmative action works.

IL: The backlash, that's what it's all about, right?

NH: Yeah, so . . .

IL: The fear of white males not getting an equal opportunity when . . .

NH: Well, they're getting a larger opportunity.

IL: Affirmative action is supposed to have leveled the playing field.

NH: Exactly. So I got to talk about that process, and Andy and Ellen got to talk about what it was like being a white writer who has some awareness of some of these race issues, writing in this space where I have invited them because they have the awareness and the talent, but the two have to go hand in hand. And it being very deliberate on my part in the challenge it put them up to. It can be done. You can make the space to have that kind of conversation happen. I have the feeling that if I hadn't been there a lot of people might have gotten uncomfortable. I don't know. So I legitimized the talk about race by being you know "raced" in that sort of racial initialized body being on that panel. When the Carl Brandon Society started, it started at Wiscon, and they were the people who made the space for us to do it. We proposed it to them, or I proposed it to them, that we do some paneling about race issues. And they said, "Well, here's some people of color, fans of color in the field who come to Wiscon who might be interested in putting together a team and start talking about programming." It all came out of that. So Wiscon sort of made the room.

IL: Pioneering visionaries.

NH: Or enablers, because the idea came from me based on something that Delany had written, which is why I say that he's still very much talking about this and it came out of an experience that had happened to him and me at Readercons. He wrote a piece about racism in the industry that was not too long ago, and I said in response to the challenge he put forward at the end of that piece which was that cons need to make room and paneling at the cons to talk about the visibility of people of color in this field. I said, "Why don't we start?" And so we did, but what we wanted, the team of us that got together, was three things, three panels, not panels but programming events that we wanted. One was a focus group that would be just people of color to talk about our own stuff. One was an open session that would have been open but just white people to talk about race in their own private space where they could say what they wanted. And then we wanted afterwards to keep the open session where everyone came together, talked about what had gone on in their two sessions and we began a discussion. Now, I know a con only has so much time and space for programming, but Wiscon does multiple tracks quite gracefully. Yet, they took out the program for just the white people, they took out the program for everybody, gave us just the focus group for people of color, and then two of their board members had a shit fit that it was reverse racism, and they were going to quit.

IL: Man . . .

NH: So they took out what we were intending, and then got angry at us for what was left. And this wasn't the whole cup of comments, just a couple of people who you know were uncomfortable essentially, who have very fair-minded thinking. The problem with fair-minded thinking is if the playing field isn't level, and you're not doing anything to make it level, you aren't actually being fair. So we've had our struggles. It was fun when the team of us, when we got this news, got together, and we wrote a letter sort of laying out what had happened and we didn't get the other two programs back, but we were allowed to keep the focus group and we went in. I was terrified, frankly. I didn't know when I entered that room who would be at the door or what kind of greeting, but there was nothing and we had our meeting and the Carl Brandon Society came out of it. And has kept going ever since. It is small, but it has kept growing. When I think about this, I think what happens particularly in the science fiction community is that so many of us were the outcasts. We were the geeks, we were the people who were too smart for our own good, we walked funny, we talked funny, we dressed funny, we're used to being excluded. You come into the science fiction communities and you're not supposed to single anybody out for any innate characteristic that they have. So when people try to talk about race, they're people, who without examining it, see that as singling a particular characteristic out see it as wrong. So they get very uncomfortable and they can be very stringent in silencing that discussion.

IL: I'm living proof of that.

NH: Oh yeah. I was at a Readercon one year, we were at a café klatch that was made up of small discussion groups, and it was Delany so a bunch of people came and just wanted to sit and have a talk with Delany for an hour. And a young man said to him, "How do I, as a Black gay man, have a voice in this literature? How do I? Everywhere I go people get upset when I try to talk about my issues." Before Chip could turn to answer, a white woman sitting next to this guy said, "I just don't see race in my life. I don't make it a problem. Everyone's the same. I don't see it." And I could see him just kind cringe. And Chip said—I will love this man forever for this—he said, "You know, if you can't see something that threatens my life daily, what kind of ally can you be for me?" PSYCHE!!! [*laughter.*]

IL: He hit the nail right on the head, didn't he?

NH: Yeah! So, you know, they're still out their fighting.

IL: Sure, I'd say it feels difficult to be one of the only people of color here.

NH: Yeah.

IL: It's like being in a sea of whiteness, and then amazingly that sea never touches you.

NH: Yeah, and what happens, of course, is the people of color find each other. I could probably tell you with a fairly close accuracy how many of us there are here right now and some of us not visibly of color, but somehow we find each other. [*laughter.*]

IL: You're right, and that's amazing that that happens in some respects. Let's go in a different direction. What sense do you have of your position in the field since your big splash with *Brown Girl in the Ring* (1998)?

NH: I think I'm seen as an important young writer at forty-four years old, which is a lovely place to be in. I get a sense that there are certain groups of people who are irritated with, and wary of, any open discussion about race and who are irritated that I do it. And there are people that are relieved as hell that somebody's doing it.

IL: Like me.

NH: Yeah. And who get it, and that's pretty much what I would expect anywhere, but I think the science fiction community has a sense of itself as being very open and accepting, but it's a microcosm of the society at large, and society at large is white-dominated culture that doesn't really want to hear you talk about race and I get that. I hear it. So I know that's out there. I know that when I put out an anthology like *So Long Been Dreaming*, me and Uppinder Mehan, it was his idea, that anthology. Some of the objection to it coming from people was that "Oh, that's all she ever does" and "it's exclusionary." Those are people who aren't really looking at what I do because *Mojo* was not just Black folks.

IL: It was inclusive.

NH: *Whispers from the Cotton Tree Root*, which people think of as being "Oh, that was the Black anthology." Caribbean people are every race under the sun, and I found as many variants as I could. The only anthology that I have restricted to one set of people, and that was Uppinder's idea and not mine, was that third one, right, but because I talk about race people seem to think its exclusionary so they aren't really examining what I am doing.

They're just having fits, but my sense is that they are in the minority in terms of the effect they can have on me. I'm still able to do the work I do. I'm still finding support for it, so I don't worry about it too much.

IL: What do you think about Afrofuturism?

NH: I haven't actually been on the listserve for ages, years and years and years ago. And that's partly because in so many ways I found it to be a different kind of conservatism in that the people who were the loudest, the most vocal, the most persistent also seemed to be the ones, for the most part not all of them, who had really retrograde views on things like gender and sexuality, and whose notions on what race was or what it could become or how it affected our lives didn't seem to go very deep. And I got tired of it.

IL: Sure, it seemed, it seemed all inclusive that all Black experience in the new world is science fictional because you know we were separated from the motherland and that to me is discouraging.

NH: People in ships came and took us away, and but that's a fine place to start. But I remember getting into a fight, me and Juba Kalamka and Ayize Jama-Everett—there were about five us—against this onslaught of people who were furious that we wanted to talk about queer issues. And this notion again that being a good African means having, you know, manual and penetrative sex in the missionary position to make new soldiers for the race . . . umm . . . is really only one way to do it [*laughter*].

IL: And yet that's all they want to do.

NH: And that's all they wanted to talk about so if we tried to complicate it at all, pretty quickly you discovered that there was no room to have that kind of conversation and then lots of other people who have a radical politic around things, race as well as around a complex of identity issues, wandered away from Afrofuturism.

IL: So that's where it breaks down for you?

NH: Yeah, I'm still thrilled to know that it's out there, and it still provides a very useful set of filters for me to look at a number of things from, but I can't do single issues and it feels often single-issued in a way that is kind of short-sighted. And that seems to be the loudest voices. I don't know if they are in the majority, but it sure feels like the majority when you're trying to take part in that particular online community that's gathered around the notion of Afrofuturism.

IL: Yeah, it seems like it's broken down and we need to break through the debris field that surrounds it because all of the major science fiction journals out there are embracing the term as if it's the only notion out there, which is fine. It's a cool term, right? And it sounds really great but it doesn't work.

NH: Yeah, but even people who have or are using it are saying "hang on." How does this connection it makes in our heads compare with futurism? But what I find interesting about the academic world beginning to take on Afrofuturism as a notion is what it feels like to me is it's starting from places that folks in the Black community have already left behind a long time ago. They at least stay current with what work is being made whereas when I hear it being talked about from the non-Black academic world it's still. . . They're talking about a Black science fiction production that they're a good twenty years behind, so they're following in the wake of this bunch of people who are keeping up.

IL: Yeah, and we need them. We need those scholars.

NH: But they're kind of feeding off, it feels like a poor copy. They're feeding off the work of the people who like Alondra, who started that whole community. That's stuff we've done and discussed awhile back. All right, we can move on now and to have the sort of non-Black academe treat it as, gasp, they've made this new discovery, which was Octavia Butler and Samuel Delany, but we already knew that [*laughter*].

IL: They're trying to bring you up to that status now.

NH: You're right, but what about that Black vampire anthology that came out last year? We know about Ramellzee—you know, what about him? Can we talk about *Blade III* now? [*laughter.*]

IL: Oh man, what a work, *Blade III*. You know, mentioning the vampire/horror anthology *Dark Dreams*, people just seem to not know about Tananarive Due or her husband Steven Barnes to some extent. And I don't even want to talk about Charles Saunders and his *Imaro* trilogy.

NH: Yeah . . . yeah.

IL: The Black Conan thing is a great series, and it just died with two more books planned.

NH: Well, he's getting republished by—I've forgotten the name of the press, but those are getting reissued and should probably already be out.

IL: So, I am wondering why does the speculative community only welcome a select few people of color into the fold?

NH: I don't know, partly I think that's an editorial choice that I don't think is necessarily a racist choice. It's a choice about when you're going into mainstream SF publishing, it's a choice about what they think will sell and what they think won't because they can't afford to lose money, oh they can afford to lose a little bit, but . . . [*laughter*].

IL: They don't want to take too many chances?

NH: Noooo, that's not even what I am saying. I am saying that, like in anything, like the man says 90 percent of everything is shit. And not everything is strong work, and so there's this dance between I'm rejecting this as an editor because I don't think it's strong and will people see you as being racist because that's a First Nations writer. And because the language, the means, the tropes, the metaphors of science fiction come from a dominant culture. If the other culture's . . . have you ever tried writing science fiction?

IL: Me, no. [*laughter.*]

NH: And coming from an African sensibility? You have to reinvent the language. You have to craft some bizarre amalgam of the sensibility you're trying to bring and a science fiction sensibility . . . you're grafting two things together that did not grow together, and it's difficult to do that successfully. And a lot of the people who try aren't doing it successfully the first few times they try it, and you take that work to a regular publisher and they're going to go, "This is not publishable," and they may well be right. But because there are so few of us, it starts to look like we are being excluded. I don't think that's always the case. Sometimes the work is not doing what the editors need. I am going to get pilloried for saying that. But I've had people angry with me for rejecting stories that I didn't think were working and I'd love seeing more writers of color in the field, but I also want to see strong stories, so . . .

IL: Well, since we're talking about editorship, let's think about your decision and desire to promote other writers of color through your editing anthologies, and we've spoken about this to some extent already, but could you tell me a little bit more about that? It had to be a conscious decision to try a project of that nature instead of pursuing your own writing.

NH: I knew I wanted to do some editing just to try it. I hadn't thought about what, 'cause editing doesn't pay the bills as well as writing does. Even writing's not making me a living wage, but I was focusing on the writing. I was here. I was at ICFA, and the folks from the then-new Invisible Cities Press approached me and asked if I'd ever thought about editing an anthology and I said yes, but I hadn't figured out what yet. And they said, "Caribbean fabulist fiction." And I said, "What is that?" And they said, "Well, we know what fabulist fiction is." So it was their idea, and I just sort of figured out what the hell they were talking about. I am not an academic, so the terms mean nothing to me. I figured out what they were talking about and made the anthology happen. *Mojo* was my own idea, and it took me a few weeks of some agonizing thinking about who I would invite. And it's a frightening thing to do because of the level of disapproval you can get in this field because people think you're doing something improper is fairly high, but I knew I wasn't asking South Asian writers, I wasn't asking Asian writers, and so I had to force myself to think through why that was because some of those folks are still friends of mine, who I'd been saying no not you, not this project. I think, like anything, you get an idea and you think, yes, this could work, and then you figure out how. And I'm always keeping an eye out for where the writers of color are because that's so important to me. What happens is I'm one person struggling to eat from day to day, and I don't always know how I'm going to, and I have only so much energy. I have a chronic disease, a disorder that makes my energy very fragile, very variable, and I have a certain level of visibility so I'm beginning to get people coming to me: can you read this, will you, can you do that, you should be supporting us, you're a writer of color. And sometimes I cannot take the time to do it. So I need there to be more people so that there are more of us who are having that kind of demand put on us. So I'm so delighted to see Tobias Buckell has got two books coming out soon.

IL: Tobias Buckell?

NH: He's West Indian, Caribbean. He's from St. Thomas. He lives somewhere in Ohio right now.

IL: Cool, so that's one of the emerging writers of color in speculative fiction that you would recommend.

NH: Yeah. And the thing about Toby is: in the Caribbean, it's much easier for him to negotiate race than here. Here, he passes for white when in fact one parent is Black. And like me, he code-switches to the point where you can't tell he's not American—well, you can tell on me, but you can't tell with Toby. And, if he's in the Caribbean, people aren't going to necessarily assume that he's white, they'll wait for clues. Here, he's white. So he never quite knows what box to take, but as far as I'm concerned, Toby is a person of color. Or he's a Caribbean person which is a little different.

IL: Sure.

NH: He's got a novel coming out, and he's got a collection of short stories coming out. And the novel uses Caribbean Creole and mixes Caribbean and Aztec culture. It's a really cool thing. The short story collection is lovely. Nnedimma Okorafor is about to have a novel, a young adult fantasy novel, come out from I think HarperCollins. She's Nigerian, Nigerian American. And I just coedited *Tesseracts Nine* with Geoff Ryman, a Canadian science fiction anthology, and how many writers of color do we have in there? A handful, it's very nice. And it's a healing thing. The company is very, very important.

IL: Sure. You know you're not alone.

NH: And to know that Charles Saunders has got a novel out there, and shopping it around, and having some of his work reissued.

IL: Can't wait to have him back.

NH: Yeah, I know. You listen out for the clues. To see that Tenea Johnson is here . . . she was at Clarion last year, that kind of thing. It's nice.

IL: Since this conference is about blurring the boundaries, do you see our presence here as people of color beginning to accomplish this task, beginning to break through the silence that this boundary tries to represent?

NH: [*long laughter.*] Hmm . . . I'm trying to disentangle that because answering one way or the other means I agree with the premises implicit in the question and I'm not sure whether I do because it sort of implies that blurring the boundaries is a good thing. And I am thinking about whether it is or not. It probably is, but the fact that, every year, I do see more people of color is encouraging at this conference. It would be nice to see more programming, and I haven't been to enough, [*laughter*] in future years. And it would also be nice to see programming that's just inclusive that isn't necessarily about race. The way I started out this discussion is you get into a position where women become the experts on gender and not even people of color, but Black people become the experts on race.

IL: Sure. That's a ridiculous notion that white people can't . . .

NH: . . . wrap their minds around it.

IL: Wrap their minds around as you're saying, Black culture and history, or not just a singular or monolithic Black culture, but Black cultures with an *s*.

NH: Hmm . . . hmm.

IL: And that's always upset me in my own classroom with my students saying stuff like, "You can't have that white guy in here talking about African music?"

NH: Why not? [*laughter.*]

IL: He's been to the African continent several times.

NH: He's devoted his life's work to it. He probably knows more about it than all of y'all.

IL: Exactly.

NH: Yeah, but also it's not just that, it's also nice to be at programming where you're not necessarily talking about race—where, not that you're not talking about it, but that you can be there as all of yourself and it's not necessarily a talk about race, where you can raise the kinds of issues you were raising and it's just part of the discussion instead of "OH MY GOD! It's an ANGRY BLACK MAN. Quick, hide."

122 CONVERSATIONS WITH NALO HOPKINSON

IL: Yeah, as if I look like that right?

NH and IL: [*laughter.*]

IL: But that's how it feels. It's very estranging in that sense. I'm willing to put myself out there and ask questions that I hope are provocative and will elicit some kind of response and then just the wall of silence.

NH: Yeah . . . Yeah . . . yeah . . .

IL: It's tough to deal with.

NH: Yeah, it is. Well, the way to deal with it is to propose your own programming. And what I was saying is just, if you build it they will come. Me and Andy proposed the thing on *Mojo* and had a full house. It was nice!

IL: So why do you think the SF community is more willing to discuss gay/lesbian issues versus race issues?

NH: Yeah, why do I think that is? Because queerness is still seen as a white issue, to the irritation to those of us who are both of color and queer. A queer sensibility or politic still ends up becoming largely white, or where it gets privileged is it gets privileged in white communities. It's still a difficult discussion to have coming from communities of color, and that's why I think there's a hierarchy. Queer is seen as whiter than Black [*laughter*], whiter than a colored anything at the bottom of the hierarchy. God, I'll be at the bottom of the hierarchy probably: the disabled and old.

IL: It's true that a critical mass has been reached for and surpassed with feminist and gender theory in science fiction that has not happened for race, which seems unusual. I've always been curious about that.

NH: Well, there are more women, so there's just a bigger critical mass to push the issue. That's part of why the Carl Brandon Society moves so slowly. Something like Wiscon, something like a feminist convention, women are 50 percent of the world, the numbers are just bigger. And in North America, people of America are what? What is the percentage? Do we know? Is it about around 10 percent? Then in the science fiction community probably even smaller because you've got to be pretty persistent to invite yourself into that because you are a person of color. Not that you won't be made welcome if you go but it doesn't look welcoming from the outside. So, the critical mass isn't there. Yeah, I'm pushing for it; I'm rooting for it. I don't know how it happens, but I'm rooting for it.

IL: So, let's play some more with an often-accepted idea in science fiction that humanity will one day eclipse notions of race and ethnicity or a post-race world. Do you think that could happen?

NH: Sure, I think that could happen, but what bugs me about that argument is it's often used as a way to not talk about race, to not talk about the power imbalances we have right now, let's just pretend it's not there, and I get into arguments about this frequently and recently did so, less than a month ago, talking about the whole notion that anything could be color-blind in a racist world. And that to be color-blind in a racist world is to not be an ally. I made someone very, very angry because she said, "Oh, no, the only way we're ever going to do this is to pretend there is no race."

IL: Sure, in a color-conscious world, even though race is science fictional, right, it is a man-made construction, a sociological construction.

NH: Yeah, but in order to do that you have to be deliberate. You can't just say, "OK, I'm now going to do color-blind casting." What you get is mostly white people because systemically they're the ones who have the most access. You have to make change. You don't just say I am now perfect. "Oh, why aren't you treating me as though I am perfect?" I get into these arguments all the time.

IL: At least in my old work, I get the idea that if we elide issues of race and just say it disappears, it will come back at us in new ways or in new kinds of racism.

NH: The thing is often what those people are describing sounds to me very homogenized, generic, and boring. I like the fact that we live in a diverse world and that that diversity may not always be expressed through some kind of fake notion of race, but I don't want that sense of diversity to go away and unless you're going to give me something to replace it with or some real human reason. We're not going to wake up one morning and go I'm going to stop doing this now. Talk to me about how this social change comes about through the work science fiction.

IL: Does reading, writing, and thinking about SF or speculative literature enable you to deal with the continually raced future in more hopeful terms?

NH: Yes, I think absolutely. I don't know that the literature I write is clearly hopeful [*laughter*]. It's becoming more so. But, I think we have got a body of work, a way of thinking, and a way of looking at making fiction that is about doing exactly that, and it's one of the beauties of it. I think it's part of the reason I'm so interested in it. I'm not always writing from a need to have a platform to speak about something, sometimes I'm focusing on a story and making a story work, but the potential is there.

IL: How has teaching SF, if that's what you were teaching, influenced your ideas about the genre?

NH: I'm not teaching literature so much because I don't have the background in doing so. I come to literature as a reader. I am teaching creative writing, and often it very definitely does give me a way to talk about some

124 CONVERSATIONS WITH NALO HOPKINSON

of this stuff because you encounter the memes, the unconscious memes and tropes. You encounter people trying to be multicultural and writing cultures that are instead sort of racially very disturbing, where you've got native, generic native cultures where all the people are blond and blue-eyed. And so it gives me the opportunity with the students to look at where does this come from, how might we tackle it better, why are you not making these people— rather why are you defaulting to white? And, ultimately it is that fear again of race: "Oh, but I'm going to be pilloried, if I'm talking about non-writers of color and then it also gives me the opportunity to." I think sometimes, just because I'm on the teaching slate, and I'm a person of color, and I'm known to talk about race, it means that people who sign up for it who might not otherwise, and that often means people of color. So the first year I taught at Clarion West in Seattle, I had to put it out there that I was going to be doing it and that was the year that any Clarion then in existence had the most people of color that they've ever had. Usually they have one or two, but there were I think six that year.

IL: Wow, that's a good impact.

NH: That's because Clarion had both me and Octavia Butler that year. And because I put it out there that I was going to be there. That might be ego on my part to think that that was why, but . . .

IL: There is nothing wrong with ego. As I was saying earlier, I really believe that when all is said and done about your career that you'll be right up there with Delany and Butler, if you're not already. I believe that, I really do.

NH: [*laughter.*] It'd be nice, but I think one of the things I know as somebody going into a space that feels like as not necessarily a safe space, I look around for signs that it might be safer than I think, and something like a teaching environment. I'll look for are there any science fiction writers on the slate. I'll look for are there any writers of color, any queer writers, any women writers, or instructors, whatever. And I think my being there for lots of different types of people helps them feel there might be somebody who at least knows what they're talking about. So it's nice to feel I can perhaps do that just by being there. It's also, I think, burdened if I feel like I am the only one, or one of two. So I am always trying to get administrators to think about tokenism, and are they creating an atmosphere of tokenism, and is there any way they can think about to stop doing it? So it can actually be as diverse as so many of them actually want to be. I mean, there are allies there.

IL: Let's move on. What would you like to see happening in the academic discussions of race and SF from an outsider's point of view to the academy? Why? Where do you see SF in five years?

NH: I would like regular discussions of SF to start including the kinds of practices and the kinds of production that are coming from people of color and that are talking about visions of the future or visions of the imagination that might get labeled sf.

IL: Sure. I just stumbled across this old book *Social Problems Through Science Fiction* at the book sale. This old, old book in 1975 . . .

NH: That's really fascinating.

IL: And it has all these great things in their about race.

NH: Oh my God. Yeah.

IL: Why is this out of print? Somebody was trying to do something in the seventies . . .

NH: They were! That's the thing, the allies are there.

IL: We just have to be able to identify them. Right?

NH: I'd like to see quilombo is science fiction courses. That thing is brilliant in the way that it takes the whole sensibility around Orisha, around Afro-Caribbean religious practice, and essentially creates a utopian vision of what a quilombo was that is fantastical as well in the way that a science fiction or fantasy reader understands fantastical. It's a brilliant piece of work. I'd like to see *Daughters of the Dust* on science fiction . . .

IL: Julie Dash.

NH: Julie Dash, yeah! Julie Dash is a huge science fiction fan.

IL: I'd like to see her here then. I didn't know that!

NH: She is, but she can't get or it's so hard for her to get the support to make her work. And, she's getting support for regular work, but for her science fiction work . . . I'd just like to see us get over some of the shit of the boxing in of what science fiction can be and what race can be. Where is our equivalent? I'd like to see support right through the various forms, the various artistic disciplines for artists of color who are interested in futuristic and fantastical visions. I'd like to see us really start to make them welcome because they bring a different vision. We bring a different vision and that will change the genre, and the genre is about change.

IL: You're right! It's changing. We're trying to get the racial skeletons out of the closet so to speak. Right? That's what it's all about.

NH: Yeah! So Julie Dash at SFRA. You know? Can you imagine Julie Dash at SFRA? I can.

IL: Well, I'd like to go to that one. It's just the funding [*laughter*].

NH: Yeah, I haven't been yet, but I will. Or Junot Díaz, who is a big science fiction fan.

IL: I just learned that name the other day.

NH: He emailed me the other day, and then he got to meet Joe and Gay Haldeman, and Junot was in seventh heaven and would like to do something like this.

IL: Sure, and they were asking me all kinds of questions about writers of color that they were interested in having a series of talks on their campus with writers of color for science fiction and I was like look in *So Long Been Dreaming* [*Hopkinson's laughter*], look in *Mojo*, and there's this Minister Faust.

NH: Minster Faust. He's a very good speaker. He's very articulate. He's been a radio personality for years. He's a sweetheart.

IL: Somewhere I heard that you stated many people feel that "SF/F/H films are the mythologies of the modern age." I was wondering if you could say more about that sensibility?

NH: I think I'm referencing Ursula Le Guin on some level with that. Mythology didn't use to be something people studied. It used to be something that your average guy in the street knew about. What's replaced that? What story telling has replaced that? It's film; film and video games, and to some extent music, and many of those have taken the kind of eyeball kicks of science fiction and fantasy to use a tricky city lexicon term, and are making stories with them. I don't always love the stories, but those stories enter popular imagination and you can find a whole culture or subculture talking about the new *Constantine* movie or the new *Blade* movie.

IL: I'm glad you're bringing up films because that's a topic that I wanted to talk about just a little bit with this question.

NH: [*laughter.*] So that's what I mean by mythology. And they're using large archetypal magic worlds, sometimes painted in such a broad stroke that it's a little irritating that the characterization is lost, but this stuff catches the popular imagination like nothing else. When I saw *Crouching Tiger, Hidden Dragon* and that first fight scene happens, I remember turning to the person I was at the movie with going this is genre. Not necessarily meaning fantasy—I was to realize later that the fact that true enough there were a lot of fantastic elements in it—but that there were a set of memes and tropes being invoked, referred to, and after a while, you get to the point where you don't need to any longer invoke them in depth. It was working off a set of metaphors that a lot of the audience already knew in other words. And I hadn't realized, even though I grew up watching kung fu movies like everybody else, that this was a pure distillation of kung fu movies into something else.

IL: It was done in a different way, a way that we have never seen. You're right. *Blade* [*Hopkinson's laughter*] and trying to get rid of Wesley Snipes's character. I'm just thinking of . . .

NH: He was almost rudimentary in the third one.

IL: Yeah because they were trying to play up Whistler's daughter and the Hannibal King role in that comedy kind of thing there . . .

NH: That was all right. What I loved was all the queer subtext. They've all met and they've all tasted my blade, I bet they had breasts [*laughter*]. The *Blade* movies, popular culture in general fascinates me in the way that it looks and doesn't look at race. My friend Ellen, who I was sitting beside just now, once referred to Jar Jar Binx as Steppin' Gecko [*laughter*]. And she doesn't remember doing it, but it was brilliant. That whole movie where it took the Shylock character, it takes these deeply embedded racial stereotypes, moves them into fantasy or space opera, and only those of us who remember them recognize what they're doing, and even then only some of us. It's a very insidious blanching of those metaphors while still using them and I know that it's still creating the prejudices because I see it in the unconscious things that the junior writers put out there. And the movies are wonderful for doing this because they can do it for millions of people at a time. It's very powerfully married visuals that way with movement. You get this very powerful thing. I have a *Blade* essay, but it's not a very good essay—it's just me ranting—but it's about the first two *Blade* movies on my blog, about the fact that they have taken a Black man, made him a metaphor for mulatto because he is mixed race. He's part vampire, part human, and they code vampires as a number of things, not just Black; they also code them as youth. They code them as a number of things, but they are the ones who have all the cool, have all the neat clothes, have all the sexuality, all the drugs, and he so hates the vampire side of himself which is coded in part as Black that he injects himself; you go through this whole seventies Black man on drugs movie metaphor where he straps off a vein and injects himself with the stuff and nods off with the whole heroin crack thing in order to suppress the vampire side of him encoded as Black. The first movie actually refers to it, where one of the white characters calls him an Uncle Tom, and that's exactly what he is. He never ever questions himself. He's trying to kill off half of himself by killing off a whole race of people. He's so internalized his own racism.

IL: Sure.

NH: And he's fascinating because of it. In the second movie, it retreats from so obvious a set of metaphors and then in doing so gets into some really weird territory. I'm already reading him, reading it as the vampire as a metaphor for Blackness. So we get into this whole African nation thing, where it is like I'm more African than them, meaning I'm more vampire than them, and he ends up having to kill off—essentially, he's the guy who kills Martin Luther King, he's the guy who kills off Malcolm X. And by the end of the movie, he's happy that he's done that. He's also killed off his own girlfriend [*laughter*] because a Black man cannot have sex on film.

IL: No. You're right, that's a question that I had for another time.

NH: That's a Steven Barnes rant. Oohh, he's much better at it than I am.

IL: But he's right though if you look at the films historically. I actually heard him at Stanford. It was great!

NH: Oh, it's amazing.

IL: But I was thinking, what do you make of the acceptance of Black actors in major science fiction films like Will Smith, Wesley Snipes, Laurence Fishburne, Angela Bassett, and Denzel Washington?

NH: It is getting better. They're no longer necessarily the second-string actors who get killed off. They are—for the most part, not yet—the heroes who make big-world change. Blade isn't out to change, he's out to make things go back to the way they were. Sadly, it's also that binary thinking too. It's also happening at the expense of other characters. I saw a movie with Angela Bassett and these three characters of color in this science fiction movie, it's amazing—you know *Supernova*? Angela Bassett, the guy who was in *My So-Called Life*, and the guy who was in *La Bamba*, are all in this movie, and only one of them lives. The woman lives and she even gets to have sex, but then she is a woman . . .

IL: But it's all right for a Black woman to have sex with a white man . . .

NH: Exactly, and on top of it the characters perhaps of color won't die, the queer characters die if the characters of color live. In *Independence Day*, it's one of the first ones they kill off: the old queen who wants to get home to his mother. Will Smith lives. So there's this weird hierarchy of who gets to be the cannon fodder, but I think we really just need to get rid of . . . like, mix it up.

IL: Yeah. Like if you go back to that great Canadian SF film *Cube* . . .

NH: Which I haven't seen. I was terrified. I can't deal with horror. It doesn't take much to frighten me.

IL: It's not really a horror film. It's more of a thriller. The Black cop guy just ends up going crazy on the five other people that are locked into this prison system, and he gets killed at the end by the slacker character, which is interesting, but the whole Black male beast/thug and rapist stereotype that he devolves into from the psychological aspect of being in this Cube where if you go in the wrong room you could be literally sliced and diced or melted by acid.

NH: Yeah, not watching that!

IL: But it's not really scary. There are no moments that make you jump in your seat.

NH: Michael Jackson's *Thriller* video scared me.

IL: Oh, no! OK.

NH: So I am really, really interested in popular culture and watching the mainstream popular culture slowly, slowly change. It's always the last one to make change. And the young folks who are going to these movies are probably more progressive than the movies themselves. Slowly they're going so we didn't kill the Black guy off. Is that OK? "Well, look you're still coming to the movie, suppose we kill the gay guy off" [*laughter*].

IL: Sure, but it's just unfortunate that most people's notions of science fiction derive from *Star Wars* and most camp films from the fifties and sixties, and you could go all the way up until today. People just aren't reading as much as they used to.

NH: Which means to me that film just has to get better. Someone needs to fund Julie Dash to make a science fiction movie. Someone needs to fund it. This notion that to be a Black artist means that you are making this genre called Black art is very limiting. Sometimes you are talking about Blackness. Sometimes you are talking about Asian-ness or what it's like to be First Nations, but sometimes you just want to make a damn movie or take a picture, or write a novel.

IL: And not worry about it being raced.

NH: Write about race, talk about race without necessarily being racialized like the difference between female and feminine. You don't have to be feminine in order to be female. You don't have to be racialized in order to be a person of color. And that's what we need to do more of I think.

IL: Do you watch any anime?

NH: I don't have a television. I do have a DVD player and a monitor, so I rent things after they come out. The last thing I saw was *Ghost in the Shell* 1 or 2. I'm not sure.

IL: I'm just curious because that's another kind of race that is coming into effect. First, it's coming from Japan, a different racial group, but it's coming to dominate television and cartoons here in America as well as video games, which I find fascinating.

NH: I saw *Spirited Away*, and loved it as well. What I have seen of generic anime, I am very curious about the fact that most of the characters to my eyes look white. And I am not really sure about what's going on there. And it may just be that you're Japanese, you don't see yourself as having eyes that are any different from everyone else. You just have eyes, but they also often have like blonde hair or green hair . . .

IL: And nice blue eyes or green eyes, and really pointy little noses.

NH: To me, that's the question about Black women and hair. That's a big boondoggle. You can just get into big trouble over it.

IL: Yeah, you can. My wife recently went natural over the past year and a half. And I wasn't sure how it was going to look. "Well, Heather I don't know . . ."

NH: [*laughter.*] Exactly!

IL: True enough, you shouldn't use chemicals. We have the good hair/bad hair discussion all the time—well, I can't help my ancestry.

NH: It's a struggle that Black women go through, and at some level we should be just able to do whatever the hell we want with our hair, but what does it mean? In this society, the straight thing means something. It's not just a fashion choice. I'd like that to be more conscious. Same thing with anime; it's like what's going on with the way you depict people. Films like *Spirited Away* and *Ghost in the Shell*—and I don't think *Spirited Away* is technically anime—what I love about them is that to me there is a sensibility that comes from a cultural perspective that I don't have. So they give me the world in a new way. And *Ghost in the Shell*, what I loved about it is that it comes from a Japanese director and he's not only playing with Japanese fantasy imagery; there was a whole lot of *Alice in Wonderland* in there. He claims it all, and he's just making his stuff and we all need to deal. Sure, the twin sisters look like the white creep from *Alice in Wonderland*. It's part of his palette, and he's got them in there with a dragon of the air and a dragon of the sea that are very Asian imagery. I'd love to see more of us just be able to not be boxed in.

IL: I'm still thinking about the issue of hair, and I'm thinking about your short story "A Habit of Waste" and the body changing. I think a hair story would be a great science fiction story or speculative fiction story.

NH: It would, but would it get recognized as such.

IL: I don't know.

NH: [*laughter.*] I think we just need to keep making the work and keep making it to as high standards as we can possibly make it. I'm also very big on the story needs to work as a story. The fact that you are an artist of color isn't enough.

Conjuring Caribbean Moonbeams: An Interview with Nalo Hopkinson

Michael Lohr / 2007

From *New York Review of Science Fiction* 20, no. 4 (December 2007): 21–23. Reprinted by permission of Michael Lohr.

Michael Lohr: Do you believe science fiction and fantasy fiction will ever receive proper respect from the mainstream? What about genre fiction in general?

Nalo Hopkinson: Maybe I should care, because I don't want to stay broke. But I'm not particularly mainstream myself, and I'm not sure I want to be. I think it'd be more fun if the mainstream joined us, rather than the other way around. Boy, there's a confusing metaphor, if ever there was one. Still, I don't mind it that my chosen genres are considered disrespectable by some. I think so many genres could stand to get more disrespectable.

ML: Does it offend you when someone says that you are "a great Black writer," or you are one of the "best women writers" around instead of just saying that you are a great writer?

NH: Depends on who's saying it, from what community, and in what context. Blackness is significant; living in Black skin, I'm reminded of it every day. So is femaleness. And queerness. And Caribbeanness. And so is writing. And so on. If my various communities (and I've only named a few of them here) want to acknowledge me as being part of them, that feels good. I'm not going to say to them, "No, I'm not one of you." On the other hand, I do get cranky when people say that because I write out of those experiences, I am limited to only those audiences. That's a crock.

ML: Have you ever considered writing a horror novel?

NH: Some people say that I have, with my first novel *Brown Girl in the Ring*. But I get scared easily and badly; we're talking no sleep for days and jumping at every shadow. For that reason, I have trouble even reading horror.

132 CONVERSATIONS WITH NALO HOPKINSON

I keep trying, because so many of the stories are so tempting. I can get through some of them. But with many of them there comes a point where I need to just close the book. I tried reading Stephen King's *IT* a few years ago. When I got to the part a few pages in where there was a sneering clown in full makeup in the storm drain, calling the little boy, I closed the book. I'm even worse with horror films—can't watch them at all, not even a little bit. Yet I do manage to get pretty dark sometimes with my own writing. My imagination can go there very easily. Perhaps that's why I scare easily.

ML: Your stories often times are peppered with Caribbean and Jamaican folklore. Is this something that you spend a lot of time researching, or is it something that was part of your upbringing and thus second nature?

NH: A little bit of both. Canadian writer Larissa Lai once said, "It always amuses me when people ask if I learned these stories from my grandmother; that desire for the authentic, wise, folklore-spewing celestial. The answer is no, I just went to the library." I laughed so hard when I read that, because I could so relate! A lot of my early exposure to Caribbean folklore came from seeing it on Caribbean television. And my mother is a library technician, so I grew up spending a lot of my life in libraries. And my father was an English and Latin teacher, and an actor and writer, so our bookshelves at home held everything from Louise Bennett's *Jamaica Labrish* to Homer's *Iliad*. And I was a bookworm, so I read then. But, of course, having been born in the Caribbean and growing up mostly there until I was sixteen, some Caribbean speech patterns, culture, and food are native to me. Now, I know that I'm not pointing this next comment at you, because I'm quite aware that sometimes interviewers ask questions deliberately in order to give the interviewee a chance to speak to a particular misapprehension. It's a difficult question to answer, because it's an odd question, if only because it gets leveled predominantly at people who are seen as somehow "Other." And it seems to presuppose that we get our artistic inspiration in a way that is different from how other people do. I must ask Kelly Link if she ever gets asked if her heritage is second nature.

ML: You once said that science fiction is the literature of social commentary. Do you still believe this to be true?

NH: I said it was *arguably* the literature of social commentary (or, if I wasn't smart enough to say it then, that's how I've phrased it since). Yes, I think it's one of the things that science fiction and fantasy can do: examine social systems and the process of social change, and how they affect individuals and populations. Any form of art or inquiry can do this. But I think that science fiction and fantasy specialize in it.

ML: You were the editor for a terrific collection of stories entitled *Whispers From the Cotton Tree Root: Caribbean Fabulist Fiction.* How did this project come about?

NH: I was attending the International Conference of the Fantastic in the Arts, in either 1999 or 2000, I think. It may have been the first time I'd attended. The editors of the then-new press Invisible Cities approached me and asked if I'd ever thought of editing an anthology. I said that I had, but that an interesting framework and a suitable opportunity hadn't yet come to me. They said, "What about fabulist fiction?" I said, "What's fabulist fiction?" And we were off to the races. The cool thing about *Whispers* is that it gave me the opportunity to approach the writers I knew of from my father's days as a writer, and to ask them to submit work to the anthology. The scary thing was that I then had to do what an editor does, and select some stories and turn away others, some of them by people who are my elders, in talent as well as years.

ML: In your short story "A Habit of Waste," your main character was a young Black woman struggling to conform and adapt to vulgar social conventions. Was this purely speculative on your part or was there a hint of self-portrayal within?

NH: This is from Frances Trollope, who apparently got asked the same question as well: "Of course I draw from life—but I always pulp my acquaintance before serving them up. You would never recognize a pig in a sausage." This is the type of question that stumps me every time. I'm a forty-five-year-old chunky Black woman, and I've been a thirty-year-old chunky Black woman. How would I go about *not* drawing on personal experience with a story like that? I got into work one morning, and I was already having a bad body image day. I said to a coworker, "I just saw someone getting on the streetcar with the body I used to have." She replied, "That sounds like one of your stories." And I realized it did. I'm not sure how much I got done that day of the work I was being paid to do. I think that was in the days before I had a computer at home, but I did have a computer at work. I am curious: in what sense are you using the word *vulgar*?

ML: I was using the word *vulgar* to mean coarse or pretentiously double-standarded. Because you are from a minority, things can be more difficult. It was in this regard that I meant vulgar. Instead of a more utopian ideal that merit and ability alone would allow you to succeed without the inclusion of biases such as ethnicity, religion, political affiliation, etc.

What was your primary emotional motivation for writing *Brown Girl in the Ring*? I know you were facing a contest deadline, but what was the creative source for your main character Ti-Jeanne?

NH: No one source. I was writing articles on health and fitness for a local Black paper at the time (I used to be a fitness instructor). In my research, I'd come across an article on schizophrenia in Caribbean male immigrant populations in the UK. So that was bouncing around in my brain. And I'd written six pages of . . . something to submit to a fiction course being taught by Judy Merril; it was the first time I'd dared try to be a fiction writer. So there was that. I think I was already reading about Afro-Caribbean religious systems because I'd recently realized that there were non-Christian religions in the Caribbean, and I was intrigued by the notion of deities that looked like me and came from where I came from. I decided to spring off from the ring game "Brown Girl in the Ring" because, well, it gave me an idea that I thought I could develop. And some time after I'd begun to try to write the novel, I decided that my three women fighting the same central evil in their lives could be three generations of women, and that made me think of Derek Walcott's play *Ti-Jean and His Brothers*, and off it went. I was stuck on that story for the longest while, until I thought to ask myself how the young woman and the old woman sitting in a cheap apartment watching bad television earned the money to do so. A few years later, I attended Clarion East, and I was very pleased when Samuel R. Delany advised us to figure out how our protagonists earned their livings. It seems self-evident to me now that one needs to do that, but then, it was a revelation.

ML: Did you find the time you spent as a writing mentor and instructor for the master's degree in Writing Popular Fiction program at Seton Hill University rewarding? Do you find most of your academic appointments rewarding?

NH: I started out as an SHU student in their master's program in Writing Popular Fiction. I was already on my third novel contract, but I figured that anything I could do to develop a teaching career on the side was not a bad idea. And I knew that *The Salt Roads* (then *Griffonne*) was going to be the biggest writing challenge I had undertaken up till then, and I was scared spitless by it. So I figured that having a mentor couldn't hurt either. As a mentor, writer James Morrow was perfect for me. He was amazing. He went several extra miles to help midwife me through that novel, and he pushed me to go thousands of extra miles myself—in some ways, literally: he helped get me invited to France for a few days as a guest at Utopiales, and I was able to do a bit of research while I was there. Once I'd graduated, Seaton Hill asked me to be a mentor in the program, which I did for a while. And I've done the Clarion hat trick (taught at Clarions East, West, and South), and I teach creative writing here in Toronto. I find teaching creative writing equal parts aggravating and rewarding. Oh, and challenging. It can be wearying to go through manuscript after manuscript and see the same missteps year after year and wonder if you're doing any good at all. It can be disheartening when you try to help someone see where they've misstepped, and you realize that you've stepped on their joy in writing. But then there's that rare moment when a light goes on in someone's eyes, and they've understood something about their craft that they hadn't before. That's a sweet moment. And the passion that the students have can reinfect me with passion for my own writing. When I'm in the zone, it's not about whether someone's writing efforts are clumsy. It's the glee of feeling a bit like a co-conspirator, because they are trying to do something undervalued and difficult, but by god, they're going for it! And sometimes I can help to urge them on.

ML: You are involved with an organization called the Speculative Fiction Foundation. Could you tell the readers about this foundation and its mission?

NH: I'm not very involved. I'm on their advisory board, and they don't much need my advice. I am much more involved as a founding member and board member of the Carl Brandon Society (CBS). The society is currently running two inaugural awards: the Carl Brandon Parallax Award for speculative fiction in English by a writer of color, and the Carl Brandon Kindred Award for speculative fiction in English that deals with race and ethnicity. Stuff has been written elsewhere about the CBS, so I'll point you to it: www.carlbrandon.org and <carlbrandon.org/blog>.

ML: You were an instructor at the Royal Ontario Museum (ROM) for the "Egyptian Art in the Age of the Pyramids" exhibition, which was an exposition for 4,500-year-old artifacts. What is your opinion on the origins of the Egyptian god Bes? I've heard some say Bes originated from Phoenicia while others say he comes from Babylon or the Hittites.

NH: I was a tour guide for high schools visiting the exhibit. We were taught about the artifacts in the exhibition, and there were experts on hand to provide more information. Honestly? I don't remember the god Bes ever coming up in the instruction I got. That doesn't mean he didn't; I may just not have been paying attention that day. What was interesting to me about that exhibit is that nowhere in the two extensive floors of exhibitions was the word *Africa* written. Even the map of Egypt showed Egypt floating in space, surrounded by nothing. I was curious about that, so in my spiel I began asking the students where Egypt was. The answers I got? "It's in India." "It's in China." "It's somewhere down south." "It's nowhere. It's just Egypt." A few students did know that Egypt is in Africa, but they were in the minority. So then I went into a bookstore, because I was doing research for *The Salt Roads*, part of which is set in Alexandria, fourth century C.E. The section for the books on Africa contained no books on Egypt; they were all filed under "The Middle East." I once heard a writer from Egypt say, "When did my country leave Africa and become part of the Middle East?"

It got even more eldritch. I have a chronic pain disorder, which at the time was giving me enough trouble that I asked to be allowed to sit in between tours. The museum provided me with a wheelchair for that purpose. And it was so cold in the climate-controlled galleries, so I always had a favorite wrap with me. When I wasn't moving around, I would sit in the wheelchair with my wrap tucked around my shoulders. I would stand when a class came in to be taken on a tour. Every so often, one of the few students who did know that Egypt was in Africa would scream when I stood, because they'd assumed that I was one of the artifacts. That part was only amusing, and it allowed me to get into the discussion that most fourth century C.E. Egyptians would not have looked like me, unless they were of Nubian background. (Handily enough, one of our tour guides was Egyptian, so I could point to him and say, "They would have looked more like him.") But then after the exhibit had its last day and the tour guides were being given a farewell party, one of the permanent staff in the ROM's Education Department came up to me and said how cool it was that I had been giving added value to the exhibit by "dressing up in African costume." I hadn't the foggiest idea what she was talking about. "Like today," she said, indicating the clothing I was wearing, "this costume." I was wearing a plain cotton dress from a local chain, a T-shirt, and my wrap, which is West African mudcloth. "You mean my *clothes*?" I asked her. "Yes," she replied. "Such a lovely costume." She went away before I could ask her if she thought of her everyday clothing as a costume, and if she thought that ancient Egyptians thought of their everyday clothing as such. Never mind how she figured that a piece of cloth from a country in twenty-first-century West Africa would somehow be a good way to teach anyone about a country half a continent away from there, and 4,500 years removed in time.

Even so, it was an amazing experience to spend four months being able to get close to art that was made by human hands thousands of years ago. There was a huge limestone statue of the architect Hemiunu that had been so lovingly wrought that you could see the folds in the man's belly button. It would probably have been painted, but the paint was 4,500 years gone. In the dim lighting of the gallery, the limestone gleamed like skin. Then there was the fragment of papyrus on which someone had written a detailed accounting of the artifacts a temple owned—including one lamp, broken. There's more on the Royal Ontario Museum's website, www.metmuseum .org/explore/new_pyramid/PYRAMIDS/HTML/el_pyramid_hemiunu.htm.

ML: A reviewer once stated that your novels have a mystical and esoteric feel to them. Is this something you set out to purposefully do or is this effect more a side effect the speculative nature of the fiction?

NH: I think it's more an "and" than an "or." You won't get too many binaries out of me. I write science fiction and fantasy; *of course* there's a mystical and esoteric feel to some of my work.

ML: You once said that speculative fiction has repeatedly reinvented itself over the years through visionscapes of feminists, cyberpunks, and queer writers. At the time, you hoped that speculative fiction would also open up to communities of color; do you still feel this is occurring?

NH: Yes, it is, and a little more every day. It's still just a trickle, but it's growing.

ML: So, what's the story about you skinny-dipping in Thoreau's Walden Pond?

NH: It was a blistering hot summer. I was attending Readercon in Boston. A bunch of friends of mine were there, and one of them had talked a lot in the past about skinny-dipping at night in Walden Pond. But the park is closed to the public at night, so I couldn't possibly have challenged him to take us there. We couldn't have made the trek down the path in the dark. We couldn't have stripped off our clothing and waded into water so pellucid that even in the dark, you could see right down to the bottom. We couldn't have heard the quiet laughing and conversation of other groups of people swimming in other parts of the pond. We couldn't have bobbed around in the water, talking about books and science fiction and heaven knows what else. When the sky began to rumble with thunder and we saw the first lightning flash preceding a rain shower, we couldn't have run laughing out of the water, changed back into our clothing, and left, refreshed. Too bad, because it would have been a great thing to do.

"Happy That it's Here": An Interview with Nalo Hopkinson

Nancy Johnston / 2008

From *Queer Universes: Sexualities in Science Fiction*, edited by Joan Gordon, Vernica Hollinger, and Wendy Gay Pearson (Liverpool University Press, 2008), 200–215. Reprinted with permission by Liverpool University Press.

Nancy Johnston: One of my attractions to your work is the "newness"— the originality and energy of your short fiction and novels, from *Brown Girl in the Ring* to *Midnight Robber* to *The Salt Roads*. (Sandra Jackson-Opoku has admired your "conjurer's art.") For readers, I think particularly for queer readers, you offer some radical and challenging perspectives, futures, and worlds. In much of your fiction, you seem to resist the conventions of a normative heterosexuality: the idea that one form of sexuality and gender performance is or should be the norm. I'm thinking of your subtle representation of pairings or group partnerships of queer men and women in *Midnight Robber*, Issy and Cleve's playful and electric role reversals in "Ganger (Ball Lightning)," and the fluid sexualities and the expression of complex desires of Mer and Jeanne Duval in *The Salt Roads*. What motivates or inspires you to challenge your readers?

Nalo Hopkinson: Sexuality gets binarized too often. Not only do I resist the idea of one form of sexuality, but the assumption that there are only two forms, and you do one, the other, or both, and those are the only possible behaviors. It sometimes seems to me—and perhaps whimsically so—that the people who are courageously non-normative in their sexualities are doing in the real world some of the work that speculative fiction can do in the world of the imagination, that is, exploring a wider range of possibilities for living.

I've realized recently that the commonly accepted spectrum of gay-bi-straight doesn't work for me, either, though in a pinch, I'll describe myself nowadays as bisexual if no other word that will be understood is available, and if I don't have time to give the long answer, which is one I'm still figuring out, but which seems to have to do with an attraction to queering gender, and to overt and principled sexual transgression. For a long while it was very painful to me to feel like I had no name for what I am. But I eventually realized that there are more options than straight/gay and almost as an afterthought, oh yeah, those bisexual people; that there are more than two binary poles around which most people cluster like magnetic filings with a few people wandering around in the middle, supposedly waiting for one or the other pole to draw them in.

When I write, I want to present as wide a spectrum as I can of the ways in which people can choose to behave sexually and in relationships, and I like representing those where possible as visible, acceptable behaviors. Because they should be, and because science fiction is about conceiving new possibilities. So yes, I find I'm constantly resisting both monoliths and binaries because I find them limiting for myself. It took a while for me even to be able to understand myself as queer, because monoliths and binaries obscured me from seeing it. Gay/straight/bisexual are all important to represent, but they aren't the only possible axes along which to sort human sexual attraction.

NJ: You have counted many SF writers as early and current influences on your work. Whose writing stimulates or challenges your work in the depiction or representation of sexuality or sexual politics? Which SF writers do you find the most demanding and rewarding?

NH: Science fiction is and has been ripe to discuss other possibilities for sex and relationships: multiple marriages, communal structures, different genders. Writers like Theodore Sturgeon, Samuel R. Delany, Octavia Butler, Elizabeth Lynn, Nicola Griffith, Élisabeth Vonarburg, Candas Jane Dorsey, Eleanor Arnason, Storm Constantine have been my touchstones.

NJ: When you talk about your early influences, you have often mentioned Samuel R. Delany. Critics have also pointed to Delany (as well as Octavia Butler), one of the most prominent Black writers in the genre, as an important model for many writers of color. He is also one of the most prominent queer writers in the genre and one who dramatically troubles all kinds of boundaries, including sex and gender. Has his work influenced your approach or opened up the field for queer writing?

NH: Yes—his work makes me see the world, including Blackness and sexuality and class, in ways that have not occurred to me before.

From Chip Delany's writing (I think that's where I originally encountered it, though I can't be certain), I got the notion that identity labels aside, if you were to look at the specific particularities of what or who people enjoy sexually, or how they end up structuring their intimate lives and their families, you'd see a lot more variance than we're led to believe is there. And I've certainly found that to be true as I meet more and more people. Hanne Blank (*Virgin: The Untold History*, 2006) calls identity boxes "umbrellas," because she says, as with umbrellas, they don't completely cover you; there'll often be a part of you that's left out in the rain.

NJ: In your fiction, including *Midnight Robber* and stories like "Fisherman" in *Skin Folk*, you portray female characters that choose to cross-dress or to disguise themselves to take up the traditional roles of men.

NH: I do? I hadn't realized that. I wouldn't call the protagonist of "Fisherman" "female." Kelly just lives in a community where there is no concept of being transgendered. Tan-Tan in *Midnight Robber* isn't wearing men's clothing, she's wearing trousers; no more remarkable in her world than in mine. You could make the weak case that Kelly in "Fisherman" is acting "like a man," but the things that Tan-Tan does are considered transgressive in her world because she's chosen to be an outlaw, and because she's emotionally out of control, even by the standards of a world where life is cheap and whole communities are way dysfunctional. It's not because she's female. But I am intrigued by the stories of women and men in history who have cross-dressed.

NJ: Are there historical models or folk stories in which women take on the dress or gender roles of men? Are you responding to traditional stories, in which protagonists are forced to abandon various kinds of disguises (or take up their old "skins") to reintegrate into their societies or return home? Can you discuss the significance of impersonation and cross-dressing in your own stories?

NH: I'm not sure that I can, because I haven't written the story yet. I am planning to, though. I'm not sure why it interests me so much. Gender-bending's sexy, so maybe that's one reason. And limiting people's actions based on their genitalia is kinda asinine, so maybe that's another reason. But I don't want to psychoanalyze myself on this topic too much before I actually write the novel.

NJ: In describing "Fisherman" to readers, some critics are challenged by the "graphic" depiction of sexuality. Do you intentionally challenge descriptions of sexuality? Do you view your stories, especially those depicting same-sex or alternative sexualities, as "graphic" or explicit?

NH: I hope that my vanilla and het sex scenes are graphic and explicit, too! I write. It's an art form. Why would I make the effort to describe a meal or a sunset in a way that's detailed and responds to all the senses, but not do so for a sex scene? Why are "graphic" and "explicit" good in descriptions of walking through a field of lavender in full bloom, but not for a character coming so hard that his eyes roll back in his head? I don't make a distinction between porn and erotica; I use the words interchangeably. I do make a distinction between well-written stories meant to turn the reader on, and poorly written stories meant to turn the reader on. And that's to some extent a subjective judgement. I don't try to make the same-sex or alternative sex scenes more striking than the het or vanilla scenes (and it even kinda bugs me that I'm implicitly pairing "het" and "vanilla" by wording them the way I just did). Science fiction and fantasy are about looking at the world through a different lens. So whatever I write, including sex scenes, I may first think, how can I cause myself, and the reader, to see this differently? What can I do to challenge, delight, surprise, unsettle?

NJ: Your fiction offers a breadth of female and male characters, and sexy, desirable women populate your fiction. The characters who most embrace their bodies and sexuality seem to exhibit the most power, whether personally or fantastically. I'm thinking, for example, of your early story, "A Habit of Waste," where you draw attention to how culturally prescribed Western representations of ideal female beauty are. How important are these questions of body image and representations of beauty, as themes?

NH: The prevailing mass culture message that the only beautiful female body is young, white, straight-haired, and thin with a flat behind can destroy a woman's healthy body image. The protagonist in "A Habit of Waste" started out Black, kinky-haired, and curvy, and has internalized a lot of self-hatred. She has undergone a procedure to discard her voluptuous dark-skinned body for a more acceptable thin, white one; however, she finds herself jealous of how a stranger wearing her cast-off body is broadcasting confidence and self-love. So many women live in a state of induced neurosis around our bodies. I know how damaging it is, because I have to fight it daily. I once belonged to a health club at my university. The first time I used the changing room there was the first time I saw women of all ages, sizes, and shapes walking around naked. There was beauty all around me, and only a small proportion of it was conventional beauty. It finally occurred to me that the wide range of human body shapes, heights, and sizes can in no way be expected to fit into the narrow range of "acceptable" body types and clothing sizes. And perhaps that's the point; if everybody can be one of the in crowd, how in the world would we know who's on the outs? It would be a disaaaaster! (Yes, I am speaking tongue-in-cheek.)

I know—we all know—women who have become emotionally and physically ill sometimes to the point of death, trying to fit their societies' narrow beauty and behavioral standards. We know of women who have been hurt or killed because they have not. It's happening increasingly to men, too. It's criminal and wasteful that that should be so. So if I can present all kinds of bodies in a positive light in my writing, perhaps it's a way of modeling another point of view. There are any number of ways I could do that, but science fiction and fantasy excel at it.

NJ: In your introduction to "Riding the Red" in *Skin Folk*, you used the metaphor of shedding the skin: "Throughout the Caribbean, under different names, you'll find stories about people who aren't what they seem. Skin gives these skin folk their human shape. When the skin comes off, their true selves emerge." Can you elaborate perhaps on how your characters in this collection are "people who aren't what they seem"?

NH: Those stories all got written and in most cases published independently of each other, with no thought to collecting them. I didn't write them with any connection amongst them in mind. When my editor said she would like to collect some of my short stories into one volume, I then had to figure out what to call the collection. So I looked at all the stories and tried to discern a common thread from which I could generate a title. I thought I was being so clever when I noticed that a lot of the characters change from one thing into another. But I later realized I hadn't come up with anything novel. Fiction is about taking a protagonist through some life-changing moments, and science fiction and fantasy can literalize that change into actual bodily transformations. In any case, I went with something I'd found in a few African diasporic folktales; when the soucouyant can't get back into her skin because someone has rubbed the inside of it with hot pepper, she says to the skin, "Kin-kin, you don't know me?" (something like, "Skin of mine, don't you recognize me?"). I liked the idea of kin and skin being the same thing. I liked the idea that people changed into different things by taking off their skins. Hence, *Skin Folk*. It was after the collection was published that I discovered the Black American proverb, "All my skin folk ain't my kin folk," which adds some more layers to the imagery.

NJ: In both *Brown Girl* and *Midnight Robber*, your protagonists are young women at the point of a transition into adulthood roles (or rites). This transition is ultimately liberating, and opens their access to a potent sexuality and even supernatural power. What interests you in this transitional moment for adolescent and young women to adulthood?

NH: Mostly because I was one once, and it sucked. It's like a message back in time to my twenty-two-year-old self, to let her know that it'll get better.

NJ: How does sexuality as a thematic thread inform *Midnight Robber* or *Brown Girl in the Ring*?

NH: Not so much, I don't think. At least, nowhere near as much as *The Salt Roads,* or some of my short stories. But even though they're my first two published novels, some of my natural bents are already evident: in *Brown Girl in the Ring*, the grandmother is an older woman who's not written as asexual; I believe (can't quite remember) that one of the gang members is queer—and male, and macho, and Black, and Caribbean—because I wanted to push at the misapprehension that the first attribute cannot or shouldn't coexist with the remaining four. The characters come in a few different sexualities, and I portray that pretty matter-of-factly. Still, I was too shy to actually write a sex scene between the protagonist and her ex-boyfriend. People reading my current work might be surprised to know that I was once shy about writing sex scenes. I do a similar stirring up of sexual conformities in *Midnight Robber*, with the addition of a couple of different versions of polyamory. I don't make it front-and-center, but I was interested in creating a world in which there wasn't a monolithic expectation for how sex/love/marriage relationships would be constructed. I wanted a world in which people co-created the individual relationship structures that seemed to suit them. Whatever you wanted out of a relationship you had to articulate and negotiate for, including monogamy. It felt risky to use Caribbean characters to examine different kinds of sexualities and sexual relationships. I think that we (Caribbean people) are so used to protecting our sexualities from prurient gaze that we've built up these huge taboos against many types of sexual expression; I've been affected by those taboos, too. So for me, the fact that I was finding it so difficult to depict two Black Caribbean men publicly wining each other down (the only translation that comes to mind is "dirty dancing") meant that I had to portray it, as an act of freeing up my own mind, as an acknowledgment that it happens in the real world, as an expression of my joy in the knowledge that human beings love and lust after each other. For me, it's part of my avowal that Black people and Caribbean people are human, in the face of a world that continually tries to convince us that we are not.

NJ: Are you interested in troubling notions of desire, or portraying unconventional relationships and sexualities?

NH: Yes. It's fun to do. And it's scary to do. It makes me push at some of my own biases. When I wrote *Brown Girl in the Ring*, I was, as far as I knew, straight. I was also younger and less aware than I am now. When I told an acquaintance that I had just had my first novel published, he said, "Oh, yeah? And how many queer people are in it?" I had a moment of sheer panic until I mentally went through the roster of characters and came up with, I think, seven. Or five. I can't remember all the characters anymore. Then, at some point, a sweetie of mine pointed out that one of those characters dies as his boyfriend holds him, and they could be seen as the stereotypical tragical queers—you know, well of loneliness stuff. Up until then, I hadn't been consciously aware that there was a trope. I was mortified to think that I might have replicated it as a result of not examining my own unconscious assumptions. Weighed against the handful of other queer characters in the book, two of whom are partnered and having quite happy lives together, I don't think I did play into the trope, but I only avoided doing so by happy accident, not by intention. Sometimes I've not been so fortunate; some years ago, I lost a friend over an argument we had about a male whore-cum-thief I had written into an earlier version of *Brown Girl in the Ring*. I hadn't the first idea what the life of someone like that might be like; the closest thing I had in mind was a character from the Thieves' World series; not a great idea to try to create a fully rounded character by basing him on a fictional one! It's sort of like making a third-generation photocopy. I thought he was fun, but what I wrote was hugely offensive. My friend did know people working in the sex-trade industry. He chewed me out, and I gut huffy, and though we both made nice a few days later, our friendship has never recovered. Interesting, though; a few days after that, I complained to a fellow writer about the incident. He, trying to reassure me, told me that he'd read what I'd written and he wasn't offended; he said that he was a straight, white male, and he figured people like him would form most of my audience, so it didn't so much matter what this other person thought. That was when I began to feel uneasy. Because it very much did matter to me. I had more in common with the guy who got angry with me—a politicized First Nations man—than with someone for whom identity politics were irrelevant. Perhaps straight white men are the largest part of my audience. Fair enough, but I already knew that I had no interest in contributing further to the erasure of people whose experiences are already marginalized; quite the opposite, in fact, if only because doing so would be to do psychic damage to myself. I still didn't understand why my (ex)-friend had gotten so upset. But if I didn't know how to fix the offending character, I could do the next best thing; I took him out altogether. A few years and a bit more experience and wisdom later, I understood that that man had had every reason to be furious. I had the occasion a few years ago to tell him that he'd been right and I'd been wrong. Every time I put my work out into the public, I risk putting something out there based in my unexamined and unrecognized assumptions. That's part of the game.

NJ: In *The Salt Roads*, you avoid idealizing or sentimentalizing same-sex partnerships. Your haunting depiction of Met, an enslaved woman and plantation doctor, and her love for Tipingee, is followed, in the same novel, by the more casual lovers, entertainers Jeanne and Lisette, in nineteenth-century Paris. Why is that important to you?

NH: I think my reasoning goes a little like this: people will love each other, no matter what circumstances they are in. Some of those loves will be of a type not commonly accepted. How might that play out? Mer and Tipingee have this horrible life that can injure or kill them at any moment, and that deliberately works to break their spirits, yet they find ways to love each other and other people, because that's what keeps human beings going. Everyone in their community of slaves knows that they making *z'anmi* (an old Trinidadian expression for women in an intimate sexual relationship with each other; the root word is *amie*, i.e., friend), but because they are necessary to a community in chronically dire straits, and because they preserve outward appearances, they are pretty much left alone. It's not that people necessarily approve. It's that they know they may need Mer and Tipingee's medical services someday. And because the two women have the compliance of Tipingee's husband Patrice, they can all partially shelter under the "umbrella" of the convention of polygyny, which is a familiar one to their community. Tipingee, Patrice and Mer aren't exactly doing polygyny (Mer and Patrice aren't lovers), but it looks enough like it from the outside that they're able to preserve appearances. There's also the convention of homosociality, which means that their community accepts and expects that people of the same sex will form strong friendship and social bonds; again, a partial umbrella, since those bonds aren't expected to be sexual in nature. But since any of the slaves on that plantation can see that Mer and Tipingee are good friends, they may not question the nature of the friendship.

In nineteenth-century Paris, Jeanne and Lisette aren't exactly having a picnic either; they are essentially sexual servants who know that the only way out is to use their beauty—while they still have it—to attract the attentions of rich gentlemen; and Jeanne knows quite well that because of her Blackness and her lack of "breeding," none of those gentlemen will ever

146 CONVERSATIONS WITH NALO HOPKINSON

make her his legitimate wife. Jeanne and Lisette love each other—perhaps Jeanne loves more than Lisette—but they never question that their love can only ever be casual; it's simply not possible in their place and time, for women of their station. If they were both independently wealthy, white society women, perhaps. So yes, I'm trying not to be simply reactionary in the way I portray same-sex relationships, but I'm also trying to be realistic about what's possible for the characters in their context.

NJ: You have written candidly about sexuality and sex in short stories and especially in your recent fiction. In *The Salt Roads*, you linger delightfully over one woman's frank appreciation and intimate pleasure in the taste and smell of her female lover. Has this openness been received well by readers and critics?

NH: By some, not by others. Some people find it disgusting. Some people find it liberating. My mother's just alarmed. Generally, reception has been fine. A few readers have been put off by the explicit sexuality in *The Salt Roads*, and I suspect it's at least partly because the sex is non-normative. The other part of what people may find shocking about the non-normative sexuality is that I involve a respected historical literary figure in it (Charles Baudelaire), and I also show Black people doing kinky sex. There are all kinds of reasons why it feels particularly taboo to do the latter. For one thing, we ("we" in this instance meaning Black people) are too often the victims of having white sexual fears projected onto our bodies, often in dangerous ways. So we can be cautious about making any room for that to happen. But I think there's a cost when Black communities keep too opaque a veil over the fact that Black people's desire and sexual inclinations are as varied and human as anyone else's. I was thinking about that when I wrote *The Salt Roads*. So I show a Black man and woman who both enjoy dressing him up in women's clothing when they have sex. I show a famous white poet in bondage, bottoming to his Black female lover. I show two nineteenth-century women, one Black, one white, having oral sex. I wouldn't have thought that would be particularly shocking; by contrast to the other two, it's pretty daily sex. But I do tend to try to evoke all the senses in my descriptions, and that may be more than some people are comfortable dealing with. I use explicit words for sex. A lot of the characters in the novel are sex-trade workers, so they have bawdy, streetworthy, specific language for sex and sexual acts. That's the kind of language I tried to put into their mouths. *The Salt Roads* has received a more mixed reception than my other books; for all kinds of reasons, not just the sexualities. The novel is also nonlinear with multiple viewpoints, and there are differences of opinion as to how successful that was. But even so, the overall response has been positive. I haven't heard a lot of Caribbean response yet; a hardcover book priced to the American market is an expensive thing in the Caribbean, so I suspect that it hasn't been that widely read there.

I am aware, though, that there is no accounting for how people will perceive what I've written. One reader was disturbed by what he saw as my depicting Black women as indiscriminately ready for sex with anyone, any time. He wondered at my playing into the stereotype of the rapacious Black or mixed-race woman. That reading surprised me, because I was actually trying to write against the stereotype by depicting the characters as people with full lives who find ways to make choices, good, bad, and indifferent, no matter how constrained their circumstances.

NJ: You said that you had wanted to tackle Saint Mary of Egypt . . .

NH: Yeah, I also wanted to play against the traditional depiction of Saint Mary of Egypt, who has struck me powerfully from the first time I encountered stories of her. She's sometimes called "the dusky saint" or "Gypsy Mary" ("gypsy" as in "Egyptian"). So here was an expression of Africanness that I had not seen before in Catholic orthodoxy—an African saint! (I'm deliberately not saying a "Black" saint. Egyptianness does not necessarily indicate Blackness.) Her Africanness and her "duskiness" were intriguing, that potential for a rare reflection of self in mainstream mass culture. But when I investigated the stories about her, she was depicted as so consumed with sexual desire that she became a prostitute at the age of twelve so she could have sex with a lot of men. Seems to me that the last thing you would do as a means of enjoying sex is get sold into prostitution. So I had a look at what was happening in North Africa in that general time period. There were a lot of famines, and farmers in particular often ended up selling themselves and/or their families as bondservants because drought had destroyed their livelihoods. If you were female, you could end up working as a serving girl in a tavern, where you could be expected to turn tricks. It made much more sense to me that Gypsy Mary might have ended up a prostitute because she was bloody well hungry.

The Catholic lore further goes that Gypsy Mary became sanctified when she accepted shame and not only gave up her sexual self, she gave up her appetite entirely; she stopped eating. These were the times of ascetic Christianity, where there were people who were mortifying the flesh in order to glorify the spirit: people who lived in caves and never bathed; people who climbed to the tops of pillars and lived exposed to the elements for years. Intriguingly enough, I found that one ascetic practice was to have sex with anyone who asked. That too was a way to mortify the flesh. So looked at through one lens, prostitution was the ultimate in self-indulgent debauchery. But through another lens, it was a practice of subduing the wills of the flesh in order to elevate those of the spirit. The hypocrisy made me kinda cranky on poor Gypsy Mary's behalf, even though she may never have existed. So I tried to interpret her story in a way that felt more grounded in how a human being might experience the events that she experiences. And I decided that the redemption she finds for herself would not be one based in self-loathing. She never does think that it's demeaning to be a prostitute. It's not her choice, and it's difficult, and not particularly pleasant, and sometimes risky. It's not fun. But it's her job, and she feels about it the way that many of us feel about our jobs. It's a means to an end, and when she knows that she's going to have to somehow earn her way back home, she quite matter-of-factly decides that she's going to whore to do so.

NJ: The tone in the Jeanne Duval section is humorous, even bawdy.

NH: Yes, it is. I'm glad you see it that way. Not everyone does. I was going for a bawdy humor, comic in the more antique sense of the word. I think the cover artist captured the comic sensibility really well (though I still have issues with him having given nineteenth-century Jeanne straightened hair. And she was much lighter-skinned than the cover image shows). Nineteenth-century Paris was very sophisticated, but it was also a big city, and as with any big city, management of water and waste was a challenge. You had to draw water from wells, which meant going outside, which (particularly if you were a woman) meant the bother of getting decently enough dressed to do so. The catalogue of the layers of clothing that went into dressing a nineteenth-century French woman made my head spin. So I could absolutely see why you would use your chamber pot until it was overflowing, and put off bathing until it was absolutely necessary. I didn't want to so romanticize the time and place that I omitted dirt and piss-pots.

NJ: Do you see your work, or a particular work, as addressing or redressing negative stereotyping of queer issues or people?

NH: I do enjoy using my work to challenge unexamined norms and binarized conceptions of human sexuality and gender identity (and race, and class, and . . .). Does doing so address or redress negative stereotyping? I don't know. For readers who are ready to be convinced, or who are hungering to see themselves represented, or who like having their assumptions challenged, maybe I can provide some of that. But for others, people can react negatively to anything if they're determined to do so. For some people, the mere fact that a story of mine contains a description of Baudelaire's

Black mistress tying him up and butt-fucking him—to both their enjoyment, I might add—is disgusting simply because it's there. In fact, someone tried to have my novel *The Salt Roads* banned from an American public library system on the basis of that scene. Apparently, women, and especially Black women, would never do something so depraved. I'm probably not going to change the mind of someone like that. Though I do note that the scene is halfway through the book, which meant that she'd gotten past the scene where Baudelaire is clumsily mauling his mistress about during sex and she's not much liking it; the scene where a plantation master skins a slave alive; the one where Jeanne is listening helplessly while Baudelaire's mother mocks Jeanne's dark skin; the one where a woman loses a baby in childbirth and two other women help her bury it; and the lesbian cunnilingus scene accompanied by hashish smoking, tampon removal, blood, and pissing. She didn't complain about any of those things, but the scene of a man and a woman enjoying the (admittedly kinky) sex they're having with each other was apparently "filth."

NJ: Can you tell me something about your new novel, *The New Moon's Arms*?

NH: I was thinking about the story of the Green Children of Woolpit, which was originally written down as history, not a folktale. And about the "aquatic ape" theory of evolution. I was also thinking about poltergeists, and the theory that it's not caused by ghosts; that it's telekinetic energy driven by the sublimated sexual expression of a young girl about to enter menarche. I decided that if menstruation can be magic, then menopause can be magic, too. My protagonist Calamity is a fifty-three-year-old woman whose mother disappeared when Calamity was ten. Calamity's life from that point on has been hard and full of trouble. Now, without realizing it, she's going into menopause, and every time she has a hot flash, something from her past materializes. Not always something she's happy to confront.

NJ: Finally, some parting thoughts. You said in your earlier essay, "SF Writers of Color," that you found SF to be a malleable genre, one that has the potential to subvert political and social boundaries. You said, "Speculative fiction has reinvented itself repeatedly at the hands of the new wave, feminist, cyberpunk, and queer writers. Perhaps idealistically, I believe that it will also open up to fantastical expressions from communities of color." Do you still have the same idealism about speculative fiction's potential to subvert or bend boundaries and categories? How open do you find the genre, especially readers, to presenting diverse perspectives on sexuality and queer identities?

NH: Well, I find that we in the SF community sometimes like to think of ourselves as more progressive than other people. And while there's a lot of fodder for that argument, I'd say it's also true that we are reflective of the larger communities to which we also belong, and as those communities struggle with sexism, racism, queerphobia, classism, ableism, ageism, etc., so do we. And it shows. Sometimes the SF community can be quite oppressive and close-minded. But it's also a place that values openness and critical thought and exploration and the notion of diversity (even though we still have a long way to go to practice that last one more). SF/F/H [science fiction/fantasy/horror] is perhaps the only community I know where an editor can put out a call for submissions for a queer anthology and have straight writers wanting to submit stories largely without the defensive posture of "I'm straight, but. . . .". Science fiction as a literature probably helped to save my life. I suspect I would have self-destructed without it, and without the people I have met because of it. So even when I'm critical of it, I'm very happy that it's here.

AE Interviews: Nalo Hopkinson

Paul Jarvey / 2011

From Aescifi.ca, *Canadian Science Fiction Review*, March 14, 2011, https://aescifi.ca/nalo-hopkinson/. Reprinted by permission of Paul Jarvey, Editor in Chief, AEscifi.ca.

AEscifi.ca: What first drew you to the work of Theodore Sturgeon? It seems almost every fan remembers the first Sturgeon story they read vividly.

Nalo Hopkinson: Theodore Sturgeon is one of my touchstones both as a writer and as a reader. I think my favorite of all his stories is *Godbody*. It was probably the only thing I've ever read that made Jesus make sense—which means it was probably not very popular [*laughs*]. I grew up in a fairly religious household, and [Sturgeon] seemed to be looking at religion with a hard eye that I had not seen before, which was a relief. He talked about the things that are taboo to talk about. Did Jesus have sex? Did he want to? And he was fearless—the fearlessness in his writing is one of the things that I really liked. He was writing stories about queer rights before the rest of the genre knew what to call it. He was writing gender bending stories . . .

Anyway, Noel Sturgeon approached me at ReaderCon in Boston this summer, where I was the guest of honor, and asked me if I would like to participate in this reading and of course I leapt at the chance. The cool thing about this job, about being a science fiction writer, is getting to meet the people you idolize, but Sturgeon was never one I met. I have heard stories from people who knew him, and from the stories they tell it sounds as though he would have lived up to the image that I have of him in my mind. I mean, the man actually did run away to join the circus. Rockin'! He's an actual ninety-pound weakling that ran away to join the circus . . . you can't not love him.

AE: Could you tell me a little bit about the story that you will be reading tonight?

NH: I'm reading from "Crate" tonight, in which Sturgeon does the novel thing of taking a bunch of working-class kids who are essentially in a juvenile home, and treating them with respect, like people. The story doesn't talk down to them. It's written in something approaching a vernacular style, in the way someone like that might speak. He's looking at a lot of the things that concern the real world and he does so in a way that is very egalitarian for writers at the time. And he's just a hell of a lot of fun to read; I mean, the man is a stylist. The language just bops along—it really makes it pretty in the mind.

"Crate" is set in a future where instead of juvenile detention, kids who are under the age of majority get shipped off to planets where they do hard labor, except that they can expect to become colonists. So it's a bunch of kids who have been shipped off . . . their parole officer has decided to go along with them, but they don't like her. They think she is just a witch of a woman. Their shuttle crashes and many of them die. A handful of kids are left having to hike to the nearest settlement, on an alien planet where they know nothing about what to expect. And it's essentially about how they manage. It does this sort of microcosm of looking at social relationships and how they shift and change, and the kinds of tensions that you will get amongst people who are teenagers—you know, everything is very important. And, of course, in this story it is. It could kill them if they don't get there. It's just a lovely story, beautifully written and heart-wrenching. It's a very nice piece.

AE: Nice, and not in a *Lord of the Flies* way . . .

NH: Exactly. It's much better. I didn't have to read *Lord of the Flies* in school—I got to read it for entertainment—so I never had the trauma of having to read it in a classroom. I was the geek kid who, when the new year came around, was reading all my books for English class before the start of the class, so luckily most of them weren't ruined for me.

AE: When did you first start reading science fiction?

NH: I started reading it as a teenager, living at that time in Jamaica where I was born. My mother is a library worker, and I would finish my day at school and walk over the library on Tom Redcam Avenue. They separated the library into adult and children's sections, and you could not read in adult if you were a child. But my mother gave me her library card and so I started reading science fiction from the adult section. I remember the first book I looked for was *The Andromeda Strain*. I wanted to read it as a book because I was too young to see it as a movie, which had just come out at the time. And I just kept reading in the genre. I found it way more interesting than straight-up fiction.

AE: That interest has brought you a long way!

NH: Indeed it has. And now I am doing what I love: writing. Plus teaching, and doing some arts consulting. I really do whatever I can to bring in a few bucks . . . I will say it's a privilege but not a luxury [*laughs*].

AE: I remember Peter Watts speaking sentimentally about the moment when he was able to put aside his technical writing and engage in fiction full-time . . .

NH: I remember that moment for me. I quit regular work far too early . . . but I would probably do it again [*laughs*]. At the time, I was working for the Toronto Arts Council [TAC] as a Grants Officer. It was a great job. It was technically part-time, but there were days when I was there till two in the morning. It gave me a grounding in the arts; it gave me a sense of how artists survive; and it gave me the courage to become a writer. It gave me the permission in many ways. I went to the Clarion Science Fiction and Fantasy Writers' Workshop, which meant the TAC had to give me six weeks off. Well, I mean, they didn't have to, nobody has to, but they did. Being an arts organization meant that they understood why it was important, and they really enabled me. When I did finally quit, I remember my boss talking about the time I came in to ask to take two months off work to finish a novel for the Warner Aspect first novel contest and she thought I was just blowing smoke . . . but then I wrote the novel, won the contest, and started my writing career!

AE: Many of your novels share a Caribbean setting and focus on the adventures of a young person in a strange land . . .

NH: It's kind of a natural theme to science fiction and fantasy, being in a place where you can't take anything for granted. Writing about it from a lived experience makes it both easier and harder. Because I'm not writing autobiography—there are spaceships in there—it is a very different story. And you need that distance to be able to take the stuff and compost it and cherry pick from what we know and turn it into story. But it also means that you really understand the experience of writing.

AE: You also play with ideas about what the role of a host country should be, and how living within a new country can or should be. Does this also reflect your experiences immigrating to Canada?

NH: In "A Habit of Waste," which was my first short story, that was the kind of thing I was very explicit about. Writing *Midnight Robber* allowed me to go back to a place where Caribbean culture is the majority culture, only this time it was a whole friggin' planet. It allowed me to do Carnival on a large scale. It allowed me to speak and write the way I grew up speaking and writing. Even though it's an invented vernacular, it's a style that I know. So there's a freeing up that happens when I can go into that storytelling mode, because Caribbean culture very much has a storytelling component to it. And the idea of the robber king, which is where I base the mask that

[*Midnight Robber*'s protagonist] plays, is about how well you tell a story. It isn't about how much sense you make, it is about how compelling you are. And the robber king holds people up, and makes them hold still in order to tell them a story. So it allowed me to move into that role of orator, very dramatic, and writ large. That was the fun of it for me.

AE: Tell me more about the vernacular of *Midnight Robber*. It seems that the language of the book, although it's fictional, is very organic. The invented vocabulary feels very natural.

NH: When you grow up speaking a vernacular people are very quick to tell you that it's incorrect, it's wrong. But Caribbean language has its own roots, its own linguistic integrity, its own modes of speech. Part of it is that writing in vernacular helped me to understand what speech does and to see what has happened to English, having been imposed on the Caribbean people and then the Caribbean people taking it and making it their own. Hence the quote inside the front cover, which was written by my partner: "I stole the torturer's tongue."

That novel has been translated and is about to be published in Chinese. It's the first time any translator of my work contacted me when they weren't sure about a word. I can't speak to the actual language, but the efforts of the translator are reassuring. And the cover has a visibly Black woman on the front—which is not always true of my translations. They made it look kind of a cross between steampunk and something tropical. Oftentimes people don't do that with my work. They exclusively tropicalize it, even when it's in an urban setting and far in the future. There is this notion of the Caribbean as a place that knows no technology.

AE: Cultural tension goes alongside the linguistic tension in your novels. Do you think that fiction helps people negotiate environments where there is cultural tension, in places like Toronto, for example?

NH: I think it can if they are willing to see it. For example, I went to see *Avatar* with my partner. At the time we were sharing an apartment with two guys. One had the critique I expected, but the other thought we would love it and was very surprised when we both came back ranting. Eventually [my partner] said, "Well, did the movie make you feel good about protecting the environment?" And our flatmate said yes, it made him feel really good. My partner replied, "So you paid your twenty bucks, you saw the movie, now what are you going to do about it?" And our flatmate replied, "Well, if I could I would . . .," which was when I piped up. You could stay in your apartment and find two hundred things that would help. But what the movie told him was that you need to be a hero in order to make a change.

You have to be the big guy. And if you aren't, you have no responsibility to do anything. So some people will take away a message about how to live with people and some won't. You can't control that.

That is one of the puzzlements and delights of writing. Once a woman came up to me at an event. She had just finished reading *Midnight Robber* and loved it. We had a few moments before the next session and she asked me if she could ask a few questions about the book. And while talking to her I realized that she had not read the same novel that I had written, in no way, shape, or form. Nothing that I had put down there was what was coming out of her mouth. But she loved what she read, and I'm not going to say to her, "Well, you're wrong!" I hear from teachers and professors as well. One told me about a paper they had received about how the novel was an argument that Orisha [the Afro-Caribbean belief system] was evil. I think my face went weird and the prof said, "Well, that's what she wanted to get." And, of course, I was thinking that the meaning was totally the opposite.

AE: Your writing is very fluently symbolic—it seems to come to you very naturally. How do you choose to encode different symbolic meanings into your work?

NH: When I went to Clarion, one of the first stories I read by one of my fellow Clarion-ettes was by Kelly Link. It blew me away, just blew my mind. I finished reading the story and thought, "This is so good, I should be so jealous." And that story was "Survivor's Ball," where she builds metaphor on top of metaphor, changes them and then just shoots them. I perceived the technique and I started trying to use it.

Wilson Harris is a Guyanese writer whose mind works at the depth and intensity of Samuel Delany. I republished a short story of his once. In the course of going through the story line by line, I began to understand what he had done, which is to build an architecture of metaphor. It was a technique I really admired. And my dad was a Shakespearean actor, my mother was a library worker, so I have a huge palette of symbols from different kinds of literature. It's fun to draw on them and see who gets the references.

On the other hand, twice a year, spring and fall, I get an email from someone who says, "I'm reading your book in class, I'm really enjoying it, but can you tell me what the relationship between X and Y characters symbolizes, and can you give me page numbers please, and can you do it before next Tuesday?" They think I'm just off the banana boat [*laughs*]. I get some genuinely respectful questions, and I get some that think the novel is a big quiz with right and wrong answers. And I admit to no understanding of the symbolism in my work. As you just saw talking to me about it, you the reader will get different things out of it than I will put into it. So I say, no, I know nothing of the symbology of which you speak. They hate it! And I never hear back from them.

AE: I don't doubt it. What's in the pipes, any new work?

NH: It's been slow. On top of a few other things I had gone and developed debilitating anemia and didn't realize it. The funny thing about your brain getting no oxygen is that you can't do anything. So I pretty much couldn't write for a while. Of course, this meant I had two books under contract that I hadn't finished. But I've been working on them, and I'm writing my patootie off right now. I just finished a young adult fantasy novel that is currently being called *T'aint*. It's a working title, and I'm waiting to hear back what the publisher thinks. It's very exciting because it's the first novel I was able to finish in four years. I'm working on another novel and hoping to finish soon, so I'm cranking ahead. I'm really enjoying being back in the saddle again and able to keep thinking through the end of one sentence to another. For a while I couldn't even read an email, much less write an email. For a while I thought I wouldn't write again—so it's a very cool thing to find I've still got it.

"Correcting the Balance": Outspoken Interview with Nalo Hopkinson

Terry Bisson / 2012

From *Report from Planet Midnight* (PM Press, 2012). Reprinted from *Report From Planet Midnight* by Nalo Hopkinson. Published by PM Press, pmpress.org.

Terry Bisson: Your work is often described, even by yourself, as "subverting genre." Isn't that against the rules? Or at least rude?

Nalo Hopkinson: Science fiction's supposed to be polite? Dang, maybe I'll take up poetry instead. To tell the truth, I kinda rue the day I ever let that quotation out into the world. I used it in a Canadian grant application fifteen years ago. In that context, when not a lot of science fiction and fantasy writers were getting grants from the arts councils because many of the jurors thought science fiction and fantasy were inherently immature, it worked. It allowed me to come out swinging and get the jury's attention. But as something said to science fiction people, it just sounds presumptuous. I don't remember how it got out of my confidential grant application and into the larger world. It was probably my own doing, and my own folly. Now the dang thing keeps coming back to haunt me. People quote it all over the place, and I can feel my face heating up with embarrassment. Science fiction and fantasy are already about subverting paradigms. It's something I love about them.

And yet. If I'm being honest, there is some truth to that piece of braggadociousness. No one can make me give up the writing I love that's by straight, white, Western male (and female) writers, but at a certain point, I began to long to see other cultures, other aesthetics, other histories, realities, and bodies represented in force as well. There was some. I wanted more. I wanted lots more. I wanted to write some of it. I think I am doing so.

158 CONVERSATIONS WITH NALO HOPKINSON

TB: Does the title of your debut novel, *Brown Girl in the Ring*, come from the game, the song, or a wish to connect with Tolkien?

NH: Tolkien? Ah, I get it! One brown girl to rule them all! Well, no. The song comes from the game ("There is a brown girl in the ring, tra-la-la-la-la/ and she look like a little sugar plum"). It's an Anglo-Caribbean ring game, mostly played by girls. I used to play it as a little girl. All the girls hold hands to form a ring, and one girl is in the middle. When the other girls sing, "Show me your motion, tra-la-la-la-la," the girl in the center does some kind of dance or athletic move that she figures will be difficult to copy. The rest try to copy it. She picks the one whose version she likes the best, and they switch places. And so on.

In my first novel, Ti-Jeanne, the protagonist, is surrounded by her life dilemmas and challenges, and things are getting worse. She's the brown girl in the ring, and she is young and untried. She herself doesn't know what she's capable of, but she needs to figure her skills out and employ them, quickly, before she loses everything she cares about. Tra-la-la-la-la.

TB: Who is Derek Walcott and why is he important?

NH: Derek is a St. Lucia-born poet, a playwright, a Nobel Prize winner, and a master wordsmith. These words are his, from his poem "The Schooner *Flight*":

> I'm just a red nigger who love the sea,
> I had a sound colonial education,
> I have Dutch, nigger, and English in me,
> And either I'm nobody, or I'm a nation . . .

Doesn't that last line just fucking give you chills, coming hard on the heels of what preceded it? *Goddamn.* Much respect. Derek started and for many years was the artistic director of the Trinidad Theatre Workshop. My father was one of the actors and playwrights in the company. He and Walcott eventually fell out and stopped speaking to each other. But in a way, that's beside the point. Walcott and my father are two of many talented Caribbean wordsmiths whose work I was absorbing as a child.

One of Walcott's early plays was a fantastical piece called "Ti-Jean and His Brothers." I believe it was modeled on a St. Lucian folktale. Ti-Jean ("young John") is the youngest of three brothers who set out to beat the Devil, who appears in the play as that archetypical monster, the white plantation owner. The two elder brothers fail, and it's left to Ti-Jean to save the day. At some point during the writing of my first novel, I realized that since I was writing about three generations of women who were all facing the same central evils in their lives, there were parallels with the basic framework of *Ti-Jean and His Brothers*, so I used the parallels to inform my plot. I wanted to make Walcott's influence evident, so I gave my three characters feminized versions of the brothers' names, and I embedded brief quotations from the play into my story. Walcott generously gave me his permission to do so.

Folktales are great for learning dynamic storytelling and how to structure the resonant echoes that give a plot forward motion. It wouldn't be the last time that I modeled a plot upon the shell of a preexisting folktale. I've discovered that it doesn't matter whether your readers recognize the folktale. It may not even matter whether the folktale is real, or one you invented. What matters is that it has structure, echoes, trajectory, and style.

TB: *Skin Folk* won a World Fantasy Award, and there was talk of a movie. What's up with that?

NH: The movie project isn't mine. The director who optioned it is the visionary Asli Dukan, of Mizan Productions. I believe the project is currently in the development stage, which means raising the money to make the film. That is the stage at which most film projects die stillborn, so if anyone who wants to see the final product is of a mind to support Asli with some hard cash, I know she'll appreciate it. Particularly when I speak at schools, people in the audience want to know whether there are going to be films of my books. Myself, I'm more jaundiced. I've seen what can happen when text-based science fiction gets zombified by Hollywood. Look at what happened to Gibson's "Johnny Mnemonic."

TB: I know. I wrote the novelization of that unfortunate script.

NH: My condolences! I've also seen what can happen when mainstream American film and television try to depict Black Caribbean people. You get the likes of Kendra the vampire slayer, Sebastian the crab from *The Little Mermaid*, and the eternal disgrace that is Jar-Jar Binks. Seriously, would it be so hard to hire actors who can do accurate Caribbean accents? Though that wouldn't solve the depiction problem; mainstream American media seem to believe that Caribbean people are little more than simpleminded, marijuana-steeped clowns who say "de" instead of "the." In any case, my work isn't going to make it to the big screen any time soon, given the types of characters that are in it. It'd be a lot of money for producers to invest in a project when they're not sure there's a big enough audience out there for it.

And because people are always quick to jump down my throat whenever I talk about institutionalized discrimination, let me acknowledge that there have been a few SF/fantasy films and television programs with Caribbean

160 CONVERSATIONS WITH NALO HOPKINSON

characters that weren't stereotyped. Actor Sullivan Walker as Yale in the short-lived series *Earth 2*, for example. Geoffrey Holder's voice as the narrator for the 2005 *Charlie and the Chocolate Factory*. There are probably one or two more, but not many at all.

Some people hear me talking like this and get pissed off at me. They don't tolerate critique of the things they love. They miss the fact that I may love those things, too. I just don't think love should be blind.

Anyway, we were talking film. When directors option my stories, I'm more confident if they are independent artists with some personal connection to some of my communities (science fiction, Black, Caribbean, Canadian, queer, women, etc.). There are two other novels of mine in development: *Brown Girl in the Ring* by Toronto's Sharon Lewis, and *The New Moon's Arms* by Frances Anne Solomon of Toronto's Leda Serene productions. Both women, like Asli Dukan, have roots in the Caribbean.

TB: You once identified the central question of utopia as "who's going to do the dirty work?" (Ursula Le Guin would agree.) So how would you describe *Midnight Robber*'s planet Toussaint, where work is a sacrament (to some)?

NH: A sacrament? Did I do that? Not trying to dodge the question. Just that my memory is poor, and it's been a long, busy, often stressful few years since the time it published. I'm trying to remember back to when I finished the novel, perhaps sometime in 1999. I suspect I hadn't come up with the notion that the big dilemma of science fiction is who's going to do the dirty work. I may have just begun asking myself that very question . . . ah.

I do remember this: the people of Toussaint have a maxim that back-breaking labor isn't fit for them as sentient beings. They've come from a legacy of slavery, of having been forced to do hard labor, and they're not about to forget it. But manual labor still needs to be done. They mechanize it as much as possible. The machines that do that labor are unaware extensions of the self-aware planetary artificial intelligence that sustains their various support systems. So how you gonna keep your machine overseer down on the farm, once she's crossed the Turing threshold? They *program* her not to mind doing all that work. They make her like her servitude. When you think of it, our brains are also wired to respond in certain ways to certain situations. But do we get to make that decision for other creatures? You could argue that we do so all the time, through domestication and by breeding other living things for specific traits. You could argue that that doesn't count, since other animals aren't self-aware. But anyone who's ever lived in close quarters with another animal for an extended period of time can present convincing evidence that many animals are indeed self-aware. You could argue that it's OK to mess with creatures who are less intelligent than we are. But as someone with a couple of cognitive variances and as someone Black and female, I have reason to be suspicious of intelligence tests. I'm not sure that we understand enough about cognition to be able to measure cognition effectively. For one thing, we're measuring it against human markers of intelligence. I wonder whether those are the only markers.

So, in *Midnight Robber*, there is a powerful human-manufactured sentience that we have programmed to love us and to want to take care of us. Was it wrong of us to do that to her? Ethically, it's a conundrum. That was deliberate on my part. The planet of Toussaint isn't exactly Utopia. I didn't solve the problem of who does the menial work. I just put it into the hands of a being that's been designed to accept those tasks. I may have had some of the human citizens voluntarily take on forms of manual labor as part of a practice of ethical mindfulness.

TB: These are the people I meant, who see labor as a sacrament.

NH: It's their way of acknowledging that work that looks after oneself and others isn't really beneath them. You know, something like the old proverb attributed to Buddhism: "Before Enlightenment, chop wood, carry water. After Enlightenment, chop wood, carry water."

I still haven't answered the question of who does the work in a Utopia. I have an alternative history fantasy novel in progress in which I'm exploring the idea that everyone in a municipality is assigned menial tasks in a rotating schedule. But in practice, my characters have all kinds of ways of slipping out of their turn taking out the town's night soil or working on the building site of that new community center. In the novel, it's a cooperative system, but not politically socialist; I'm trying to build something a bit different than our current political paradigms. I'm not quite happy with it yet as a world-building element.

My partner tells me I need to wrestle with systems of exchange in return for labor, money being the primary one that we use in this world. I need to look at effective alternatives to money. I'm daunted by that, but he's right.

TB: You have a lot of uncollected short stories. Any plans for them?

NH: Un*collected*, yes, but all but one of them has been published. I've actually collected them into a manuscript, which I plan to submit to a publisher soon. Honestly, it's the formatting that's slowing me down, the thought of writing intros to each story. Maybe I don't have to do that last bit.

TB: You often speak of putting the "threads" of a story into a "weave." Not uncommon, yet from you it seems something more than metaphor. How did you get into fabric design?

162 CONVERSATIONS WITH NALO HOPKINSON

NH: On a lark, thanks to a company called Spoonflower which came along to take advantage of new technologies of printing with ink on fabric. Spoonflower's website democratizes the process and makes it easy for someone with basic image editing skills to dabble in fabric design. They've built an online community of people interested in cool fabric. We range from hobbyists to professionals. We talk to one another, vote on one another's designs, and buy fabric to sew. It's like print-on-demand for fabric.

I sew as a hobby; have done since I was a teenager. When I hit the fashion-conscious teen years and my desire for new clothes outstripped my parents' income, they bought me a sewing machine. My mother taught me how to use it. It was an extraordinarily frustrating learning curve for someone with undiagnosed ADHD. Once, I glued the seams of a blouse because I was too impatient to stitch them. My mother was horrified. But I did learn how to sew, and how to get to a place of patience around it (plus some time-saving tricks that kept me from going supernova). Since then, I've always had a sewing machine. I have an ever-growing collection of clothing patterns, some dating back to the 1930s. I'm a big girl, almost always have been. There was a time when attractive clothing at reasonable prices just wasn't available for larger women. Being able to sew meant that I could make my own. It's easier now to find non-hideous off-the-rack clothing in my size, but when you make it yourself, the fit can be better, the clothing more unique.

Now that I can design my own fabric and have the designs printed, I can create and use iconography I don't find on store-bought fabric. Ever since I was a child, I've been hesitant to wear images of non-Black people on my body. Not because I hate white people, or some rubbish like that, but because I wanted to be able to love Black people and my own Blackness. Nowadays, you can find fabric with images of Black people on it that doesn't make you want to go postal, but good Lord, , does it ever tend toward the twee! I prefer images with a bit more bite, a bit more perversity, and a bit less saccharine.

I can make science fiction and fantasy imagery, too, that isn't all unicorns with flowing manes on a background of rainbow-colored stars. I adapt a lot of historical imagery, and my own photographs as well, and sometime I draw. I know nothing about design, and I haven't conjured up the patience to learn. I make fabric designs by trial and error. Some of them are hideous. Some of them are just OK, and some of them are successful. I'm always a bit surprised when someone who doesn't know me buys fabric from my online Spoonflower store: http:// spoonflower.com/profiles/nalo_hopkinson.

I make stuff. I was a craftsperson and did a lot of my own cooking long before I took up writing. I have my mother to thank for showing me that it was possible to make things for pleasure, for sustenance, and to save money. Come the zombie apocalypse, I know I'll have some survival skills to offer.

TB: You have edited several anthologies (*Mojo: Conjure Stories, So Long Been Dreaming*, etc.). Is this part of a plot to wedge more Black and female writers into the genre until they outnumber, overwhelm, and eventually drive out men? Or not?

NH: Good lord, you've sussed out my cunning plan for world domination! Excuse me for a second while I go work some obeah to keep you quiet. Please ignore the toad and the padlock lurking behind the curtain. OK, I'm back. That toad's never gonna croak again. So. How does trying to foster a more representative literary field translate to wanting to exclude white male writers? How would that be representative? I mean, I'm bad at math, but I'm not that damned bad at it.

Just now, once I was done burning a candle of a particular color and padlocking a toad's lips shut, I glanced at the pile of books beside my desk. Among them are titles by Gene Wolfe, Steven Gould, Rudyard Kipling, China Miéville, Stieg Larsson, Hal Duncan, Charlie Stross, George R. R. Martin, Kim Stanley Robinson, and a certain Terry Bisson.

Whew. Frankly, you gave me quite a turn with the intimation that white male authors were in danger of extinction. If that were true, we'd have to immediately start the Society for the Protection of White Male Writers. We'd get a board of directors together, and we'd do a fundraising drive on Kickstarter, and make depositions to all the major publishing houses, and hand out T-shirts with our logo on them, and infiltrate government, media, the churches, and the multinationals. We'd become so ubiquitous that pretty soon, people would cease referring to us by our full name—TSFTPOWMW is so unwieldy, don't you think? Instead, they'd just refer us as Society. Oh, wait . . .

TB: I get it. You would have the status quo.

NH: You said it, not me. Anyway, beside my bed are also books by Liz Hand, Ursula K. Le Guin, Samuel R. Delany, Madeleine E. Robins, Nisi Shawl, Ivan E. Coyote, Ayize Jama-Everett, Barbara Lalla, Olive Senior, and Rabindranath Maharaj. That list comprises some women, some Black folks, white folks, multiracial folks, South Asian, queer, Canadian, Jamaican, and Trinidadian writers. They are for the most part books I had to go a bit out of my way to find, which meant that I had to figure where to look.

There are a lot of readers who pride themselves on not paying attention to the identities of their favorite writers. Some of them think this means that they're not prejudiced. I don't know anyone who isn't, myself included. But let's just say for argument's sake that those particular readers in fact are not prejudiced. How many books by writers of color do you think you'll find on their bookshelves? I'd lay odds that if there are any at all, they will be far outnumbered by the books by white authors. Not necessarily because those readers are deliberately choosing mostly white/male authors. They don't have to. The status quo does it for them. So those readers' self-satisfied "I don't know" is really an "I don't care enough to look beyond my nose."

And that's cool. So many causes, so little time. But don't pretend that indifference and an unwillingness to make positive change constitute enlightenment. If you truly want to be a colorblind, unprejudiced reader, you can't do so from a place of being racism-blind, or you'll never have the diverse selection of authors you say you'd like. Why get pissed off at people who are fighting for the very thing you say you want?

Yet I don't think there's some conspiracy of evil racist editors. There doesn't have to be. The system has its own momentum. In order to be antiracist, you actually have to choose to do something different than the status quo. People who're trying to make positive change (editors and publishers included) have a hell of a battle. Fighting it requires a grasp of how the complex juggernaut of institutionalized marginalization works, and what types of intervention will, by inches, bring that siege engine down.

We're in a genre that is heavily invested in the romance of the individual villain and the lone hero who defeats that villain. We want to know who the bad guy is. Dammit, we want someone to blame! And there are people who say and do racist things, consciously in ignorance. You can try to change them, or to limit the harm they do. These are useful and necessary actions. But pulling the weed doesn't destroy the root system, and what do you do when you realize that we are all in some way part of that system? I don't know all the answers. I'm sure that some of what I say here is going to come back to haunt me with its ignorance or naiveté. Remember when Robert Silverberg published that essay about why the stories of James R. Tiptree Jr. (pen name of Alice Sheldon) could only have been written by a man? I'm impressed by how graciously he later acknowledged that he'd been wrong. That's a grace to which I aspire. I have a feeling I'll need it.

There are those who fear that if books get published according to some kind of identity-based quota system, literary excellence will suffer. What seems to be buried in the shallow grave of that concept is the assumption that there are no good writers in marginalized communities. That huge prejudice aside, there is some validity to the fear. If you want to vary your diet, you put a larger selection of foods into your mouth. You don't toss vitamins into the toilet. The latter would be attacking the problem from the wrong end.

TB: So to speak. So what would be attacking the problem from the right end?

NH: A few years ago, when I was about to put out the call for submissions to the anthology *Mojo: Conjure Stories*, I had two equal priorities that the received wisdom in this field says are antithetical: I wanted to choose stories based on the quality of the writing; and I wanted to end up with an anthology (about an African diasporic form of magic) that would actually contain a lot of stories by Black writers.

It took me some hard thinking to figure out the flaw in the logic that leads people to think that antiracist diversity and literary quality are mutually exclusive. This is what I came up with: there are many steps to editing an anthology, and they have different priorities. Efforts to broaden the representation have to happen at the beginning of the process, not at the stage where you're selecting for literary quality. If I wanted Black writers to send me their stories, I'd have to specifically invite them. And in an effort to right the systemic imbalance in numbers, I'd have to invite more of them than of anyone else. If I wanted the participation of non-Black writers (and I did), I'd need to invite the ones that I felt were creatively up to the task.

I knew that statistically speaking, if you invite people to something, one-fifth of them will attend. I knew that I had room for roughly twenty stories in the anthology. I multiplied that number by five, and so decided I would solicit stories from more than a hundred writers. "More than" because I knew I would reject some of the stories as unsuitable.

Then I made two lists of writers to invite who I thought could handle the material well: one of writers I knew to be Black, and one of writers I knew to be non-Black, or whose race I didn't know for sure; after all, some writers don't place a focus on their racial identities, and that is their right. I listed twice as many Black writers as those in the second group. In a way, you could say that I deliberately did the opposite of what would have happened in our current context of institutionalized racism if I hadn't thought about who I was inviting. Some might call that reverse racism. I think it was more in the way of revers*ing* racism (grammar's so important, don't you think?), if only for a small space of time in a temporarily and very conditionally autonomous zone.

I sent out the invitations, crossed my fingers, and waited nervously until the submission deadline. There was a chance it wouldn't work. The law of averages means that efforts to even out that kind of imbalance work in the aggregate, not necessarily in every single instance. I had to take that chance, and to also take the chance that if it didn't work out, I'd face disapproval from some of the Black readers in the field. Part of the job. At least I could say that I'd tried.

Once the stories were in, I read them and picked the ones I thought were strong, no matter who the writer was. Much of the time I willfully disremembered the writer's name until I'd read their story; my natural forgetfulness comes in handy that way. I tried to read cover letters only after I'd read the attached stories. I didn't pay much attention to who was going to be in the anthology until I'd assembled the stories I wanted in the order I wanted. I believe that in fact I didn't assess it until I'd submitted the anthology to my editor and she'd accepted it. I'd have to recheck in order to verify this, but I think that about 50 percent of the contributors to *Mojo: Conjure Stories* are Black.

I'm glad it worked. It was probably my first lesson that de-marginalization has to start at the organizational/systemic level. Trying to do it person by person is starting too late in the process. Individuals are going to have a hard time making change if they're not receiving organizational support. You start as early on in the process as you can.

To certain white male writers, I'd like to say, "When those around you try to wrestle with issues of entitlement and marginalization, please don't give us the tired trumpeting of 'Censorship! No one can tell me what to write!'" True, people *shouldn't* tell you what to write, but people will try to, for bad reasons and better ones. Your mother will try to tell you what to write or not write. Your husband will. Your editor, your government, your church, your readers, your nosy neighbor. Humans are an argumentative lot. Dealing with that as a writer comes with the territory.

Those books by my bedside? They include a book written by a white man about a white woman, one by a white man about South Asian people, one by a white woman about a Black woman, one by an American about a Londoner, one by a Black woman and a white woman about, oh, everybody; I could go on. Write whatever the blast you want, and if you live in an environment where doing so doesn't endanger your life or career, count yourself blessed.

When I hear a (usually white and usually male) writer trying to shut down a discussion about representation by bellowing that no one should tell him what to write, it sounds very much as though he's trying to change the topic, to make it all about him. To him I'd say: Why not try to further the discussion, rather than trying to, um, censor it? What do you think needs

TERRY BISSON / 2012 **167**

to be done in order to make publishing more representative? Nothing, you say? The doors are already open but we just won't come in? Women, Black people (and purple polka-dotted meerkats) actually "just don't write much science fiction"? Or their books are "only relevant to their communities" (which is often code for "those people are incapable of producing anything of real literary merit")?

Funny, how every one of those statements boils down to not being willing to change the status quo. You do realize that you're even drowning out the white voices amongst you that are trying to make some changes along with the rest of us? You do realize that a more representative literary field would be representative of all of us, yourself included?

Sure, there are people on both sides of that discussion who are full of crap. But as a smart white man once said, "90 percent of everything is crap." The crap doesn't invalidate the discussion.

Oy, I'm ranting again! This is what happens when you ask me to be an "outspoken author."

TB: In *Midnight Robber* the naming (and renaming) of things seems to be an important part of the story. (Granny Nanny instead of "electronic overlord" or some such.) What exactly are you "subverting" here?

NH: In my novel, Granny Nanny is a supercomputer that loves us. That's not new. She's like a planet-sized Tardis. The difference may be that the way in which I describe her is culturally specific. Granny Nanny is named after Nanny of the Maroons, a seventeenth-century African freedom fighter from Jamaica. She is one of our national heroes. In a West African diasporic linguistic context, Granny/Nana/Nanny don't necessarily designate a sweet, harmless old lady who bakes you cookies. It's a term of respect for a female elder, for a woman who has more years and more life experience than you do. Granny Nanny—the woman, not the A.I.—led an insurgency that fought off British soldiers and eventually gained freedom for a Maroon community in the hills of Jamaica. The soldiers were convinced that she could catch their bullets between her ass cheeks and fart them back like a machine gun. She was an Afro-Jamaican woman guerrilla strategist on horseback, and I enjoyed invoking her memory in a science fiction novel. A lot of the time, all I'm trying to do is put some of my specific ethnocultural touchstones into science fiction and fantasy. When white writers do that, it's barely remarked-upon. And sometimes it should be, because it's often wonderful.

TB: Your literary background runs both wide and deep, from Russian lit to Shakespeare to classic SF to Caribbean folklore. How do the artist and the scholar get along in Nalo's head? Heart?

168 CONVERSATIONS WITH NALO HOPKINSON

NH: I'm not a scholar. That implies in-depth, perhaps guided study. I skim. I'm more along the lines of a knowledge geek who's been exposed to a lot of different cultures. They all get along well in both my head and my heart, but it often means that people don't pick up on all the references I'm making. I try to be aware of that when I'm writing. Sometimes I try to make sure that it doesn't matter if a reader doesn't get all the references. Sometimes I try to make it a bit of a game for the readers who don't know a particular reference, as well as a kind of in-joke for those who do.

TB: Do you read comics—excuse me, graphic novels?

NH: I do, whatever one calls them. My partner and I are verrrry slooooowly working on creating one. Some of my favorites are *Love and Rockets, Bayou, Finder, Le Chat du Rabbin, The Invisibles, Dykes to Watch Out For, Fun Home*, and *Calvin and Hobbes*. The superhero comics from the Big Two mostly make me twitchy and cranky, though I'll usually go to the spin-off movies. The films make me equally twitchy and cranky, but there's my fannish pleasure in watching impossible science and impossibly beautiful people blow impossible shit up real good. And they give me lots of food for thought and ranting about everything from bad physics (when I can pick up on the incorrect science in a film, it's *really* fucking incorrect) to messed-up gender politics. Comics thrill me. They make me wish I were a comic artist.

TB: You are often called a magical realist. Is that just a euphemism for fantasy, like speculative fiction for SF? Or does it actually get at something?

NH: I haven't read tons of magical realism. I don't have as informed a feel for what magical realist writing does as I do for fantasy and SF. I sometimes feel that in magical realism (in literature, not in art), the supernatural elements are conceits that don't have to be followed through as rigorously as we demand from fantasy. It seems to me that in magical realism, the story as a whole takes precedence. The supernatural elements are only one of its parts. In fantasy, the fantastical elements are as central as plot and character. I think.

TB: I love your description of geeks as people who "know too much about too many things that other people don't care about." What then are literary snobs?

NH: I think the main difference is that all geeks aren't snobs, whereas all snobs are snobs.

TB: Do you read V. S. Naipaul? Do you like Naipaul?

NH: I read his earlier short story collection *Miguel Street* over and over when I was a kid. I really liked it. I think it still holds up fairly well, but I haven't read his newer work. He is, of course, notorious amongst his fellow Caribbean writers and everyone else for his outrageously racist and sexist statements. I don't like those. But I find him easy to ignore.

TB: What kind of car do you drive? (I ask every author this.)

NH: I don't have a car. You don't need one in Toronto. I believe the last time I owned a car was twenty-three years ago. I don't remember what kind it was. It was red. I hated it. I don't like cars. I don't like the expense, the maintenance, the danger of driving them, what they've done to the planet. Now that I spend part of the year in Southern California, I may have to get a car. This part of the world is built around the assumption of people having cars. It's difficult to get around without one, and I have fibromyalgia. I get tired.

TB: James Joyce never went back to Ireland. Do you see yourself growing old in Canada, or in the Caribbean? (Or growing old at all?)

NH: I don't know where I'll grow old. Perhaps moving back and forth between a couple of places. The Caribbean is the home of my heart, but no one place has everything I'd want as a permanent home. Wherever it is, it'll probably be a big, socially progressive city with lots of cultural, linguistic, ethnic and racial variety, lots of Black people, a mild climate, and a large body of water nearby. I haven't yet found a city that has all those things. I do plan on growing old, and I'm simultaneously terrified of it. I'm fifty-one years old, and the past few years as I entered what may be the latter half of my life were hellish. I experienced escalating illness, which led to destitution, homelessness, and a near loss of my career as a writer. Things seem to be stabilizing now. I'm addressing the health concerns that can be addressed, I'm writing again, and I now have a professorship that is going a long way toward stabilizing my income. My primary (life) partner and I not only stayed together during those horrible years, but I think our relationship came out of it stronger. That in itself is a miracle, and unutterably precious. And yet I'm constantly aware that it's all temporary, that getting older will probably bring more and perhaps worse physical affliction to me and to my loved ones. Certainly, the longer I stay alive, it'll mean losing more and more of the people I love. I think of those afflictions and losses to come, and it makes me frantic with terror. I'm trying to remember that there will also be lots to gain in those years: new friends, new experiences, new competencies, new joys.

TB: When you teach writing, what do you teach? What do you un-teach?

NH: Nowadays, I'm all about architecture and integrity. A story has to be given a deliberate shape that hopefully has some structural integrity and architectural wonder and it has to be in dynamic movement along a trajectory. Is "dynamic movement" a tautology? I mean, there should be pacing. I'm also all about allowing the reader to inhabit the body of a point-of-view character and experience the physicality of her or his world. I try to un-teach the notion that a story is something told to a passive listener. I try to get my students out of the point-of-view character's head and more into that character's physical sensations. I try to model my love of words and meaning. I try to show them that editing is the fun part. It's the part where your word baby develops fingers and toes and eyes and starts looking back at you and reaching for things.

And being me, I'm now thinking about just how ableist a metaphor that is.

TB: Did you initially see SF and fantasy as a gateway, or as a castle to be stormed? How has that perception changed?

NH: That's a fascinating question. As neither. I think. You can breach gateways and storm castles, or enter gateways and inhabit castles. Maybe this is trite, but science fiction is a universe.

TB: You totally work magic with titles: "Greedy Choke Puppy," "Ours Is the Prettiest," etc. At what point in the creative process does the title come to you?

NH: Thank you! Often before the rest of the story. The title's sort of the distilled version of what the story wants to be. Before I quite know what the story is, the title whispers hints to me.

TB: I like that. Now here's my *Jeopardy!* item. I provide the answer, and you provide the question. The answer is: because they can.

NH: Why do cops routinely brutalize people? Why do bumblebees fly? Why do humans make art?

TB: In the postscript to your ICFA speech, you took someone to task for separating Art and Labour. True, both are work. But isn't there an important difference or two?

NH: Both are work, and both can be art. Hopefully, you're being paid for both. (And thanks for granting me that "u" in "Labour.")

TB: Are you a Marxist?

NH: No.

TB: Three favorite movies?

NH: *Quilombo* by Carlos Diegues. *Pumzi* by Wanuri Kahiu. *Lilies* by John Greyson.

TB: You seem to have stolen from Shakespeare (literature's master thief) in "Shift." What does a reader who hasn't read *The Tempest* need to know?

NH: Let's see . . . in the play, Prospero is a rich white duke who's been exiled to a small island with his beautiful daughter Miranda. There he finds an ethereal fairy Ariel who's been trapped inside a split tree by a white

Algerian (African) witch named Sycorax. Sycorax had been exiled to the island earlier, while pregnant with her son, Caliban. Sycorax has died, leaving Ariel imprisoned and Caliban abandoned. Prospero frees Ariel and requires her servitude in return, but promises to release her eventually. Prospero takes Caliban in and teaches him to read, but when Caliban attempts to rape Miranda, Prospero makes him a slave (as in, no promise of release). Ariel gets all the flitting-about jobs and Caliban gets all the hard labor. Prospero repeatedly ridicules Caliban. Ariel helps Prospero and Miranda get off the island, and thus wins freedom. I think we're supposed to identify with Prospero and Miranda, but I was disturbed by Ariel's servitude and Caliban's slavery; and even though Prospero eventually pardons Caliban, I had trouble with the play's relentless mockery of Caliban as a "savage."

A few years ago I was visiting Kamau Brathwaite's literature class at NYU, and they were discussing Caliban. I had the insight that Ariel and Caliban could be seen as the house Negro and the field Negro, and I proceeded to mess with the story from there.

TB: Someone once defined a language as a dialect with a navy. Would you agree?

NH: I don't know if I agree, but it's hilarious! Whoever it was has a point.

TB: Do you read poetry for fun? How about science? History?

NH: Although my father was a poet and I know much of his work, I used to think that I didn't read a lot of poetry. But then I had occasion to check my bookshelves and discovered that I owned more poetry than I thought, and had read most of it.

I'd forgotten about children's poetry ("The more it snows, tiddly pom . . ."), not to mention Louise Bennett and Kamau Brathwaite, and Marge Piercy and Homer, and Lillian Allen and Dennis Scott, and, and, and . . .

There are poems I can recite by heart, and as a kid I read the *Odyssey*, the *Iliad*, and Dante's *Inferno* for pleasure; read them over and over, in fact. I don't think I could struggle through Homer nowadays, but I was more persistent as a child.

I do end up hearing a fair bit of poetry, as readings or spoken word or dub poetry performances, and as music. It's rare that I'll read a whole book of poetry from end to end as fun, but in sips and nibbles, I do read it. And I read science and history for fun as well as for research.

Michio Kaku. *African Fractals. Death in the Queen City.* I also read critical theory for fun, and to find out what the hell it is that we writers are doing when we write. When it comes to fiction, I mostly read science fiction, fantasy, and comics, plus the occasional mystery or erotica/porn piece. But my nonfiction reading is more catholic.

TB: Do you think the World Fantasy Award should be a bust of someone other than H. P. Lovecraft?

NH: I have one of those. In appreciation for the merit of my work, the World Fantasy Award committee has given me a bust of a man who publicly reviled people of my primary racial background and who believed that we are by nature inferior to other humans. It is way creepy having racist old H. P. Lovecraft in my home looking at me.

I don't like the fact that the bust is of him, but I love having the award. So I console myself in a number of ways: it was designed by Gahan Wilson, and how freaking cool is that?

Lovecraft's own (part-Jewish) wife and his friends thought his racism was over the top. I gather his wife frequently called him to heel when he made anti-Semitic remarks; and I like imagining that Lovecraft is spinning in his grave as he's forced to view the world through the eyes of his statuettes placed in the homes and offices of the likes of Nnedimma Okorafor, Kinuko Y. Craft, S. P. Somtow, Haruki Murakami, Neil Gaiman, and me.

I think the award should represent a fantastical creature, perhaps a different one every year. (I know that's probably too expensive, but since I'm fantasizing here . . .) A kitsune. A troll. A chupacabra. Anansi. A fat, happy mermaid with fish in her hair.

TB: Do you outline plots, or just wing it? Ever write in longhand?

NH: Nowadays, I have to write proposals for unwritten novels in order to sell them. I don't outline, at least not whole novels at a time. I tend to do it when I get stuck. I rarely write longhand. I type much more quickly. Plus, I lose paper, whereas I rarely lose my computer or laptop.

TB: Do you have trouble with copyeditors, or rely on them?

NH: Both. Being copyedited is an occasion for taking a lot of calming breaths when I encounter wrongheaded or ignorant suggestions, but also for gasps of relief when the copyeditor catches something unfortunate in my text, or makes a suggestion that lends a clumsy line grace. It also gives me an early insight into how my story is being understood, which means I still have time to make small adjustments. In my new young adult novel, *The Chaos*, I invented (I thought) the name of a pop star. The copyeditor thought to Google the name, and discovered that it's the performance name of a porn star. Not an issue for me, except that she was not the character in my novel. I came up with another name.

TB: You once described a first draft as clay. I like that. Can you describe your general procedure in writing fiction? Do you try to always sit in the same chair?

NH: I don't. Sometimes I don't even have a desk at which to sit. I write and edit on my computer or laptop. I try to write in the early part of the day, since my mental energy peters out towards night-time. I try to start with a solid meal before I take the ADHD meds which help my concentration. If I don't eat that first meal, the meds take away my appetite (but not my hunger), and by early afternoon my brain is so overclocked it's like bees buzzing in my head and I'm so ravenous I'm dizzy, but food tastes like ashes in my mouth. I usually need my surroundings to be relatively quiet. I generally can only go for short bursts, between fifteen minutes and an hour. I spend way more time trying to make myself sit and write than I do actually writing. It's pretty painful, but I give myself less grief now that I know it's how my brain is wired. The meds do help me to stop procrastinating and to focus. I've heard lots of people say that they fear that ADHD meds will ruin their creativity, but for me, they are creativity aids. They help me to slow my thoughts down enough to register new ideas, and they give me enough concentration to write those ideas down.

I write scenes more or less in sequential order, but if I get stuck, I'll jump ahead to a scene that feels more tasty. If required, I'll backfill the rest in later. It's interesting, how often I find I don't need to backfill.

Another thing I do when I get stuck is to step away from the laptop and go do something physical that I don't have to think about: wash dishes, go for a walk. My mind goes musing and I often come up with solutions that way. Or I'll try to describe the problem to someone. Sometimes the very act of doing so helps me solve the problem before I can finish articulating it to the other person, who's then left frustrated as I waft back to my computer in a creative trance. I use manuscript organizing software such as Scrivener. That allows me to see all the scenes at a glance, and to map out, shape, and move elements of the story around until they click into place. When I'm in Toronto, I'll often meet my friend, writer Emily Pohl-Weary, at a local library. She's the granddaughter of Judy Merril and Fred Pohl, and a bitchin' writer in her own right. We'll take our laptops and each work on our own stuff for about three hours. We do goof-off, but I get a fair bit of writing done in her company. I miss Emily.

TB: Clute? Delany? Steampunk? Butler? Le Guin? Each in one sentence please.

NH: Clute's critical writing makes terrifyingly astute art.

Delany: All hail the King.

Butler: I wish more people would talk about the ways in which she messes with normative sexualities, and I miss her very much, and I don't care that that's really two sentences masquerading as one.

Steampunk: Cool gadgets, cool clothes, but whose hands assemble the materials?

Le Guin can make me cry with the simplest, seemingly inconsequential sentence.

TB: You once said, "Fiction is NOT autobiography in a party dress." OK, then what is it?

NH: It's what happens after you grind up a bunch of your personally received input, everything from life experience to that book about spices you read ten years ago, compost it within your imagination, and then in that mulch grow something new. I think that could even apply to autobiographical fiction.

TB: You claim to have grown up in a culture without strict boundaries between literatures. Really? Not even between "high" and "low" art?

NH: Yup. You can absolutely find that kind of snobbery in Afro-Caribbean culture, but it feels mostly toothless. The borders aren't as strictly policed. It's possible to have a literary conference in which both Nobel laureate Derek Walcott and dancehall singer-songwriter Lady Saw are headliners, plus bell hooks. In North America, there's no way that what I write would be considered in the same breath as, say, Michael Ondaatje's work. In the Caribbean, genre distinctions seem less important. Part of it might be that we don't have "alternative" culture in the way that it manifests in Eurocentric cultures. As far as I know, there is no Caribbean equivalent of the hipster, or the science fiction fan, or the zinester. Perhaps that's because we're already marginalized from dominant Western culture, so we don't need or don't have the luxury of subdividing along minute genre fractures. There aren't enough publishers to have that kind of specialization. The focus tends to be more on what each work is trying to achieve than on what genre it's in.

TB: Your SF background seems heavily post-New Wave (1960s). Did you ever read the "Golden Age" all-guy crew like Heinlein, Clarke, Simak, Bradbury?

NH: Absolutely, and still do. One of the proudest days of my life was when I got my mother to read Bradbury's *R is for Rocket*. Her verdict? "But it's not about rockets and robots, it's about people!" I agreed.

TB: You could easily (well, maybe not easily, but brilliantly) teach modern literature as well as writing. Given the choice, which would you prefer?

NH: Thanks for the compliment. I couldn't, though. Geoff Ryman, now, he's brilliant at both.

TB: In New York, I worked with some taxi mechanics from Guyana. Saturdays, they drank Teacher's and played cricket in the parking lot. What's the deal with cricket anyway?

NH: Lord alone knows. My dad was a big cricket fan. Cricket to me is golf as a team sport, with better outfits, that goes on for what seems weeks. Just give me the Teacher's. Lots of it, if you're going to make me watch cricket. Yes, I am a bad West Indian.

Interview: Nalo Hopkinson

David Barr Kirtley / 2013

From *The Geek's Guide to the Galaxy* podcast, https://www.wired.com/2013/03/geeks
-guide-nalo-hopkinsons. Reprinted with permission of John Joseph Adams and
David Barr Kirtley.

David Barr Kirtley: Your new novel is called *Sister Mine*, and it's about a pair of sisters, Abby and Makeda. Could you just tell us a little bit about those characters and how you came up with them?

Nalo Hopkinson: I've been trying to remember that, and I'm really not sure. Part of it is because I've always been intrigued by "Goblin Market" by Christina Rossetti. It's from the nineteenth century, and it's about two sisters, one of whom saves the other from goblins. I wanted to write about two sisters who were very, very close, as these two were, so I came up with Abby and Makeda, who were born conjoined. They got separated at birth, and when you separate conjoined twins, often they've been sharing some part of their body, so one gets it and the other one doesn't. So, when Abby and Makeda get separated, Abby gets the magic and Makeda doesn't.

DK: They belong to this family of demigods called the Celestials. Are those characters drawn from folklore or did you just make them up? Where did those characters come from?

NH: The characters are kind of a kind of a riff on the deities from the Afro-Caribbean belief system, which is rooted in West Africa, and you see various versions of it throughout the African diaspora, wherever African people landed up, West African people specifically. So they are sort of based on them. Beyond that, I departed a bit and had a bit of fun and used a bit of imagination, but . . . people will be able to identify who's who.

DK: Could you talk a little about a couple of them and what sort of spins you put on those characters?

NH: Well, I have Grandmother Ocean, who is loosely based on Oshun, who is a riverine deity; she's associated with bodies of waters, such as rivers.

I made her into the grandmother of the lot, and put a pun on her name so that "Oshun" became "Ocean." I have General Gun, who is very loosely based on Ogoun (again, a pun on the name), and Ogoun is a blacksmith, but can also be found on the battlefield, where he has a tendency to go into berserker mode. So I did a bunch of playing around with Ogoun and who Ogoun is as General Gun, that kind of thing.

DK: Makeda and Abby's father had fallen in love with a mortal woman, and so they're half mortal, and so they're kind of on the outs with their family. Does that have a history in folklore, that that sort of thing might happen?

NH: Sure, there's a history in science fiction and fantasy, the idea of the biracial savior of two races, or what a sweetheart of mine calls "not so subtle race allegory science fiction theater," so I did some of my own. And the idea that they're on the outs with one half their birth family is just the kind of thing you can see in life everywhere, where the circumstances of somebody's birth, their family doesn't approve of it, and so decides that they aren't really one of them and finds subtle and not so subtle ways to keep them feeling ostracized, so I sort of drew on human foible.

DK: The magic system in this book is called hoodoo. Is that just a variant spelling of voodoo? Is it different in any way from what people think of when they hear the word *voodoo*?

NH: It is, and it isn't. They are related. Getting into the specifics of how they are and are not related could take up most of this podcast and needs somebody with more training in it than I have, but they are definitely related, and I think I called it mojo.

DK: I think both terms appear in the book.

NH: Yeah, I do use them. I throw in a bunch of terms, but I call magic specifically mojo.

DK: Is there a difference between hoodoo and mojo, or is that also too complicated to get into?

NH: Yeah. [*laughing.*] *Mojo* feels to me like a broader word, and most of us know the blues line, "I got my mojo working." That sense of "got game" is one of the ways you'll hear people use "mojo," and hoodoo is something specific that's a specific set of practices.

DK: One example of the magic in this book that I really liked was one of the characters was once one of Jimi Hendrix's guitars, and he was turned into a human being. How did you come up with that idea?

NH: Totally written randomly. I was writing, and I don't do well with outlines. I have to outline in order to be able to have a project I can sell to an editor, but the outline's always very vague, and once I've done that, I just start writing. So I was writing that scene and got to a moment where Makeda asks something about Jimi Hendrix, and the guy leans forward and says, "I used to be his guitar," and that just came out of my fingers. I was just typing and there it was, and then I thought, "OK, that's cool . . . what? How did that happen? Did Jimi Hendrix even have a British guitar at any point? (Because this guy is British.) What did I just do?" So then I had to do some research and figure out a bit more about Hendrix and his music and his guitars, and it also went into and informed the story. That one was completely random.

DK: It's funny, there's a part in the book where Makeda sort of zones out and creates this powerful magical artifact, and I saw a clip with you where you said you have this tendency to sort of zone out and don't ask you how the toothpaste ended up in the refrigerator and stuff like that. I was just wondering, is that part of your creative process? To sort of zone out and then come to and kinda look at what you've written and you're like, "Where did this come from?"

NH: It can happen. It hasn't happened reliably for about five or six years now, partly because I spent five or six years quite ill, and couldn't concentrate on anything for more than a few minutes, so zoning out in a creative way did not happen much. But I have ADD, and part of that means that sometimes you just kind of lose track, either because you're hyper-focused on one thing, or because you're not focused at all and struggling to focus and sort of taking in *all* the information all at once, and getting too confused to make any good sense of it, and so I know the sense of—I have had lovely moments that feel like moments where I'm writing and writing and writing, and I'm quite aware of what I'm doing, then I look up, and it's four hours later when it feels subjectively like only a few minutes. They don't happen often enough. Because they're fairly easy, or—they're not *easy*, writing's never easy—but they're exciting when they happen. But I've heard other writers describe going into that kind of creative vortex where you sort of get lost in the work, and everything else kind of fades away for a while, and then you look up, and you're surprised, almost, that you're back in the world.

DK: A lot of the characters in this are artists and musicians and things. There's this wonderful, I think, bohemian atmosphere to the apartment complex that Makeda moves into. Did you have a background in arts grants or something? I was just wondering if you had experienced that sort of environment or is that a sort of dream life or . . . ?

NH: A little bit of everything. My dad was a poet, a playwright, an actor. A lot of his friends were writers or actors, some of them artists, so it's a world I kind of grew up in, but not like Makeda experiences it. I have been in a warehouse, I've lived in a warehouse, but it was awful and filthy, and it didn't feel bohemian so much as just really not any fun at all. But this is fiction, so I can have fun, and because I worked in the arts in Toronto, because I still tend to work in the arts, I'm very much used to that surround, so I was very much able to draw on it, and also had people I could ask for advice, like when I didn't know anything about how an electric guitar works, for instance. So it's a little bit of experience, a little bit of drawing on the experience of others, and, you know, I would love to move into a building that was never intended to be a house and make a home into it. I want to live in a fire station, I want to live in a silo, I want to live in an old church or an old mosque and make it my own. It's a dream. I don't think it will ever happen, but it's been a dream for a very, very long time.

DK: You mentioned that this was sort of inspired in a way by the Christina Rossetti poem "Goblin Market," and there are actually excerpts from the poem scattered throughout the book. I was just wondering, why did you decide to include those excerpts in here?

NH: The poem itself is gorgeous, and it manages to simultaneously be very innocent and very sexual. It's these two sisters who have such a strong love for each other that they're physically affectionate as well as just loving, and some of the lines in the poem read like sex scenes—they aren't, but they read like sex scenes—and I just couldn't help but include some of that gorgeous, gorgeous writing of Christina Rossetti's, and some of the lines that it is possible to twist, and read as perverse if you have a mind like mine.

DK: Well, no, I think that the sexual subtext of the scene, particularly where the two sisters smush fruit all over, and the fruit is running down—

NH: Sucked juice off the other's body! I mean, that's, *really?*

DK: And there's a scene very reminiscent of that in here where the two sisters are kind of smushing oranges on each other—

NH: Oh, yes.

DK: That was the one I noticed. Were there other scenes like that, pulled out of the poem or . . .?

NH: I don't want to give away too much, but there's stuff that I refer to that refers back to the poem, between the two sisters, between my two sisters that I created for the novel, and I tried to sort of evoke their closeness with the line about "like two birds in one nest," where they're sleeping in the same bed, so there are a few bits where I sort of refer backhandedly to things.

DK: The title of this book, I saw, was originally *Donkey*. How did that change to *Sister Mine?*

NH: That was my editor. [*laughing.*] Editors get to change your titles. I mean, you have to agree, but they'll work really hard to get you to agree. I called the novel *Donkey* because when the sisters were younger, one of them, Makeda, was a little more physically healthy and developed quicker than the other, and she would occasionally carry Abby on her back, and because Makeda is the one without the magic, she's grown up with this notion that the family thinks that the only thing she is good for is for carrying her talented sister around. And so she thinks of herself as the donkey, and, in fact, some of the other relatives think of her that way too. So that's what that came from. My editor thought that the title *Donkey*, though apt, was sort of ugly in what it referred to, and they didn't want to turn people off the book before they had started reading it, and I figure the marketing department knows their job better than I do, so I was OK with it. The neat thing is, when I was most of the way through the first draft, I discovered a pair of sisters, Black girls who were born into slavery, Millie Christine, who were born conjoined, kind of back-to-back and side-to-side, and who became singers, where one was physically stronger than the other, and actually the weaker one would sometimes sort of kite her legs up into the air, and the stronger one would walk around with her. So I went and found singing Black sisters where one was stronger than the other *and* they were conjoined. I had not known about them before then; my friend Ellen Klages, who is also a writer, told me about them.

DK: Makeda collects photos of conjoined twins. Did you do a lot of research on conjoined twins?

NH: Yes, I did. Not so much on the modern day aspects of them, although there's a little bit of that there, but the way they have been treated in history is interesting to me because of how they have often ended up being put on display and having to be treated as one person. When you read references to Millie and Christine, they're called "Millie Christine" and referred to in the singular, as though they were one person. So I did a lot of research into various types of ways that human beings can be born attached to each other, and some of them were fascinating. The whole idea of the parasitic twin, where it's not even a whole person, it's a body part that's sort of attached to the child when it is born—just some amazing stuff our bodies can do.

DK: You also have a YA book out called *The Chaos*, and they made you change the title for that one too, right?

NH: You've been doing your research! Yes, that one I was calling *Taint*, and I was getting pushback on the title from the very beginning because of some of the street names, what "taint" means on the street, and I kind of liked that meaning, so I wanted to keep it, and had tried to sort of modulate it by putting an apostrophe after the T, so that it could also be kind of a thing like "t'aint no sin to take off your skin and dance around in your bones." But when I handed in my manuscript, the editor wrote me back and said, "Look, my sales managers are giggling every time, can we please change it?" So I did. That whole thing of changing titles, I've learned now to have second title in reserve [*laughing*], because frequently I seem to come up with titles that make editors' hair fall out.

DK: *Sister Mine* is very sexual, and I would imagine a book called *Taint* might be as well, although it is a YA book, so I wonder . . . is there sexuality in *The Chaos* and what sort of—

NH: There is. The protagonist is sixteen; she is sexually active. That's barely there in the story. It's obvious that it is, but I don't make a whole lot of it. For me, part of what was going on in *The Chaos* is that when she was younger, before she was sexually active, she was in a different school where she was being slut-shamed by the other girls in the school, that kind of phenomenon where girls will spread rumors about each other, or they'll find one of their own to pick on and spread rumors about awful things they're doing with the football team, or sometimes will physically attack them as well. I wanted to talk about that, because it will happen regardless of whether the girl they pick on is actually sexually active, so I have a moment where my protagonist in *The Chaos* remembers the other girls sort of passing around notes or something that said that she had been giving blow jobs to the whole football team, and she's at this point maybe thirteen, she doesn't even know what one is, she just knows it's not good. So I wanted to talk about that phenomenon and what happens to her, what happens to girls who have this visited upon them, because often they're the ones who are for some reason cast as an outsider. They might be different in some way, or they might be newly come to the school when all the others know each other already. There's usually something like that going on, and I did a lot of looking into the lives of girls who had been slut-shamed.

DK: Well, actually, one of the Amazon reviews complained specifically about that line about blowing the football team, that it was too graphic or something. Have you gotten—

NH: Yes, but that review . . . I sympathize with the reviewer. She's a woman who has two girls, two daughters of her own, and she's sort of alarmed at the notion they might be reading stuff, not even about blow jobs, I don't describe a blow job, I don't—there's no sex on-screen in the book at all—but the notion that they might be reading words like that, and she was also alarmed that my protagonist often disobeys her parents; that one made me smile. I mean, I have sympathy for the woman, but the fact is her girls might be dealing with this stuff as we speak, and they'll need to be able to come to her and tell her. They need their parents to be allies, not so afraid of the world that they won't deal with it. So I'm of two minds, and it was how I was going to write it anyway.

DK: Back in episode seventy, we interviewed Junot Díaz, and I asked him if he was familiar with your work, and he said, "Of course, I mean, Nalo's my girl. I saw Nalo just a couple of days ago," so I was just kind of curious how you guys know each other and how often you hang out and stuff like that?

NH: Well, I knew his work because he was making such a splash for himself with his very first short story collection, *Drown*, and I did not know him, but turned on my email one day to an email from him, basically saying hi, how much he loves science fiction, and how much he wanted to write it, and we kept in touch. We finally met—oh, I can't remember the year—but he and Joe Haldeman, who both teach at MIT, engineered having me go to visit MIT, and that's when I met Junot. I'd known Joe before because Joe was a teacher at the Clarion I attended, so that's when I met Junot in the flesh. We've kept in touch. We tend to see each other across crowded rooms where two thousand people have gathered to hear Junot speak and we wave. He's a wonderful, wonderful man. I teach his work in my creative writing classes now, to give students a sense of voice and language and just fierce honesty in your writing.

DK: Yeah, could you talk about that? You started teaching fairly recently, right, at UC Riverside?

NH: I've been teaching all my entire writing career, off and on, but usually one-off things like a Clarion or that kind of thing, and I mentored at Humber College in Toronto, where it was an online mentorship, but a few years ago in 2009 I was offered a position teaching creative writing, specializing in science fiction and fantasy, at the University of California, Riverside. I don't think there's another job like this in the world. I mean, a lot of people teach science fiction and fantasy, but they're usually not in a creative writing department, or there isn't a position created specifically for it. This university has the Eaton Collection, which, I'm told, is the largest science fiction archive that is open to the public. It's a glorious, glorious collection, and there are three profs here who are part of a research cluster, a science fiction research cluster, and a lot of our work is sort of centered around the Eaton Collection. I've been to the collection and sort of touched some second editions of Thomas More's *Utopia* and first editions of Mary Shelley's *Frankenstein*. For science fiction writers, it's like going to church.

DK: You mentioned that you've had health problems. I saw you said that you hope this job will provide you a bit of economic security, and I think some of our listeners were just sort of wondering just how you were doing.

NH: Oh, bless them. I love science fiction. There are ways in which this community kept me and my partner alive through some very, very bad years, and I will always acknowledge that, so thank people for asking. I'm doing a whole lot better. A regular paycheck is magic. It's a pretty decent paycheck, though I'm still struggling with a lot of stuff. Climbing back out of a hole of not just poverty but homelessness takes a whole lot, but I am starting to believe it's going to hang around, that the good stuff that's happening is going to hang around, my health is coming back, my creative focus is growing again, I'm making a home for myself here. I'm not forgetting Toronto and keep making a home for myself there, but basically I am now eating regularly and back on medication I need to be on, and doing better and better every day.

DK: Ah, that's great.

NH: Yes!

DK: Another book you had just come out recently was that you were one of the featured authors in Terry Bisson's Outspoken Authors Series. Can you just talk about that series and how you got involved with it?

NH: *Report from Planet Midnight.* Terry approached me while . . . see, partly my memory's bad because of the ADD and the learning disability and the fibromyalgia, but put it through then five years of destitution, and it gets even worse. So I remember Terry approaching me, I don't remember when or how, whether it was in the flesh or whether he sent me an email, but he told me about the Outspoken Authors Series that he edits, that are chapbooks where one author is sort of featured. They will have a story or two in there, an interview with Terry, and an essay. And I said, yes, I thought I could do that, and we worked on it. Terry was very, very patient as I went through homelessness and clambered my way back out to sort of having a home to really having a home to being able to think about writing at all, and, bless his heart, he kept waiting, and he remained patient, but kept on at me until we had *Report from Planet Midnight.*

It's got two of my short stories; I didn't have the brain to write new ones at the time, but I picked two that most people would not have seen because they got published in such obscure places. One of them wasn't even published as a short story, and it wasn't published under my name. Then he did the interview, and I took an address I had given to the International Conference on the Fantastic in the Arts (ICFA). I was the guest author in

184 CONVERSATIONS WITH NALO HOPKINSON

a year where the theme of the conference was race in the literature of the fantastic. It was about a year and a half after RaceFail, so I knew it was going to be touchy, and I did part of the address as a performance piece that talked about translation, about what we mean when we say, "I'm not racist." So all of those are in the chapbook, which I really liked. I really loved the work that Terry did, the editing he did, the way he put everything in context, I loved the way the book looked, I loved working with the editor and the publishing house, but since it was a chapbook—and I know, particularly in this genre, we're size queens; a book's not a book unless it's at least four hundred pages, preferably twice that—I figured it would mostly be of academic interest. To my surprise, people have been buying it and reading it and talking about it and it's got legs, it's doing quite well. I'm very pleased. I'm proud of having done it, proud of the fact that Terry asked me. Terry's been an outspoken writer for a very long time, and that he thought what I had to say was important enough to be heard is a lovely thing.

DK: In this performance piece you mentioned, you actually enacted it as if you were sort of channeling an alien intelligence. Could you talk about why you decided to present your remarks that way?

NH: I knew almost two years ahead of that particular ICFA, that particular year of the conference, that I was going to be a guest author, and I had been trying to write my speech for most of that time, and you know how touchy things got around RaceFail, and the kinds of stuff that was happening, and I'd start trying to write it, and I'd get a combination of scared and furious, and I'd go take a walk around the block, and plus I was still homeless and hungry. No, by then I actually had an apartment, a room in somebody's apartment, but the words weren't coming in a way that felt strong to me or felt like people would find them "listenable to." Until it was the day before the conference, I was actually already at ICFA, and I took my notes down and started going over them again, and it may have been something my partner said that made me start writing in that mode of a translator from another planet, and I was mixing all kinds of modes because I have the translator sort of inhabit me, so we have the very science fiction/fantasy notion of possession, but the notion of possession is also one that you find in the Afro-Caribbean spiritual systems that I talk about in my writing. Only it's not a scary possession, it's not a ghost taking you over so that they can vomit out every fluid you've ever had in your body; it's in the course of a religious service, you open yourself to the deity, you invite the deity, one of the deities, to come down and inhabit your body for a while so they can talk to their parishioners, so I was evoking both simultaneously, because I can't . . . my world is a hybrid one, my references are hybrid references, so I just really worked that. And I had this translator from another planet inhabit me as a horse, which is what you'd call the person in the spiritual service who has a god riding on their head, and he and his team of translators have been listening to transmissions from Earth and having to translate them, and they're not sure they're really getting them because the translations they're getting aren't really making sense to them. So he's asking for clarification, and when they tried to translate "I'm not racist," they got something like "I can swim in shit without getting any of it on me." And he looked at their own translation and thought, "That doesn't make any sense. What sensible race would say this?" So they've come down to ask for clarification, always with a confession every so often that, you know, "sure you guys do some crazy things, we do some crazy things too," because I didn't want to give people the notion that I was standing there with some notion of purity, of being unaffected by racism. And it was a fascinating performance to give. I was shaking; I was shaking because I knew who attended ICFA, and I knew that some of the people who were there would not be fond of what I was saying. But I could also hear the supportive people in the audience who did get it and who encouraged me and I actually cut it short as a speech, because I just couldn't bring myself to keep standing up there feeling as vulnerable as I did, but to my surprise, when I stopped, I got a standing ovation from the audience. So Terry had me take that speech and put it in context for people who don't know the science fiction community and for whom RaceFail would not make any sense just as a phrase, and then I put the speech in with some additions.

Um, I have forgotten your question.

DK: The question was just, I guess, why did you choose to present as an alien being, and maybe is there some synchronicity between feelings of alienation and extraterrestrials and race relations and stuff like that?

NH: Mm-hmm. Well, you look at science fiction, and look how often it talks about being alien, being alienated by the Other. Look at the numbers of blue people!

DK: Yeah, that was funny, you mentioned all that—

NH: *Avatar*, looking at you. And it is now easier to find people of color in science fiction literature and media, but the issues of representation are still really, really troubling. The way they took, for instance, *Avatar: The Last Airbender*, that was in a pan-Asian world, and made the protagonist white. Neil Gaiman talking about—I believe it's *Anansi Boys* or *American Gods*— getting an offer for a film production of it, then having the producers say,

"Well, of course, we're going to make everyone white, because Black people aren't interested in fantasies," the kind of thing you'll hear white writers say about not wanting to write any people of color, for one reason or another, but it all boils all down to "because I don't want people to be mad at me." So the issues are still very, very much there. Even though we talk about race a lot in the literature, there's still this idea of, "Well, if we make this person blue and give them pointy ears, then we don't have to actually talk about what's happening in the real world." And those of us who live in racialized bodies feel that lack, we feel that erasure, so yes, there was something quite deliberate in my doing half the speech as an alien.

DK: I think actually a lot of our listeners don't know what RaceFail was, so do you want to maybe just explain that for them?

NH: Yes, I believe in 2009, discussions on race and racism in science fiction and fantasy in literature and community blew the hell up on the internet. There are some ten thousand posts that have been archived, with people of color in the community talking about what our experience has been, with white people in the community talking about what their experience has been, with lots of people who are very proud to say that they're colorblind opining very loudly on why the people of color were talking nonsense. It just got very productive, and I use that word deliberately because a lot of good came out of it. For one thing, people of our color began to see that there were [others out there], we made contact with each other. Often, you go to a con, and it can still happen that you're the only, or one of the handful of people of color there. When Octavia Butler was alive, it was the experience of all the other, maybe four, Black women science fiction writers in the community that we would go to a con, and someone would assume that that's who we were, to the point that Toby Buckell suggested that we call ourselves "The Butlerian Jihad." [*laughing.*] I want T-shirts!

So a lot of the buried and not-so-buried systemic racism in the science fiction community became laid bare. Lots of people denied it was there, but how could it not be? We're part of the rest of the world. Like I said, you can't swim in shit and not get any of it on you. This idea that the worst thing that could happen to you is for somebody to say "That was racist," and that you should react virulently against the very notion that you can be affected by your own society. People began to talk about that, and people began to make space to talk about it. One of the lovely, lovely things that came out of it was a publishing venture that's going quite well and got supported by the community beautifully. And out of it came this sort of Fifty Books Challenge where a lot of the readers realized that they weren't reading writers of color and started challenging each other to read fifty books by writers of color in a year. And they're doing it. It's a lovely thing. There's still this notion that you are somehow morally superior if you don't know anything about the background of the writers you read, and I maintain that writers have every right to not talk their backgrounds, that's fine, but when people do and it's important to their work, to not know doesn't mean you're morally superior, it means you are indifferent. And so there's just all of that going on, still going on, still getting challenged, still arguments going back and forth. It's a very rich time, I think, in the science fiction community, and a lot of nastiness has come out of it, but a lot of change, I think, is beginning to come out of it, and it's, at base, a hopeful time for me.

DK: If people want to embark on that Fifty Book Challenge you mentioned, what would be five or six they should start with that you would really recommend?

NH: Oh my God. [*laughing.*] You want me to get hate mail? Five or six? OK, let's start with one on my desk: *The Best of All Possible Worlds* by Karen Lord. It's her new one. I am reading it now and really enjoying it. Something I'm teaching my students: Thomas King's *Green Grass, Running Water.* He's a Canadian First Nations author. Umm, that's two. Samuel R. Delany: pretty much anything. That's three. Hmmmmm . . . *The Hundred Thousand Kingdoms* by Nora (N. K.) Jemisin. Charles Saunders: pretty much anything. And *Love and Rockets* [by the Hernandez Brothers], which is a graphic novel/comic, as well as *Bayou* [by Jeremy Love], which is another set of graphic novels. There! Off the top of my head.

DK: Actually, speaking of graphic novels, I saw you said that you were very slowly working on a graphic novel. Is there any—

NH: Progress? No, but I'm still collecting research. It's something that my life partner and I were working on together, and he's gone back to school, so it's on hiatus. But I'm still collecting research and notes for it. I don't know when it'll happen; it's nowhere near imminent.

DK: Can you say what you're researching or what the overall topic is or . . .?

NH: Part of what we're looking at it is discussions of what constitutes a human being at a time between sort of the Second World War and a few years afterwards, where we had the suffragist movement where women were fighting to be recognized as people, we had corporations being designated people under the law, that kind of thing. But I'm also looking at a particular African supernatural creature and the history of Black men on the railroad in North America. You know, it can't be just one thing. It all comes together, I promise you, but I just don't know when.

DK: OK, so that pretty much does it for the questions. Are there any other projects that you're working or have coming up that we haven't touched on yet?

NH: Yes, I am back to working on *Black Heart Man*, which is a novel that I've mostly finished and had to put aside, so I will be working on that over the summer. I am shopping around a new short story collection, and just generally getting about the business of learning to become a full-time professor and getting back into my creative brain. So that's where I'm at.

Somehow Déclassé:
Interview with Nalo Hopkinson

Gary K. Wolfe and Jonathan Strahan / 2013

From *Paradoxa: Studies in World Literary Genres*, no. 25, Africa SF (2013): 289–302.
Reprinted by permission of *Paradoxa*.

Gary K. Wolfe: Congratulations on the publication of *Sister Mine*. I had a lot of fun with it, and it looks like you did too!

Nalo Hopkinson: As much as I have fun writing—which I mostly don't—yes, I did.

Jonathan Strahan: The publication of *Sister Mine* and *The Chaos* signals a very active return for you after a long period of not writing. That must be enormously satisfying after a presumably frustrating time without a lot coming out?

NH: Yes, I had a lot of unfinished work and I have been finishing it as quickly as I can, which creates the happy circumstance that I've had three books come out in the past year and a bit. It is very satisfying. I'm no longer as worried that I have tanked my own career by being sick. It's been a very good thing.

GKW: You have indeed had some hard times. I recall you were working on *Sister Mine*, then called *Donkey*, about five years ago?

NH: Yes. That is very, very true. That book was so hard to write. I couldn't finish a sentence—neither reading one nor writing one. I'm still finding little snippets of things I wrote during that five year period that I have no memory of writing. The only way I know they're mine is because they are in my notebooks, in my handwriting, and in my particular style. So I was still writing, dearly, but not able to connect the dots.

It started to turn around for me finally in 2009 when my partner and I were actually house-sitting for *Locus* right after editor Charlie Brown passed away, so that meant we had housing for a couple of months and a little bit of money for food, and my brain started to come back to me. I had by then figured out what was wrong, and was dosing myself for the extreme anemia that made it impossible for me to think. So, in 2009, my health began to return. I'm still having moments of "Oooh! Here's a thing I can do now that I wasn't able to do a few years ago!" For example. I read a couple of books on the plane on the way to the Octavia Butler celebration at Spelman College this spring. I actually read books from cover to cover! It's been a while. (It helped that they were good books.)

GKW: I remember you being an unofficial writer in residence at *Locus*. To you it was house-sitting; to us it was an honor!

NH: It was wonderful place to be: to be surrounded by like-minded people and be in such a beautiful part of the world. It is something I will always remember. Also all the little memories of Charles that were around. At one point I realized that on the desk I had been working at for months there was a box that had his ashes in it. At first I thought, "Oh, this is just an empty box." Then I pushed it and it was way too heavy so I thought—that would be Charles in there! And I knew that if he were round, he'd be giggling at the cosmic joke of it.

GKW: You also had a really nice academic position at the University of California, Riverside, come, and then go away, and then come back again, which must have been rather nerve-wracking?

NH: Well, I hadn't actually been looking for that teaching position. In fact, while I was on the mend, people kept sending me the emails about the job and of course I knew very little about how academia works (and still don't know that much). To me, tenure was a vague concept. Of course, it means a whole lot more now, but the people I knew who were teaching in universities had no time or space to do anything else. And so I'd get the emails and say, "No. I'm on the mend, I can do one thing; I can either write or I can teach, and I know which one I'd rather do!"

This carried on until I heard from the selection committee. I was one of a few people they had asked specifically to send in applications. So that provided enough adrenalin for me to sit down and be able to read the job call properly. I interviewed and got the job in 2009, and then their funding got pulled and they had to withdraw all outstanding job offers. They had warned me that was a possibility and so although it was a shock, I didn't feel hard done by. But bless their hearts—they got permission to hold the job until they could offer it to me again. I started in 2011.

JS: That sounds like a precarious, difficult time.

NH: It was horrible. It was a few years living in constant panic mode. Waking up in the morning and not knowing how I was going to survive, and it was happening to both me and my partner. I would not wish that on anyone.

JS: Is it coincidence that you came out of that period of time with a novel called *The Chaos*?

NH: You would think so! But my original title for that novel was *T'aint*. However, my editor didn't want me to use it because of its colloquial meaning. It's slang for "perineum," i.e., t'aint your butthole, and t'aint your junk. It's the part in between the two. My title was making her sales reps giggle.

GKW: That brings up an interesting point about your use of language. I think my favorite new word from *Sister Mine* is *claypicken*. So I thought I'd check that out and I googled it and all it does is come back to *Sister Mine*. You just made that up, didn't you?

NH: I did. It was originally *mudpicken*, but that seemed too much like *mudbloods*, so I changed it.

GKW: Essentially it is used to talk about muggles . . .

NH: Yes, exactly and that's why I didn't use *mudpickens*. *Mudbloods* is a pejorative term they use in Harry Potter novels for people like Hermione, who are born of regular human stock. My word incorporates a West African word for children: in Jamaica we say *pikni*. In Nigeria, I believe they say *picken*, but it basically means *small*—"small children."

GKW: So that's where *picaninny* comes from in American Southern use?

NH: Yes. I often get people who are slightly disturbed when they see the word *pickney* in my novels and realize where it comes from. They're used to hearing it used as a pejorative, but in Jamaica it just means *children*.

GKW: One of the things that fascinated me in reading your fiction is that once you started using all these terms that nobody had seen in SF and fantasy, such as duppies and *soucouyants*, you can just make things up and people will think, "That's probably authentic because all the other stuff has checked out."

NH: Exactly. Even though they generally don't make the same assumption about the inventions of white writers. I'm somehow presumed to be less inventive, more "traditional," less able to depart from existing lore. To be fair, that comes in part from a lack of familiarity with African diasporic folklore, but there's also a certain amount of stereotyping going on. I've had it happen in reviews where people just assume that if something in my work feels folklore-ish to them and they don't know it, then it must be Caribbean. And sometimes it's not; sometimes it's German!

I do make stuff up as well. I also use uncommon words. There's a word in *Sister Mine*: knobkerry. I didn't need to make that one up, because it already exists. It's a type of club with a knob at one end. I love words. I collect them.

JS: *Sister Mine* brings you back to a certain place in your work; back to a fantastical Toronto—which is not uncommon in feel to *Brown Girl in the Ring*.

NH: Toronto is kind of magical—for all that many people who live there think it's a very mundane place, it is a very unlikely place from my perspective. It's a lovely place in which to set a fantasy story, because there are people from all over the world, so everybody's folklore is there in a way.

JS: Does it give you a location where you can blend folklore in new and different ways in order to create stories?

NH: Very much so—it meant I didn't actually have to do a lot of hand-waving as to why the Trinidadian nature deity Papa Bois is in a care home in Toronto . . .

JS: My experience of Toronto is that it is a rich, multicultural place, with a lot of people who did what your family obviously did—they came up to Toronto from Jamaica.

NH: My family is complex; I and my mother are Jamaican, and my brother and father Guyanese. We moved around the Caribbean for a while. I think we were living in Guyana when we made the move up to Canada in the 1970s. There is very definitely a wave of Caribbean immigration to Canada that started, I believe, in the 1950s. It is ongoing, but there are all kinds of waves of immigration to Toronto, from all over the world.

JS: But presumably not typically bringing all of their gods with them?

NH: People do bring their gods with them. There was a documentary made at one point by a couple of Montreal filmmakers called *A Lot to Share*. It was about a stretch of street in Toronto where there is a mosque, a Jewish synagogue, a Buddhist temple, a number of Christian churches and a Zoroastrian temple, all within walking distance of each other. The mosque and the synagogue share a parking lot. The documentary showed the imam of the mosque and the rabbi of the synagogue talking about peace and interaction. In other words, where people go, so go their gods.

GKW: How much do you get treated as a Canadian writer? I know in Canada you are certainly celebrated, but do general readers see the Canadian connection as being that important? I think you are right that it is a kind of melting pot that isn't the same kind of melting pot we get in the US.

NH: No, it is not. It's not a melting pot at all. It's more like a stew. There isn't the notion that you come to Canada and you become Canadian, which means you have to forsake all others. It's more that you bring everything you are to being Canadian. So I can be Jamaican Canadian, I can be Africanadian, I can be Black . . . there isn't the same sense that you have to abandon your previous culture.

I do get seen as a Canadian writer. I think in the US I get seen as "Other" and people aren't always sure which "Other" it is. Sometimes they say Canadian and sometimes they say Trinidadian and sometimes they say Jamaican—which is only partly true. None of it, however, is untrue. Sometimes they say African American, which isn't true of me at all.

GKW: I wonder if people are doing doctoral dissertations on you yet in relation to issues such as postcolonialism? I ask because there is an obvious connection that academics could not resist, which has to do with your father, Muhammad Abdur-Rahman Slade Hopkinson, and Derek Walcott, and the whole Trinidad Theatre Workshop, which gives you a kind of "royalty" connection to what most Americans think of as magic realism.

NH: There was an extended essay that Mary Hanna, a Jamaican academic, wrote about me quite a few years ago that was published in a Jamaican newspaper, and that was the angle she took. Most Caribbean people in the literary field make the connection, but to them it is not an unusual connection; other people don't mostly.

GKW: You had met Derek Walcott a few times?

NH: Oh, yes—for a while when I was a kid, my mother would drive me to his home every day in the mornings and I believe his [then-] wife Margaret would take me and their daughter to school. So I knew them quite well. And I'd been at rehearsals at their place. When *Brown Girl* was coming out, I needed to get permission to publish the excerpt from his play *Ti-Jean and His Brothers*, so I called him. He was quite wonderful about giving his permission.

GKW: One of the things that some of us collect in the backs of our heads for no rational reason, is Nobel Prize-winners who seem OK with the fantastic. There's Doris Lessing, and if you go far enough back there is Rudyard Kipling, and then there is Derek Walcott.

NH: I don't know why the current literary disdain for the literature of the fantastic has such a strong hold. Sometimes I suspect it's because those novels actually sell. Of course, I'm being facetious. But I did not grow up with any kind of suspicion that what I was reading was somehow impoverished literature; I didn't discover that it was supposed to be such until I'd begun publishing it!

JS: What attracted you to writing SF and fantasy?

NH: It's what I always read: SF and fantasy, or in some way literature of the fantastic. My dad was teaching English and Latin in senior high school, plus being a playwright and an actor and a poet. So the books on our bookshelves were things like the *Iliad* and *Gulliver's Travels*, collections of folktales and just a lot of literature of the fantastic. Some of that stuff I could not read now. I'd probably find it too difficult. But as a child you just suck it all in and take what you can from it. So that is what I read in preference to the more mimetic fiction. Because mimetic fiction felt a lot like real life and I felt like I was having one of those and I wanted something more.

GKW: So you read genre SF and fantasy, not the classics? But you did a master's degree in Russian literature?

NH: No—my undergrad degree is in Russian and French languages, which meant I had to take Russian literature. I managed to skip French literature, I'm not sure how! It's a deficit I must mend. My master's was in Writing Popular Fiction through Seton Hill University. By then I was on my third novel, though. My master's thesis was under contract then to my publisher when I started attending SHU.

GKW: There is a sense among many people I know involved in MFA programs—mostly mainstream MFAs—that anyone who actually has a contract and an advance on a book and possibly a marketing campaign is so alien to their experience that they can't get their heads around it.

NH: I didn't find that at Seton Hill so much, since the program was specifically in writing popular fiction. At that point, I was the most published student there (perhaps even more so than some of the profs). Anyway, the ways of mainstream publishing were not unheard of. People expected it could happen to them. But I get the feeling from other places in the academy that it is somehow déclassé to be a commercial success in popular fiction. I see some of this academic bias when it comes to certain of my colleagues assessing the quality of a student's writing. If the writing is demonstrably bad and it's SF or fantasy, they defer completely to me, with the clear inference that perhaps inept writing is OK in my genre. Mind you, there are times when they should defer to me, but not to the point of abdicating all judgment! Because it becomes pretty clear when we talk about it that we have the same assessment of the student's level of craft. I may know the canon better, but it's clear to us all what is and is not working in a piece on a craft level.

JS: Yet some academics continue to filter it through that perspective—that genre is something different?

NH: Yes. However, there are plenty of closet SF and fantasy fans in academe—people who you don't have to scratch too deeply before they are happily talking about their favorite SF with you—but it's not what they have been able to do as writers in academe. I gather it can actually hurt your career. I'm happy that UC Riverside has taken steps to become a thin edge of the wedge.

JS: If it's not an atmosphere where people are admitting to reading SF or fantasy, then they are not going to be accustomed to a dialogue about it in a detailed or rich way?

NH: That's why it is lovely being here at UCR because my position, and Rob Latham's and Sherryl Vint's were built around the Eaton SF and fantasy archive run by Librarian-in-Chief Melissa Conway, so there are all kinds of cool things happening. There is the Eaton conference that happens every other year. There is an SF and fantasy reading group initiated by Rob. It's informal, mostly grad students. So there are places to begin having those conversations. I still think we have a long way to go.

One of the things I've found (and this might be just my bias) is that for a lot of people who set out to try to write SF or fantasy, the learning period seems to be longer. Their writing initially feels less mature than those of their peers who are writing in other genres. I think that stands them at a disadvantage when it comes to things like applying to grad school. Luckily, you don't need a degree in order to be published!

GKW: I remember talking to Daniel Keyes, who taught at Ohio University for many years, and everybody wanted to study SF with him because of *Flowers for Algernon*, and he wouldn't let them write SF till the second semester. He said that in the first semester they had to learn to write a decent story: they had to learn story structure, character, all the details of writing a good story, and then in the second semester they could write SF and fantasy because it's harder.

NH: It *is* harder. I'm finding that a lot of my undergrads who are wanting to write SF and fantasy—through no fault of their own—no longer have the sort of base in various types of language use, historical references, literary references, that are in the genre. They haven't been exposed to them and haven't yet discovered communities where they can talk about the literature they love, so their writing has a long way to go. Or it takes the students—especially the grads—a very long time to break out of the mold of "we must be able to see the happenings in the story as metaphor," because it is so dinned into them that it is not worthy fiction if the fantasy creatures are real.

JS: Is this a problem with their fiction, or an example of genre being exclusionary? That attitude of "you must be well read in the field . . ." Is it a material thing or just an exclusionary tactic?

NH: I think it's both. There are people who are very invested in policing the boundaries. I've seen it happen to women writers in the genre and it certainly happens to people from elsewhere. So being Black and female and from the Caribbean means that every so often at my readings somebody—usually male, usually white, who has been reading the SF classics for a long while—decides that it is his job to quiz me in whether or not I know them. And then to try and point out that Heinlein was doing this before me. As though this is news! Though there are some things that Heinlein was *not* doing before me.

So there is very much that policing of the boundaries. Yet I think art is, in part, a conversation that builds upon what came before, as well as having lots of room for new takes on things and new ideas. So if you don't know some—you can no longer know all of what came before—but if you don't know *some* of it, you tend to not be part of the conversation.

GKW: One of the things I have learned in discussing the growing multiculturalization of SF over the last fifteen or twenty years is how many people have read Heinlein—people like Karen Lord in Barbados. You don't have to be part of that classic white male establishment to have read those works.

NH: When I was on tour with my second novel, one of my stops was a big bookstore in some American city. The person working behind the desk simply found me astonishing. They made a point of coming out from behind the desk and taking me up and down the shelves, saying, "This is Le Guin, have you heard of her? This is Asimov, have you heard of him?" And I thought, "What is this person doing?" As far as I'm concerned, you can see in my writing that I do, of course, know the genre. Yet because my audience crosses genre lines, every few weeks I have to deal with somebody who is not an SF and fantasy reader who is trying to prove to me that my writing is not SF or fantasy because it is, to quote one audience member, "good."

GKW: I have colleagues who are happy to look at you in another tradition but want to ignore the whole SF/fantasy thing.

NH: True. I also get it in a different, in other words positive, way from Caribbean academics; they might not know that much about genre, but they recognize what I'm doing. In the Caribbean, there aren't the same minute genre boundaries, partly because the publishing industry is a lot smaller. We don't have the luxury of subdividing twelve ways from Sunday and getting into fights about whose work is really literature.

JS: So when you get into a situation where everything is broken down so much, does it become too separated?

NH: I think it does. I think that really works against the whole project of literature. Because writers talk across supposed artistic and genre boundaries; those who pay attention, anyway. It seems as though our [writers'] canon is not the same as the academic canon. I'm pulling from everything when I write; pop fiction, "classic" literature, visual art, film, poetry, liturgical narrative, music videos, hipster slang . . . I'm used to getting a certain amount of snobbery from people who think there's "high" culture and "low" culture and that the former should only incorporate the latter ironically, if at all. I'm a fan of dance for instance, and there are forms of current dance that to me feel very much—I don't know the academic terms—that feel very apt to me to be studying as an SF/fantasy writer. I once said to someone in the dance department, "I love ballet, I also love the television program *So You Think You Can Dance?*" I got such a rolling of eyes in response! But there is useful material for me there. There is something that informs my own practice and teaches me about narrative and flow. There is beauty there and content and criticality. You watch some of the master krump dancers, and there is a whole narrative in evidence about Blackness in the face of racism and about anger and traditions of movement and ritualized insult going back centuries. And, of course, in any artistic form there is a whole lot of schlock. But there always is.

JS: Is part of your mission as an SF and fantasy writer to bring things into the context of the genre that weren't there previously? To broaden the context of the genre in order to encompass them?

NH: That's part of it. I find myself as I am teaching, bringing in children's picture books, for instance, and having my students be very surprised that they are every bit as meaty to read and to assess as a full length novel. So that is part of it: to say that SF can and does do all these things, and get over it already! It just makes the writing richer. The people whose work I love have been doing that forever.

GKW: So whose work do you love, and who did you read growing up?

NH: Chip Delany, always, always. I like China Miéville's work. Ursula Le Guin. Remember you are talking to someone who for five years couldn't read, so there are huge holes in my reading. Shaun Tan, I love his work so much! Kelly Link . . . I could go on forever.

Growing up I read what they gave me in school to read. I remember reading *The Lion, the Witch and the Wardrobe* in my first year of high school in Trinidad. When we read the section in which Aslan the lion awakes Narnia, the teacher let me read the part of Aslan, which was wonderful. I can still quote it. I read the books on my parents' bookshelves, which included some of the European classics, but also included folktales, a lot of poetry, a lot of plays. Anything I could get my hands on. I recently did a little documentary

198 CONVERSATIONS WITH NALO HOPKINSON

for the Eaton science fiction and fantasy archive. They filmed it in the Eaton collection, and I asked one of the librarians to bring out the January 1968 issue of *Playboy*, where Kurt Vonnegut's *Welcome to the Monkey House* was serialized. I read it when it came out, because I somehow got my hands on a copy of *Playboy* at the age of eight. I didn't know or care about all the naked ladies—I mean, they were pretty, but whatever—but I really liked the strange stories. My reading was lot broader in scope as a child than it is now.

GKW: At some point you must have read something by Asimov, something by Heinlein, something by Zenna Henderson—you must have started reading genre SF at some point?

NH: When I was about fourteen my mother was working as a clerk at the Kingston Public Library on Tom Redcam Avenue in Jamaica, and I would walk there after school. Because they divided the library into adults' and children's sections, you had to be a certain age to get an adult card. But I was already reading at an adult level, so my mother engineered for them to give me an adult card, and I went looking for the kinds of things I knew I liked. And the SF and fantasy shelves was where I found them. I remember reading *The Andromeda Strain*, Harlan Ellison's *Shattered like a Glass Goblin* . . . I think it was later when I discovered Henderson. And I remember reading collections of Hitchcock horror and scaring myself horribly. I still can't read horror. That's when I started to read genre SF because it was giving me the stuff I had been reading on my own: folktales, European classics, and so on.

JS: Your characters in *Sister Mine* and other books are Black, gay, non-American, sometimes disabled. Do you think that SF today is more inclusive than when you came into the field in 1998?

NH: Without a doubt. And built on the shoulders of a lot of people who did a lot of work before me. I think that yes, it is more inclusive. In some areas of SF, the work is there to be found. There are always certain readers who surprise me because they are not interested in looking for it. But I think editors certainly seem to me to be more interested in expanding the scope of the genre and the diversity of the genre. However, just like the rest of the world, the field is still quite racist, sexist, homophobic, classist, ablist. There's a lot more work to be done.

GKW: It is also the depth and complexity of characters that SF is willing to sustain. To take *New Moon's Arms* as an example: it features a radically unsympathetic point of view character, Calamity. She's homophobic, she's got a bad self-image, she's overweight, she doesn't deal with her kids well, she's just a horrible character in many ways and yet you make her the point of view character. And you make her a very sympathetic character in many ways by the time the novel is halfway through. That is a level of complexity of characterization that SF and fantasy has seldom seen before. I just loved that character because I didn't like her!

NH: You should have seen her in the drafts, when *I* didn't like her! I had to do a major rewrite of her. I wasn't aware as a young reader of SF and fantasy in general having thin, one-note characters; perhaps because I started out reading SF and fantasy very young, so at the time, it didn't take much for a character to feel well characterized to me. Also, I managed to skip over lots of the Golden Age SF. It wasn't making its way to the Caribbean, and when I did find it, I probably didn't find a lot of it interesting. If the protagonist hauled out a slide rule and started doing calculations, my eyes would glaze over and I'd go find something with monsters in it, or time travel. But any shift towards more complex characters hasn't come whole cloth from me, but from those who were doing it before I was, such as some—by no means all!—of the feminist writers. And people like Ted Sturgeon. The subtlety of characterization in his work is just delightful.

GKW: In the past, Sturgeon and a handful of other writers could do this as the "oddball" writers, but now it seems to be much more easy to do?

NH: I may have been lucky, I haven't really had an editor say you can't do that (with the exception of using certain swear words in certain young adult stories for certain publishers). I haven't had opposition to what I want to write. It's something that I try to talk about whenever I can: that good editors actually will work with what you've written. They are not these evil people who are there to count beans. They are doing a probably underpaid job because they love fiction.

GKW: Nobody has said to you, "You can't do Calamity, nobody will like Calamity, she can't be a point of view character"?

NH: No—I forget if it was my editor or my partner or me who said she was too unsympathetic. That was in early drafts, and it became clear I was getting stuck because I didn't like her. So I had to pull back and make her more likeable, or at least admirable. But when I handed my final draft in, my then editor didn't say a word. My editor a few years earlier also didn't say a word when I handed in *The Salt Roads* to her to be published by her SF/fantasy publisher.

GKW: *The Salt Roads* is your most ambitious novel. It's a three-era historical epic, and with the cover illustration, could have easily been marketed as a mainstream novel.

NH: Yes—it was, in fact. But it was also marketed to my SF and fantasy readers. My then-editor, Jaime Levine, took the novel to her boss who was in charge of the larger imprint, and got permission to not put SF or fantasy on the spine. But they didn't abandon the usual SF and fantasy outlets. I don't recall seeing an SF or fantasy reader complain that it wasn't genre. Some of them have been bemused, but have for the most part been willing to take the novel in their stride.

JS: With *Sister Mine* out, what are you working on now?

NH: I just turned in a short story to a YA anthology that I hope is taking it. This summer, when I'm off teaching, I will be going back to *Blackheart Man* that I got so far on and could get no further because I was really too sick to be writing. I hope to finish it. My ability to produce is never predictable, though.

GKW: Any inclination to write more SF like *Midnight Robber* sometime soon?

NH: Not soon, but I do have an SF novel that I want to tackle at some point—in the future. I don't know the core of it yet, it isn't a novel yet. It's still growing in my mind. That is going to come at some point but I don't know when. I still feel like I am clearing the decks after the previous years of havoc.

JS: You must be just about ready for a new short story collection as well?

NH: My agent is shopping one around right now. The market for single-author collections was never that great, and it seems to be worse now. The editors that Don Maass, my agent, has approached are very concerned about the fact that most of the stories have been published previously, which I don't recall being an issue before. To my mind, the point of a single-author collection is to gather up an author's work that may have been published in a bunch of different places and assemble it into one volume for easy reference.

JS: Do you have any plans to edit any more anthologies, because you have done some quite remarkable ones over the years?

NH: Thank you. I suspect it will happen, but I don't have any immediate plans for one, because that still feels beyond my energy at this point. Plus, there are so many other people now doing wonderful anthologies that I want to catch up with their work!

Writing from the Body:
An Interview with Nalo Hopkinson

Jessica FitzPatrick / 2015

From *Hot Metal Bridge* (Summer 2015), https://hotmetalbridge.org/an-interview-with-nalo
-hopkinson/. Reprinted with permission of Jessica FitzPatrick.

Hot Metal Bridge: What is "postcolonial science fiction"?

Nalo Hopkinson: I remember when Uppinder Mehan and I were doing the anthology, *So Long Been Dreaming: Postcolonial Science Fiction & Fantasy.* I knew what "science fiction" was—and that itself is a contested term—but he had to explain to me what "postcolonial" was. And, of course, it was a long explanation with many long words in it. People had been telling me that I wrote postcolonial literature, and I had no idea what they were talking about. If I were to explain it now in terms of science fiction, I would have to go to a dictionary even though I've edited an anthology of postcolonial science fiction. But to me science fiction is a sort of perfect way to be talking about colonialism and its aftereffects because that's the core story of science fiction: going to other places and meeting new aliens and taking their stuff! [*laughs.*] So when you get that awareness being brought into science fiction by writers and critics from postcolonial communities or with an analysis of colonialism and its effects, many times we already have a lot of the language for making fiction about it, a lot of the language for critiquing it, for saying here's what may result, or here's what could be different, or here's some of the possibilities, here's what this experience is like psychically. And there is some resistance in the science fiction community to people doing that, but there's also a whole lot of people going, "Hell yeah! It's about time! We've wanted to see this for a very long time." So it's a very fruitful genre to be doing that kind of work in.

It has been a genre that has been predominantly white, Western, middle-class, and male for a long time. Now it's closer to being 50–50 in terms of male and female writers, but there have been waves of people claiming science fiction for their own. There's the whole feminist wave; there are anthologies based around queer experiences in science fiction, and increasingly, anthologies based around communities of color. There's one coming out that's talking about ability and disability. And so the community's generating its own material as quickly as it can, and being that we're so internet-connected, we're very quick to take advantage of things like Kickstarter to get small things funded. And as with any small community that has been marginalized and is accustomed to activism in support of its own survival, give us any little bit of money and we can make wonderful things happen.

One of the things I'm seeing about those anthologies is often it's a younger expression. It's younger folks with not as much experience. So, for instance, one of the things you'll see is the copyediting won't be as strong as something coming out from Simon and Schuster. And I have to put that aside, to some extent, and look at the message, look at the vigor, insight, and imagination in the work. This is modern day samizdat. This is "we can now take the means of production into our own hands." And people are learning on the ground, learning from each other. When I think of a zine, I don't expect everything to be spelled correctly. What I want is the message, the challenge to my own preconceptions and those of others. When I pick up these anthologies, what I want is the story and the sensibility. And those are coming out in *droves*. There's a lot of pushback . . . but there's a lot of push-forward.

HMB: As long as it's not a Doctor Dolittle pushme-pullyou type of stalemate . . .

NH: Right! Forward tends to win out.

HMB: During your talk at Carnegie Mellon, you mentioned science fiction's relationship to our "real" lives, but also to the reality of the classroom. Does teaching interact with what you're writing, or how you're writing?

NH: It does . . . the lovely thing about teaching is that the students challenge you because they want to know why about everything. Sometimes they want to know the why of things you've never questioned. It's also quite humbling. More than once, I've found a particular literary strategy that I see failing over and over in someone's work or in a group's work—I'm noticing it because I've done it myself. So I have to confess and say, "Yeah. . . . there's a reason why I know this so well. And I hadn't even thought about it until I saw it in your work."

Because I'm teaching in a plot-driven form, I bring a different way of looking at structure to people. My metaphors for craft tend to be scientific and kinetic. (Go figure.) When it comes to teaching craft, we try to open their eyes. Which means you have to have different strategies because you never know what's going to make the lights go on for a student. I bring different strategies from our genre that many of them haven't seen or heard of before, and often they tell me it's the first time they've thought of something in a particular way. I also bring my current hobbyhorse, which is about the way that fiction really works by creating a sensory kinetic map for the reader. The sensory map is the protagonist for the reader to enter and move around *inside* the story. It's not that we receive the story, it's that we're inside the story, exploring and learning about it as the protagonist does.

HMB: Kinda like a video game?

NH: Better. Hmm. No—let me not do a disservice to video games. Good ones can do this just as well. You have to create strong sensory images for sensation and movement. So if you say, "She was angry," that's just delivering a fact. If you say, to use an old cliché, "A pulse beat in her temple," all of a sudden the reader's nerve endings are firing. A pulse may not actually beat in a reader's temple, but those nerve endings are firing. They've scientifically mapped this.

I bring a certain amount of science to the craft of writing; I bring a fair bit of magic to the craft of writing. I try to give them as many new ways of approaching it as possible. And because I also come out of a Caribbean writing tradition that has very much privileged writing in vernacular, I do a lot of getting them to practice discovering what their own vernaculars are, listening for other peoples', and trying to make sure that not every character speaks the same, or necessarily speaks in the same register as the author. It's a hard one for them to grasp at the undergrad level, I find. They've had the expository essay so dinned into their heads that they try to write fiction in bland, declarative prose, and it just doesn't work.

HMB: That type of writing sounds really ugly and horrible.

NH: I often wonder why, if you think that's what fiction is, would you major in creative writing at all . . .

HMB: Let's move away from the chilling idea of undergraduates who can't write anything but exposition and back to your idea of moving through the literary world. Science fiction and fantasy are genres that are not only plot-driven, but also world-driven; the world-building relates intensely to what can happen in the plot. Previously you've mentioned that when you write about Big Important Issues you don't want them to have an incredibly easy fix—just because you're a character in a fantastical or science fictional world, there's still no waving a magical wand and escaping from lineages of violence—

NH: No superhero can make time go backwards.

HMB: Right! So how does this avoidance of the genre-specific "easy outs" affect the worlds, the spaces and places, you build? This may lead into more general ideas about the use of literary place . . .

NH: One of the things I have to challenge frequently in younger writers is the unquestioned notion that the character doesn't have much baggage, that the character is just a vehicle for story. When in fact everything in our history creates our environments. The fact that there are train tracks running by this river that we're sitting by and that those tracks have a certain width is an effect of history. The fact of what we're sitting here eating is an effect of colonialism—we're eating *figs*.

HMB: And *marmalade*!

NH: Even though it's below freezing outside. All those things affect our experience of the world. They affect the character's experience of the world in subtle ways. It is better to avoid a long information dump on those connections, but you do have to really live inside your character to know what the world is doing to them and what they're doing to the world. I have to have people ask questions such as: "What is this person's history?" [and] "What do they do for a living?" I mean, questions you're probably asking in fiction anyway become all the more important in science fiction and fantasy because you're creating the world from the ground up. You have to choose what to put in and what to leave out. It's too easy to make protagonists into ciphers.

HMB: Writers have to ask the question, "Is the character you're writing using the steampunk gadget, or are they building the gears for the steampunk gadget?"

NH: And if you're building the gears for the steampunk gadget, how does that affect your *body*? There is, and I remember having this problem, so I can't say "youth nowadays" . . . but today there's not a very strong sense of history. Anything twenty years in the past might as well be from 2,000 years ago. I'm a voice for research. The character of an upper middle-class nineteenth-century young woman from New York is *not* wearing shorts to the market.

HMB: And if she is, that writer is doing something very deliberate with the timeline.

NH: Exactly. The writer is creating an alternate history. It's not that you can't do it, but know *why* you're doing it. And what it affects.

HMB: Including how everyone else in that world will react . . .

NH: Certainly. And I sometimes fear I'm overwhelming my students because there are so many layers of competency you have to take on in writing science fiction and fantasy. When your writing concerns only reality, there are things you don't need to question. Writing science fiction and fantasy means you need to question whether there's even a sun. And then question what direction that sun comes up in and what color it is.

HMB: Let alone how many suns there even are.

NH: And then, using the answers to those questions: What color does it mean the plants are? What is the composition of the air? Given that composition, what is the biology of creatures on the world you've created? Lots of competencies . . . It means people who are trying to write science fiction and fantasy will at first usually be very clumsy. It means, at the apprenticeship stages, science fiction can look a lot less mature than mimetic fiction because there are so many more steps of knowledge to take on and then try to synthesize. So for creative writing teachers, what I'm trying to say is to be patient; don't assume this person can't write. You may just have to bring them to the understanding of, for instance, the emotional connection to the character (we tend to focus a lot on the plot because the story falls apart if the plot doesn't work).

You have to find ways of making students see other things. I don't think he will mind me telling this story because he's told it himself on the internet, but I had a student who had been at a workshop for four weeks and was facing two more weeks. He had been told over and over again that his writing was hollow.

HMB: Hollow?

NH: Hollow. There's a particular type of journeyman science fiction writing that's just hollow. The character feels like an eggcup with legs. In his story there was a teenager trying to survive on her own with a freshly broken ankle, but he hadn't written any effects of her trying to walk on a broken ankle.

HMB: Ah-ha. Hollow.

NH: And he thought he'd had a breakthrough, but just got exactly the same feedback he'd been taking in for four weeks. So he came to me not knowing what to do next. And I said, "When you write, where are you writing from?" He said, "I'm in the character's head, and I'm thinking about what are they thinking about . . ." and he used the word *think* over and over again, and finally I said, "You need to write from their body, and I don't mean emotions—those will come through—but what are their sensations and what is movement doing to them." At first, he didn't see why it was important and was having a hard time understanding it . . .

HMB: You can't focus on anything, let alone think, when your stomach is gurgling about being hungry.

NH: Right! So he listened, and went away and wrote the next story. And he nailed it. I started reading it and critiquing it, but the whole time I was thinking, "Something's different . . . Something's different . . ." and I realized the character had just skinned his knee and my knee was burning. The character was embarrassed and I could feel my own checks flushing. I was in the story for the first time.

You might need to do that with the students writing science fiction and fantasy. They've been writing it in isolation because everybody tells them these genres are bad writing, are bad literature. If they haven't found the science fiction community, these writers are working completely in the dark. They might have one set of competencies working beautifully and miss things that to you are obvious. So bring them to it before you decide that a) the literature is impoverished, and b) the student has no talent.

HMB: I think sometimes the many-layered competencies of the genre seeps through to the demands on its readers. I just finished teaching *Midnight Robber.* The first third of the book occurs on the technology-filled planet Toussaint. Though they were reading critically, I noticed most students were also just thoroughly enjoying the differentness, the futureness, of that planet. And then the protagonist, Tan-Tan, gets banished to a *very* different planet. The class realized that, just like her, they had to reassess, they now didn't know what was going on. And then, in the middle of regaining their footing, there's sexual violence.

NH: I tried to put in signs that it was going that way . . . Much of that was done in rewriting. It wasn't so much in the first draft, but I went back in subsequent drafts and figured out where the points were that I could embed hints so that hopefully it wasn't a total surprise. Some people still were surprised.

HMB: As were some of my students before we discussed those indicator signs. However, even though they were hard to read, the students appreciated the sections dealing with sexual assault and its aftermath. Those sections invited important discussions; it let them talk about things that they wouldn't have otherwise. Your writing often allows for such conversations. I'd be interested in hearing your thoughts on hard subjects like sexual violence: How do you write about them? How do you teach about them?

NH: Writing about hard subjects, writing about sexual violence (which is the one that pushes most people's buttons the hardest), but also any kind of violence—bad relationships, fraught relationships, bad things happening to good people—I'm still learning to do. I'm really good at being explicit about sexual violence, about any violence. I'm very good at imagining what happens to the body because I write from the body, so it brings people in even when they don't want to be brought in. I'm learning when to temper that.

I don't believe in soft-coating it, but sometimes you can bring the reader in as far as they need to go and give them the mercy of looking away a little bit. I had to write a scene that had actually happened, where a freedom fighter in Haiti named François Mackandal was burned at the stake. I wrote the scene from the perspective of one of the witnesses. So, I took the reader up to seeing Mackandal tied there. I show them the flames being lit. I can imagine what happens to a live body being burned. But instead of writing that, I have the witness say, "a burning body smells like pork." I didn't need much else. The reader's already gone there. I didn't need to go through all the sensations and the screaming. I'm learning when the reader's already there with me so I don't need to grab them by the hand and drag them to the corpse. It's that sensibility I try to teach. Sometimes you do want to rub the reader's nose in things. You know that that's going to make some readers mad at you. And you might be triggering people if you're writing about a traumatic experience akin to one they've had. I think the really important thing about that is: if you're going to do it, then get it right. 'Cause it's bad enough they're re-experiencing it, but if you get details wrong then it's a little betrayal. So do your research. So now I'm trying to be just a little bit gentler on the reader, but not much.

When it comes to writing *sex*, I write all kinds of sex and sexualities. Which means I need a reader who won't be freaked out by being in a body that's not, perhaps, the one they'd want to be in, having an experience that's not one that makes them comfortable. To me that's part of the fun of it. Susie Bright, who used to publish an annual anthology of erotica, found it wasn't doing so well because it was pansexual. She tended to have more female readers than male readers, 'cause female readers are more used to that and more comfortable with it; male readers didn't want to find themselves in a sexuality they weren't comfortable with having a reaction to and, of course, erotica is there to turn you on. I like messing with *that*.

Sometimes I've had to write my way into a scene that I didn't know how to approach, or was afraid to approach because it wasn't my sexuality or it was and I didn't want to talk about it. And I found one trick would be to sort of tell it from the experience of a character I was more familiar with. Usually in a sex scene there's either an equivalence of play or there's the equivalent of pitcher/catcher, so I learned I could pick the one I felt more comfortable with and write from that perspective. I could turn off the internal censor and let myself play with the situation I was writing.

HMB: Would you then go back to the scene and do it from another perspective, or would you keep it from the slightly more familiar and comfortable one? It might depend on the story; if you needed a particular character's view . . .

NH: If it wasn't the point-of-view character, I have the point-of-view character observing those reactions. That's the easiest way to explain it. At some point you have to just kind of go for it. Tell yourself nobody need ever see this, and just go for it. Afterwards, if you find it strong, you'll want to send it out to publishers.

HMB: I know of no enticing transitions from the topic of sex scenes so, instead, a dorky question: what is one thing (magical, scientific, or somewhere in-between) you've created or greatly appropriated that you wish was real and you could use/have or just existed in the world?

NH: That might be a hard one for me; I'm not sure I tend to do that. When I was a kid I hated dolls. I hated playing make-believe. And now it's what I do for a living. So I don't have that sort of wishful thinking. I wouldn't own a magic wand, for instance.

HMB: You wouldn't want a TARDIS? Everyone wants a TARDIS.

NH: No. I wouldn't time travel. Time travel is baaaaaaad.

HMB: OK, sure: it can go wrong in many ways. It can be awful. But . . . wouldn't you just *want* it?

NH: No, no. [*shakes head.*] There must be something . . .

HMB: I want your colordot because lip*stick* is evil and devilishly hard to apply. In *Midnight Robber*, the character Ione just has to put her favorite colordot on her lips, purses them together, and has perfect lip color.

NH: Oh, like that—sure. I would like to be able to wake up every morning and choose what body I want to be in. Today, I want freckles and I want to be seven feet tall.

HMB: Talk about something that could really change the way you write and teach! What have you read lately that stuck in your head? When I ask this awful question—because it's an awful question to try and answer—what pops into your brain?

NH: It is an awful question. I'm not sure it ever helps anybody, but people ask it all the time so it must be helping someone.

HMB: Well, it gives you a name and a title to look up.

NH: Yes, it does. I think I'm currently just feeling overwhelmed, like "there's so much to read!," so I want titles but . . . [*distressed groan*].

I really enjoyed the graphic novel series *The Rabbi's Cat* by Joann Sfar. I preferred them in the French, but the English is good, too. It's set in a Jewish community in Morocco and told from the point of view of the rabbi's cat, which is a delightfully evil little beast. The cat is upset because it's intelligent, but can't speak, but the rabbi's parrot is stupid and can speak. Eventually the cat says "So one day I ate the parrot" and then the cat can talk. The story speaks about the anti-Semitism of the time, living there in a Jewish community that is literally under siege. At one point the cat wants a bar mitzvah, so now the rabbi has to figure out if a cat has a soul . . .

HMB: Especially if the cat can talk because it ate a parrot.

NH: Exactly, it hasn't stopped being a cat; it's still a hunter, it has a moral code we wouldn't think of as being good. The cat also has a huge crush on the rabbi's daughter. There are four books in the series, and it's just delightful. I've been reading a lot of graphic novels. I liked *The Invisibles*. I liked *Bayou* by Jeremy Love, another series of graphic novels that won a competition DC Comics was having. It's set in the Jim Crow era in the American South and is fantastical, so it uses the Black folklore from the time. There's a talking hound dog sheriff who has real dogs and who hunts down "bad behaved" Negroes . . . and there's a giant golliwog, but it's white, and it comes out of the swamp and eats people whole.

HMB: That sounds terrifying.

NH: It is terrifying. And so beautifully drawn; it's very childlike. There's a little girl who's trying to save her dad. They're both Black, and he's been wrongfully accused of something, and she knows if she can't stop it he's going to be lynched. So she's going through this magical bayou to get to him.

HMB: This is why people keep asking you that awful question—that's a fantastic answer.

NH: I'm going to be teaching *Bayou* in a couple of weeks. I'll see how my students react. I'm teaching them the folklore roots of science fiction and fantasy, having them come in and tell folktales from their own backgrounds, and linking folklore in modern day literature that draws on folktales.

HMB: Since you've been thinking about this for pedagogical purposes . . . other than your own writing, which draws on folktales a lot, shifts and connects and takes different parts and combines them, and other than *Bayou* . . . anything else you find really striking which uses folktales?

NH: I just reread Jane Yolen's *Briar Rose*, which was part of the fairytale series of novels curated by Terri Windling. It's still such a powerful novel. It talks about one of the places where Nazis imprisoned and killed Jewish people where nobody came out, and it does so in the context of the Briar Rose story. When people talk about fantasy as escapism . . . this story does not let you look away for a minute. It's beautiful. And it holds up very well.

I taught Larissa Lai's *Salt Fish Girl* which draws on lore about the Chinese goddess Nu Wah, because I wanted to bring in folktales from as much of the world as I could. I'm teaching short stories as well, there's a beautiful one called "I Shall Do Thee Mischief in the Wood" by Kathe Koja. It does things to the Little Red Riding Hood story that . . . are so *delightfully* messed up. You keep thinking you know who or what the wolf is, and it keeps slipping on you.

Interview with Nalo Hopkinson

Tiffany Davis / 2017

From Clarion Blog (April 2017), https://clarionfoundation.wordpress.com/2017/04/13
/nalo-hopkinson-interview/. Reprinted with permission of Tiffany Davis.

Tiffany Davis: You were a Clarion student as well as an instructor, correct?

Nalo Hopkinson: I was a student in 1995. I have been asked to teach both Clarion and Clarion West a number of times, and when there was a Clarion South for a while (in Australia), I taught the first one. I taught Clarion West either last year or the year before—I can't quite remember—but I'm going back to Clarion San Diego this summer [summer 2017].

TD: *Brown Girl in the Ring* came out in 1998. Was that after you finished Clarion, or your entry into it?

NH: I was already working on two novels, and *Brown Girl in the Ring* was one of them, and I had sold a short story. So when I got back from Clarion, I really wanted to finish a novel. I had already finished a draft of *Midnight Robber*, my second novel, but I hear it wasn't working. So I got to work on the first one, which was a little simpler and a little more standard in terms of plot and format, and tropes. So I finished that in, maybe, 1996. I entered the Warner Aspect First Novel contest and won it, and they published it a year later.

TD: Obviously, you're a writer, but you've edited or coedited anthologies as well (including *Mojo: Conjure Stories* and *So Long Been Dreaming*). Is it a nice break from writing to edit, or what is it about editing anthologies that you enjoy?

NH: It's a different break. The work is almost as hard as writing a novel. The most recent one I did was a special edition of *Lightspeed: People of Colo(u)r Destroy Science Fiction*, short science fiction. What I like about it is seeing what happens when people have a theme to write to, and seeing what both new and existing voices can do with that theme. And, of course, I like bringing a lot of work by people of color, and queer people, and women.

211

I like bringing that stuff to the forefront, to audiences' attention. And just finding new fiction, man—just seeing what people do is so exciting.

When you read a story and think, "Damn! Damn, I could not have come up with that!" So that part's really cool. And increasingly, you know, since I've been around a little while, it's often my former Clarion students. Not all the time, but enough that I get to be like a proud mama, like, "Oh! Write that! I'll publish that!" So that part's cool, too.

TD: Your Lemonade Award, which you started because you kind of want to reward people for doing acts of kindness, if I recall correctly. When are you going to start disbursing that, or have you already started?

NH: I haven't started shit. [*laughing.*] I have some offers of help; I'm collecting money to do it. I have enough to run it for a couple of years. And now, I have to start a nonprofit and pull a jury together, because it's going to be juried. Next year [2017] is when I anticipate announcing the awards for the first year. And probably not early next year, so don't hold your breath because I don't do things fast anymore.

TD: Let's talk about non-writing, because I follow you on Twitter. I notice that you do a lot of food. I teach lower-income students how to cook healthier, so your tweets interest me because I'm always looking for new recipe ideas.

NH: Oh, I would love to teach something like that, and I haven't figured out a way to do that at my university yet. I'm not really trained; I followed my mother, and I know my way around a kitchen, but this is a litigious country and, God forbid, that a student gets a burn.

TD: You post a lot of recipes, and pictures of food you've made. Is cooking another creative outlet for you?

NH: Yes. I usually don't cook anything that takes more than twenty minutes to prep, so it's the opposite of writing a novel. At the end of it, you have something, hopefully, good tasting and good for you. I do a lot of cooking and because I have fibromyalgia, I have certain dietary—they're not needs, but I feel better if I eat certain ways. And at home, it's easier to know what's exactly in my food. Plus, food is fun, you know? It's like, pretty things you can play with and then eat them. It's the best thing ever.

I do the cooking, and I've been a crafts person since I was a kid. I make stuff—if I see a technique I haven't tried before, and you can make pretty things with it, and it's fairly simple, I will try it. My practice, I think, goes beyond just the words, but I usually bring something science fictional or fantastical, and usually Afrocentric, to it. I design fabric as well—very amateur. I was an early user on Spoonflower, learning to use Photoshop, trying to make fabric designs.

Whatever I turn my hand to, even the food, a lot of it comes from African cultures, or I'm doing some kind of fusion. The other night I made *rösti* [Swedish potato pancakes], but I made it with cassava. Oh my God, it was so good!

I'm always trying to find ways to make things feel like home. So yeah, I make stuff. I make stuff all the time. The writing is the thing I do the least, actually [*laughing*].

TD: When you say "home," do you mean Jamaica or Canada? Because you went from Jamaica to Canada.

NH: I lived in Jamaica, Trinidad, Guyana, the US, and Canada. So when I say "home," you have to ask me which one I mean in that particular context.

TD: Do you ever cook anything and it triggers something in your mind like, "Hmm, this might make an interesting novel, or an interesting story?"

NH: Everything does that, so probably. [*laughs.*] Sometimes the mistakes are more likely to do that. The last short story I sold, which is going to show up in *Uncanny* magazine, it's about stuff you find in the drains because, you cook a lot, and stuff gets in your drains, and you have this kind of hair, and you have to be cleaning the drain out often.

Sometimes the ideas come when it's something I actually heard, but heard it wrong. The Easttowns [*Falling in Love With Hominids*] story came from me not hearing what the guy on the subway was saying. When he said, "Eastbound," I heard, "East Town." I thought, "All right, so what's in East Town?" It took about three years, but the story came from that.

The world is a pretty weird place and if you have any kind of imagination at all, you tell yourself stories about things. I don't tell myself whole stories because that's what I do for a living, and it's work, but I get a notion and I'll write that down. I'll put it in my "ideas" file and when I look for a story idea, I look for two or three of those ideas and smush them together, particularly if they don't seem to have anything to do with each other. The tension of finding the through line creates the plot.

TD: Quick sidebar: the tattoo on your arm—is that an *nkyimkyim* symbol [an Adinkra symbol from West Africa]?

NH: Yeah, I got it when I finished *The Salt Roads*, 'cause that novel tried to kill me! [*laughs.*] It was my celebration. I'm also a word in Shelley Jackson's performance piece/story called "Skin," a work of art where you apply to her—it's a 3,000-word story—and she gave you a word, and if you're working with punctuation, you got that too. And you had to tattoo the word somewhere on your body and send her a picture of the tattoo. So I'm the word *lace*.

TD: You get asked about writing all the time, such as, "Where do you get your motivation?" or "How did you come up with your ideas?" I'm nowhere near your level as a writer, and I get tired of people asking me that!

NH: There's no way to answer that question and actually give people useful information. I can say something, and it would sound good, but . . . eh.

TD: We're in an era where people think, "OK, so if I do X times Y, then I can write . . ." And I'm like, "It's not quite that simple."

NH: No, it's not. I get it from my undergrads all the time. They're taking creative writing but they want a job. I'm like, "You understand those two things don't actually go together?" [They ask], "What do I do to get an A?" [I reply], "Well, write the best you can."

TD: You post some good things on your Twitter feed. You posted a gluten-free cracker that looked good, so I tried it.

NH: Yeah, they tasted really good. It looks a bit like I'm pandering to them, but it's food! If it tastes good, people should know.

TD: Anything else you want to share?

NH: I guess the big thing is, that I recently became a Doctor of Letters. The Anglia Ruskin University in the UK wrote me and said, we want to give you an honorary degree. So I went over there [in October 2016] and I gave one of the valedictory addresses, and they put me in the gown and the hat and the whole bit—I looked like I went to Hogwarts. I only needed a wand.

TD: If you were in a [Hogwarts] house, which one would you be in?

NH: I would want to be able to switch houses at will. I'm a switchy kind of person.

So now I'm a doctor of letters, as a science fiction writer, which is very, very cool. And that's the thing that's in my mind right now. I also work at a university that has a science fiction archives, books going back to Thomas More's *Utopia*, so that's going back to the sixteenth century—the bootleg version; we have the bootleg version. That has been a lot of fun because I get to work with the collection, I helped to create a PhD minor in science fiction, and I'm teaching all these courses that I could have never found at university. They hired me as a science fiction writer, which is pretty cool.

TD: Who do you like to read, in any genre? Because you're a writer, so you like to read, so who are the people you like to read, in general?

NH: This summer past, I discovered Sylvia Moreno-Garcia. She's from Canada—Vancouver, I think—but she's Mexican-Canadian. I read her first two books like *psst*, and I was done! It was so good. I mean, I'd known about her but just hadn't read her work. I like [Samuel] Delany [Clarion instructor], of course, because he was my touchstone for writing in general but also for writing as a Black queer writer in science fiction. I just love his artistry, what he does with words. China Mieville. I just finished a book by Tiphani Yanique, *Land of Love and Drowning*, set in Antigua.

TD: That's all the questions I have. Thank you for taking the time for this interview.

NH: Thank you for having me! It was fun.

Waving at Trains: An Interview with Nalo Hopkinson

Avni Sejpal / 2017

From *Boston Review*, October 18, 2017, http://bostonreview.net/podcast-literature-culture
-arts-society/nalo-hopkinson-waving-trains. Reprinted by permission of Avni Sejpal.
Avni Sejpal is a Ph.D. student in English at the University of Pennsylvania.

Avni Sejpal: I would like to start by asking you about speech and orality. To my ear, your story "Waving at Trains" lends itself very well to being read out loud. Perhaps it is because speech, particularly the inflections and rhythms of colloquial Caribbean English, is such an important element in this story, as it is in so much of your work. When you write, do you consciously attempt to capture the lived quality of language? Or to put it another way, how do you conceive of the relationship between the spoken and written word in your work?

Nalo Hopkinson: I think it is integral. The way people speak, the way cultures speak, it tells you so much. Hearing it in your mind's ear, even if you do not speak with those rhythms, will give you a sense of what that culture is like. I have had people who are not from the Caribbean read my work. I find that they use whatever vernacular is closest to them. I have heard it in everything from Canadian-Ontario farm girl to New Orleans working class. The interesting thing is that it works each time. I love that flavor of the rhythms of speech, perhaps because I grew up in a theater family. My father was an actor, a poet, and a playwright, so I got to hear rhythms of speech a lot, sometimes in Caribbean English, sometimes in Shakespearean English, because that is what my dad was trained as. It means a lot to me in that tradition of the Caribbean man of words, which can just as easily be a person of words. It is very important.

Science fiction is thought of as being this North American or European thing, as though the rest of the world is somehow not involved in the future.

AS: So when you are writing something, are you also thinking about how it will sound out loud?

NH: Yes. If I am thinking in words at the time that I am writing. Sometimes I do, sometimes I don't. Sometimes I think in moving images and then I have to translate it into words. But, yes, I am always aware that at some point I might want to read the thing. And I am very aware of how characters speak, because speech does not only carry the accent, it carries the economic level of the characters, which tells you something. So whenever I have stories translated into other languages, generally they go for the standard form of the language. I find that that actually makes the translation a little bit pallid and it removes some of the nuances, so my characters end up sometimes sounding like middle-class people being petulant . . . and sometimes they are middle-class people, like the girl in this story, who are having a very hard time.

AS: Do you ever participate in the translation process?

NH: Not so much, because if something is being translated into Chinese I cannot be of help. I have had stories translated into French, and, when I have read the translations I can see what they have missed. But by then they will have published it. The type of nuance that gets lost: I have a story in which a Black het couple have been fighting, and finally the whole thing comes to a head, and the woman says to the man, "You are so withdrawn, you are so taciturn, you do not give me back what I am trying to give to you." And he says, "Look at me, I am a big Black man, I have to be careful about how I emote." He says, "I am a big Black man." When they translated it into French, they said, "I am a fat Black man," because it is the same word—further complicated by the fact that he is a fat Black man—but it completely missed what he was saying.

AS: That is an interesting cautionary note about translation. Coming back to "Waving at Trains," another aspect of this story stood out for me: the strong sense of place contained within it. The sun, the heat, the tamarind tree, the trains, the rotting vegetation. They all invoke a sensorial dystopia that is hard too hard to shake. In what ways do you envision dystopia as a somewhere, and is that somewhere always an elsewhere, or could it also be over here?

NH: I think dystopia is everywhere, as opposed to utopia, which is literally translated as nowhere. Particularly for peoples who are surviving the effects of colonialism and globalization, the apocalypse done happened already. We have been living it for centuries. I very much do like to get that sense of place. The tamarind tree, the mongooses, they were very important

218 CONVERSATIONS WITH NALO HOPKINSON

to me. In science fiction, as it is usually thought of, there are no tamarind trees, no mongooses. It is thought of as being this North American or European thing, as though the rest of the world is somehow not involved in the future, not involved in its own present. It is very important for me to put those details in. Also, I can be homesick. I evoke the idea of a tamarind tree and, even though it is not a very happy story, the tamarind tree and the mongooses help.

AS: Speaking of North America and Europe, and the obsession with stories and characters and histories that are located in imperial sites of power, how might reorienting our gaze to other sights of historical dystopia, say the Global South, amend our approach to the very concept of dystopia?

NH: What happens is that we get into thinking of dystopia and catastrophe as that thing that happens somewhere else, or that can be delayed, when it is happening daily all over the world. Hopefully one of the things we can start doing as a people is stop thinking in terms of "them" and start thinking in terms of "us." The kinds of things that were coming across my Twitter feed—as the cascade of completely unimaginable hurricanes were coming down on the Americas, and all the flooding was happening in places like Nigeria—was about people reminding people that this is all of us, that we cannot just say, "Well, it is over there," and please remember that Puerto Rico is the United States, and that Dominica and the Dominican Republic, though they are separate countries, are both being hit by this thing. The idea for me is to realize that it is happening, it is happening now, it is very real, and to not compartmentalize it.

AS: That is true, and your writing is grounded in the specific history of colonialism. I am struck by the trains that pass through this story. The protagonist and her friend can only wave at trains, but never actually board them. Trains are of course tied to the history of British colonialism, specifically to a violent colonial modernity that, in the name of progress, leaves behind more people than it brings into the so-called future. Can you speak more generally about how the history of colonialism influences your work?

NH: I am trained as a writer, and I did not go through school to do that. So when people started labeling my work "postcolonial," I did not know what they were talking about. I had to ask an academic friend who works with these kinds of narratives what that meant. But it is embedded very much in my own history. Coming from where I have come from, we are very aware of the effects of colonialism and globalization—they are ongoing in everything from the national debts of various countries in the Caribbean to the fact that we have such large and far-spread diasporas. I was just in Helsinki. I was a guest of honor at the World Science Fiction Convention, Worldcon, which this year was held in Finland, and another podcast wanted to interview me. They held the interview at probably the only Caribbean restaurant in Helsinki. We are everywhere.

AS: Well, you never know.

NH: Yes, it's true!

AS: It is interesting to think about the immigrant subcultures that thrive in places like Helsinki.

NH: Yes. Certainly at Worldcon there were more people of color from all over the world than I would expect to see at a Worldcon in the United States.

AS: Is that right? I want to ask you something about your work broadly. For readers who are just discovering your writing, how does "Waving at Trains" connect to your earlier work?

NH: It is very much of a piece. I started, originally, writing in Caribbean vernaculars. I do not always do so. My characters are not always from the Caribbean, or are not always speaking that way. But this story continues in that tradition. I tend to try to feature characters who are in some way like me, so often female. I like writing about children because children have such little agency in the world. Stories that give them agency, though not always in happy ways; all Angela can really do is start walking. But she is definitely going to start walking, even though she is hallucinating and trying to deny the fact that her friend is dead. But she is going to get moving. And that might actually work, you do not know if she gets to where someone can find her before she gets too sick. It is very much in the vein of the kind of thing I am doing. I am finding more and more what is happening, especially since the last US election, is that people are asking me to write dystopias. I do not always, but I have the same mood that very much lends itself to this stuff that says "What in the world are we going to do?"

AS: What indeed are we going to do? You mentioned the US election that brought Trump into the White House. You have been living in the United States for some time now. Do you see it influencing your work?

NH: Yes. Perhaps more in mood than in location. I have only been here six years, whereas I was thirty-five years in Canada, and was born in the Caribbean and lived there until I was sixteen. Those two places tend to show up more in my work. And of course, writing science fiction, completely invented places show up in my work. But as I absorb more of the environment here, it will start coming in. It very much struck me when I first moved to southern California, how it is both like and unlike the Caribbean where I had come from. There are palm trees everywhere, but the wrong fruits are on them, if any fruits at all. When you walk past the bushes you hear the rustling of lizards, but the lizards are the wrong color. If there is sand, and there are holes in the sand, it is probably gophers, not crabs, or rattlesnakes. But there is still a similarity of sensibility in many ways. If I go to a grocery store, often the people who are ringing up my produce are saying, "How come you are buying our food?" Meaning, "How come are you buying tamarinds and guavas?" Because there are large populations here from South Asia, from India, from Mexico. So we have this in common, and, yes, it is beginning to enter my sensibilities as I write. The political sensibility is definitely there, and has been from the beginning, because the United States is probably the largest world power, and so it affects everything I write. Very much more so now because I am watching this political disaster happen where people like me and people like the people I love are increasingly endangered. Women, queer folks, trans folks, people of color, people who are immigrants, all being treated like they not only have nothing to contribute to the country, but as though they are somehow deleterious to it. That is insane. So watching this political insanity happen that is killing people is very much affecting my work.

AS: On a somewhat less grim note, your work has always drawn on Afro-Caribbean mythologies and cultural traditions. Can you talk about using historical and cultural memory in your writing? For example, in *Falling in Love with Hominids*, you emphasize hybridity, or the mixing of traditional Afro-Caribbean myths with fabulism and futurism. What does it mean to transform cultural archives of knowledge through science fiction? Moreover, how do you use the past to talk about possible futures?

NH: I am still working that through in my mind. I know that for me it feels like healing, it feels like a balm. For one thing, I was not a great student when it came to history class. It seemed like I was learning a succession of histories of kings named George, because I was learning so much about British history. Fascinating as it is, it was not being presented to me often in a way I could grab on to as a young girl. But now when I go back, and I look at history and I look at Caribbean histories, they are like any history— vibrant, passionate, and more like *Game of Thrones* than anything else. But the very real histories now are much more compelling to me. You wonder what is behind the parts that do not get told. They say that history gets written by the victors, so you wonder about the bits that do not get told.

Dystopia is everywhere, as opposed to utopia, which is literally translated as nowhere.

I am doing a final rewrite on a novel based on the culture of *marronage*, where enslaved peoples from Africa brought to the Caribbean and to the parts of the United States would escape into the interior, into the bushes. In the United States, they were often taken in by the native people and made part of their communities. In the Caribbean, they would often make their own communities and take in people who were disenfranchised. I am fascinated by those histories and what those communities were like, so I have imagined an island that managed through fantastical means to survive. It is an island where people go in *marronage*, where the people who think they own them have tried to reclaim them and they were able to fight them off, even though they were outgunned. I have let that society grow as itself for two hundred years to see what would happen. Science fiction lets me do crucibles like that. I had to come up with a Creolized, eighteenth-century Caribbean nation that has been itself for a couple hundred years. I have people that were the original inhabitants, I have Taíno people, I have people who are clearly of African descent, people who are clearly of English descent, but working and farming class, because they were brought over as indentured labor and as overseers as well, and not always willingly. So I am able to bring those three communities together and then tell a story there. I decided to riff on the griot tradition of making history be something that is not on paper but is remembered through song, because you can pass that down. They have an archive that is actually a human archive of families of griots who memorized books and passed the tradition down, because this is a culture that knows that books get burned, and books get destroyed. I am able to pull together all these things. When I think about the original library at Alexandria, as a writer, it hurts to know that those books were burned, and in some cases libraries have been destroyed quite deliberately in fire because they are a way of killing culture. And that happens in big and small ways here as well. Libraries are forever fighting for their existence and they are vital.

AS: I read somewhere about your digital collage project, which entails collecting non-racist images and photographs and illustrations of people of color from the Caribbean and from the Americas. Can you tell us a little bit about that project?

NH: I am not sure that it is one project. I collect the imagery as part of my research, my ongoing research for my writing. I also do small scale soft

222 CONVERSATIONS WITH NALO HOPKINSON

sculptures and collages. Some of my work has made its way into amateur fabric design. There is a mom and pop outfit in North Carolina called Spoonflower and it is essentially fabric print on demand, so I put my designs up there. I ended up looking for historical imagery I could use that did not make me want to go postal. I am not sure you can actually say non-racist, not because the images are necessarily racist, but because racism influences how they got made, when they got made and why they got made. But images that seem like someone actually looked at a person of color and drew and painted how we look rather than how they want to make fun of us. Again, that is part of the healing. I am working on a graphic novel now with artist John Jennings. It is set in the time between the two world wars on the railroad in the United States. My character is a porter, or looks like a porter, a Black porter. I have been looking for the historical artifacts of that time and place and of people who did that kind of work. Having the imagery around me, again, feels soothing and healing. Also, being a science fiction/fantasy person obsessed with those images, I am sometimes collaging them into fantastical creatures. We are supposed to not own imagination, particularly people of African descent in this part of the world. The fantastical is something that we are not really expected to have much to do with—so, damn it, I am making Black mermaids. In parts of West Africa, two of the most important deities are riverine or ocean goddesses. So I am making them in that light, and I am making them sometimes fat, because what else would a mermaid be? And why is that not beautiful? I am making their hair be the way our hair looks. That kind of thing is also just playful. But I think inserting yourself into a place where you are told you don't belong, when you know quite well you do, is important work.

AS: So who are some of the other writers doing this work right now? Who are some of your favorite dystopian and science fiction and fantasy writers?

NH: Nnedi Okorafor. Nnedi Okorafor is Nigerian American. She, with her first novel, which I think was a children's science fiction novel, won the Wole Soyinka prize for literature, which is Nigeria's highest literary award. She has a series of novellas out now called *Binti*, about a young woman from a small tribal community in Africa who gets accepted into a university that is off planet. Nnedi's work is imaginative and rich. The concept is that it is organic, literally, the concept is that a computer is an organic thing that you are given as a child and it grows along with you. She is talking about a part of the world that, although my features tell me my ancestors came from, I do not know a lot about, and she is extrapolating it into science fiction. Samuel R. Delany is and always will be one of the most important writers, in my mind, to science fiction or any literature, and in literary criticism. He is an African American man, a Black gay man, a multiple-award-winning author, whose work is, linguistically, just gloriously, rich, and his ideas are challenging. He talks about race and sexuality and power in ways that, when I was first reading his work as a younger person, were a revelation. Ursula K. Le Guin from Portland. Science fiction, fantasy writer. Ursula can write a simple, simple sentence, and I will find myself in tears. She has always been thinking about issues of power and race and how they play out. There are so many! I recently read *The Ballad of Black Tom* by Victor LaValle, that takes H. P. Lovecraft—that very, very racist writer—and reinvents one of his stories. I think it is about to be made into a television series. There is N. K. Jemisin. There is so much vibrant work coming out, and more and more of it beginning to come out from, and depicting, a broader range of humanity. I was recently involved in a project by *Lightspeed Magazine*, which is a science fiction fantasy magazine, that has started doing special editions in response to a backlash that has been happening in the science fiction community against any kind of identity-based sensibility in the literature. John Joseph Adams, the managing editor, is doing what I have come to call the *Destroy* series. He started with *Women Destroy Science Fiction*, because that is what gets leveled at us—you know, you let the women in, and all of a sudden, there goes the neighborhood. He asked me to be the fiction coeditor for *People of Color Destroy Science Fiction*. We found stories from the Caribbean, from Africa, from Australia, and recently the issue received the British Fantasy Award.

SLF Portolan Project Interview with Nalo Hopkinson Los Angeles, California, 2019

Mary Anne Mohanraj / 2019

From *Speculative Literature Foundation*, June 3, 2020, https://speculativeliterature
.org/portolan-project/interviews/nalo-hopkinson/. Reprinted by permission of
Mary Anne Mohanraj.

Mary Anne Mohanraj: Hi, I'm Mary Anne Mohanraj. I'm here at the World Fantasy Convention in Los Angeles 2019 with the Speculative Literature Foundation and we're here interviewing Nalo Hopkinson. She's the author of *Brown Girl in the Ring*; *Midnight Robber*; *The Salt Roads*; *The New Moon's Arms*; *The Chaos*; *Sister Mine*—those are all her novels—and then anthologies and collections, she has *Whispers from the Cotton Tree Root*; *Skin Folk*; *Mojo: Conjure Stories*; *So Long Been Dreaming*, which is the postcolonial science fiction anthology; *Falling in Love with Hominids*; etc. So it's a very long list. I've read almost all of it, I love them all. And what I really wanted to ask Nalo to talk about today is her use of language, which I think is exceptional. And it's something that, as a writer, I struggle with a lot in my own work these days. I think especially as someone who has done both sort of literary fiction with a focus on prose and language, and now recently have been writing, trying to write more commercial fiction—and more genre fiction. And sometimes I find that when I am working with rocket ships or dragons, and fast paced plots and lots of dialogue, I feel like I'm losing my hold on finely crafted language and beautiful speech. And that's something you do so well. So I was going to ask you to read the opening of *Midnight Robber*. I'm going to ask her to read the opening of that, and then maybe we can just talk a little about how you approach that in your work.

Nalo Hopkinson: OK. So this is a mostly Trinidadian English vernacular, with a little bit occasionally of Jamaican and some bits of Ghanese thrown in. And this is from the introduction.

[reading] "It had a woman, you see, a strong hard-back woman with skin like cocoa-tea. She two foot-them tough from hiking through the diable bush, the devil bush on the prison planet of New Half-Way Tree. When she walked, she foot strike the hard earth *bup!* like breadfruit dropping to the ground. She two arms hard with muscle from all the years of hacking paths through the diable bush on New Half-Way Tree. Even she hair itself rough and wiry; long black knotty locks springing from she scalp and corkscrewing all the way down she back. She name Tan-Tan, and New Halfway Tree was she planet."

Mohanraj: Thank you. I know when I first read that I was super-struck by it. I love hearing you read it because I think initially I'm encountering, as a reader, a sort of a dialect I'm not familiar with, a way of speaking; it's going to be a little intimidating. When you read it, I think it comes very clear. But even on the page, it doesn't take me very long to fall into the rhythms and to be able to follow. I know you teach a few hours from here, you're at—

Hopkinson: The University of California, Riverside—--

Mohanraj: —at the University of California, Riverside. So I don't know whether this is something that you work on with your students, if you have approaches that you give them—just how you think about it when you're working with language in these texts.

Hopkinson: First of all, I come out of a literary tradition in the Caribbean of privileging common speech. And that's a movement that started when my father, who was a poet, a playwright, an actor, was still alive, and there's people like Kamau Brathwaite, like Louise Bennett-Coverley who are saying, "We speak like this." It is not "bad English." Linguists who are discovering it [say] has its own grammar rules, it has its own logic. And so there began a movement of writing the way people speak. So I already have permission, is what I'm saying. And also everybody's speech is beautiful. I mean, if you listen, just listen to people talking on the street where they're not trying to censor themselves for an English class, they flow. So one of the things I will do is put myself back in that space. My Caribbean English is middle-class English, it still has its own stuff, but it's not as, it's not as deep, it's not as basilectal.

Mohanraj: Wait, I'm sorry, I don't know the word you just used.

Hopkinson: There's three words I've learned from linguistics and they are *acrolectal, mesolectal, basilectal*. And it's a way of not getting into the trap of saying "This is upper-class speech, this is lower-class speech." So they actually go to the center. And they measure speech by how far it is from the center.

Mohanraj: Oh, that's super-useful.

Hopkinson: Yeah, yeah, yeah. So basilectal is sort of what we think of as working-class, farming-class, common speech. Mesolectal is more like what you would get from—sort of white-collar—and acrolectal is what we sometimes think of as BBC English. So I have permission, is what I'm saying, and I have the fortune of having grown up with an actor and a poet in the house. And also you can hear language being used, everywhere. You listen to hip-hop, you listen to rap, you listen to any sort of music that comes out of an everyday tradition. And you can hear people using speech beautifully as working speech. So I try to tell my students to listen to themselves and to each other and when they're in class. So they think I want proper English. And—have you read me?

Mohanraj: And this one thing I ended up saying to my students often when they're writing papers. The writing on the pages is very stiff and very, very—it's missing words, often they lose verbs, and so on. I try to remind them: you speak beautifully in class. Right? When we're in conversation. Everyone can understand everything you say, you speak with passion and with, you know, emphasis. And that's all I want to see on the page.

Hopkinson: Yeah, somehow they think you don't want that. I know. I say, "Well, you know, I don't actually want to be bored." Sometimes I don't even understand what they're aiming for. They're trying so hard to make it, you know, so I say, "What were you trying to say?" And they tell me! And I say, "Write that down." [*laughter.*]

Mohanraj: Write that down! I think I just had that conversation last week as we were revising papers. [*laughter.*]

Hopkinson: And then we have to get out of the trap of thinking that it's bad language. There is no language that is bad language. And all language is beautiful.

Mohanraj: I asked a question—you went in a direction that is actually now more interesting to me than my question. But I think I can connect them. So in the novel that I've recently finished working on, I have some working-class characters. I come from a middle-/upper-middle-class background, right? So a good half of my characters are working-class, and they're in that community. It's science fiction, it's set 100 years from now, so I can't exactly just like go and spend time in that community, right? I have to imagine it and invent it. And I wonder, what would you suggest as a way for someone like me to do a better job of representing that? Would spending more time listening to working-class voices now give me access?

Hopkinson: Yes, it would. Because then you know what you're extrapolating from. But also, I asked Samuel R. Delany when he was one of my teachers at Clarion, and I was working on this novel and struggling with how to put a whole novel in an invented, well, cobble a hybrid vernacular. And he said a little of that goes a long way. And I promptly proceeded to ignore him [*laughter.*]

Mohanraj: Tobias Buckell said something similar on a panel we were on at one point, where he was talking about how he uses Caribbean speech patterns in his space opera series. And I think he said 10 percent, right, like he tries to put in about 10 percent of what you would actually hear in conversation. And that's enough to give people the sense of it without being a barrier to those who are completely unfamiliar.

Hopkinson: Yes, yes. And I think that works—it is what I will do, when I'm not trying to, you know, experiment with speech in a whole novel.

Mohanraj: Well, and in *Midnight Robber*, you don't do the entire book in that either. Right? You switch.

Hopkinson: I switch—

Mohanraj: Somewhat?

Hopkinson: I switch—valences, I do, switch—and sometimes it's a deeper register than others. But I don't think I ever go to straight up Standard English. But yeah, a little, a little bit of it, of particular phrasings. I remember reading, I believe it's Emma Bowles[?]—it's a novel that's set on a university campus, and there's a lot of Shakespearean English floating about. But she doesn't use a lot of it. She picks one or two phrases. And I remember "I cry you mercy" shows up every so often.

Mohanraj: I know what you thinking of; it's Pamela Dean.

Hopkinson: Oh, sorry. Sorry!

Mohanraj: That's OK, that's OK. Only because I happen to love that book. It's *Tam Lin*.

Hopkinson: Yes, yeah.

Mohanraj: And she does, she does a great job with those like little moments of Shakespearean English slipping in.

Hopkinson: Yeah, yeah. So you don't have to be an expert in that particular language form to write it. You have to know it well enough to pick some choice phrases and repeat those and that will give your readers the flavor. You talked about tackling my book for the first time and not knowing the vernacular, but somehow getting the pattern. I have heard that book read in New Orleans working-class French-inflected English. I've heard it read in Ontario, Canada, farm girl. I've had people fall into whatever vernacular they're familiar with and it sort of fits. So it's not as though the reader has to be an expert. They just have to understand that people speak in different ways.

Mohanraj: One text that I find is helpful for getting my students and myself into, to pay attention to language a little bit, is Ursula K. Le Guin's *Steering the Craft.* And the first sections she has just these various exercises on sentence-level work and she has these passages—example passages. And she has one by Twain—I think she may even use two examples by Twain— one is from "The Celebrated Jumping Frog of Calaveras County." And I think what's interesting is that I have the students and myself read these pieces out loud in class. And even though I have actually spent almost no time in the South, but when I read this work out loud, it puts me in these rhythms, right, and, you know, I almost have sort of a bad Southern accent by the end of the piece, right? And, like, then I want to keep talking like that. You know? And so I think, I think the text—you know, there's this, there's maybe an anxiety that if I, if I write like this, the reader will not be able to find their way in. But you're kind of teaching the reader how to read this as they go, right?

Hopkinson: They're science fiction, fantasy readers; they're used to learning the text as they go. The thing that I do sometimes hear is people [feeling] distanced from it because they say, "Why would you want to write in bad English?" And in the UK and the US, there are traditions of writing the way people speak. But I have a former student who's teaching English in Korea and he tried teaching this novel—I mean, he managed. But they don't have a similar tradition so students couldn't understand why a writer wouldn't want to prove that she could manipulate language in the standard form. So you get that contempt, or people thinking I'm trying to express contempt for the characters.

Mohanraj: That's really interesting. There's a short story—do you know "The Goophered Grapevine"? It's in *Dark Matter,* Charles Chesnutt, where he switches registers between very, very formal Standard English and, and the language spoken by the Black slaves on the plantation. Right? And if I'm remembering right it was one of the first published short stories in America by a Black man. And he encountered a lot of resistance from people who didn't want to believe he wrote it, that he could write it. And I thought it was, it was an interesting choice to have, like, here I will prove to you that I can do Standard English. And then put the best lines and the joke of the story, the point of the story in this other voice, and you're going to have to follow me there to get it, right? It also reminds me of *Borderlands/La Frontera* by Gloria Anzaldúa, which she writes in TexMex. And again, it's this, almost a demand that, I'm not going to make this—I'm not going to translate this for you. You come to me, right?

Hopkinson: Yes, yeah. And that is another question, is how do you represent it on the page? So "The Goophered Grapevine," there's lots of apostrophes and leaving the ends off things, and that's fine. That's the way he did it. I don't. I write in, as much as I can, Standard English spelling.

Mohanraj: Right, no, that's interesting.

Hopkinson: But I keep the rhythms and the vocabulary. It's mostly not that hard to do except you get some words that just aren't translatable. There's the Jamaican word *mauger*, which means skinny, like skinny: too skinny. And, of course, comes from *meager*, but you put down *meager*, it's just not going to work.

Mohanraj: It doesn't have the feel. Right?

Hopkinson: Yeah, you have to somehow come up with a spelling for *mauger*, which means some readers won't get it unless you're very careful about how you put it in context. And I find I don't worry too much about those readers! There's Google!

Mohanraj: There's Google, right? They'll get there. *The Bone People* is one of my favorite books. And she just puts all the Maori in there, and you cope, right? And she gives you enough in Standard English that you can follow even if you don't look up any of the Maori. If you do look it up, it adds so much, right? And I actually have to admit, I do appreciate that there's a glossary at the end of my edition.

Hopkinson: Me too. But I hate glossaries. And so I try [to] read the whole book at first without using it at all.

Mohanraj: Yeah, I did too, actually, the second time through I looked at—I started looking things up.

Hopkinson: Yeah, [unknown name] and I had a conversation—he's a Canadian writer, had a conversation about—he was talking about readers who expect texts to be penetrable, who sort of assume that the text has to lay itself bare for them. And the difference between that and sort of going with what you have on the page, and I had way more fun with *Bone People* just going with what was on the page. And then afterwards, if I wanted to explore more, I did.

Mohanraj: Right. What was that little bit there that I missed? There's another example of this in Dorothy Sayers—so at the end of this trilogy, big climactic romance, she, the character writes a letter to her uncle in France. And he writes back to her. And so now there's this long letter in French that is central to what's happening and the decision she's about to make. And I think Sayers just assumes that anyone reading her novel at that, in that era in the nineteenth century, early twentieth century, would, of course, also speak fluent French. And I first encountered the book when I was twelve or thirteen in a library in New Britain, Connecticut, and I was like, there was no Google, I had no way to access the English and it was deeply, deeply frustrating. I was like, "What did he say to change her mind?" You know?

Hopkinson: What little I know of Dorothy Sayers, I suspect that she actually didn't care whether you spoke French or not! [*laughter.*]

Mohanraj: Maybe not. And maybe that's the way to go, right? That is, that that letter needed to be in French, and so it was in French.

Hopkinson: Yes.

Mohanraj: So, we are sadly running out of time. I could talk to you forever, but I'll ask you, maybe, one more thing. I do think it's laziness, maybe, for me. Maybe that's not the right word, but approaching language on the sentence level with this kind of care, I find challenging. I wonder, what would you say to a student who's handing you something and you're like, "Ah, the language is—could be better, right?" Like, are there any tips, any suggestions you give to get into the work in a better way?

Hopkinson: And do you mean someone who's trying to write in vernacular or just struggling with language in general?

Mohanraj: Maybe struggling with language in general? Yeah, I think to get themselves to slow down and—

Hopkinson: I have them practice writing dialogue, and writing it without. I remind them that nobody's seeing what they're putting on the page. They can always decide, "No, I'm never going to show this to anyone." So there's nothing stopping them from just playing. And writing is experimentation. In academe, they call it research. And it's not that you have to go look things up, it's that the writing is the research. The only way to do research is to put things together and see what goes boom!

Mohanraj: I think that ties into a whole 'nother conversation about perfectionism and revision, so we'll have to just come back and do this again. I want to thank you so much, Nalo Hopkinson. And if you could just tell everyone, what are you working on now or what you'd like to point people to of yours that they should take a look at?

Hopkinson: My second short story collection, *Falling in Love with Hominids*, came out a few years ago. But right now I'm actually learning how to write comics, by writing for one of the most popular comics franchises in the world, *The Sandman*, which is rebooted with a new house in the Dreaming, and I am writing that story.

Mohanraj: That's amazing. So I have just bought my copy and am super-excited to read a new graphic novel of the Sandman as interpreted by Nalo Hopkinson. So thanks so much.

"Fresh": A Second Conversation with Nalo Hopkinson on Life, the Academy, Race, and the Science Fiction Community

Isiah Lavender III / 2021

Unpublished interview.

Isiah Lavender III: How would describe your experience of the COVID-19 pandemic?

Nalo Hopkinson: Dismay, panic, horror.

IL: No doubt. So, what do you think of academic life now that you've been ensconced in it for a while now? The move to UBC is impressive as one of the top global universities after all!

NH: The tenured professorship at UCR was my first full-time academic gig. I was offered the position at a time when my life partner and I were ailing, broke, couch-surfing, and living hand-to-mouth. That position was a life-saver. I landed in a very friendly place; so many excellent, supportive colleagues, a glorious science fiction archive, one of the most racially and culturally diverse campuses on the continent, and warm weather. And yet I discovered all the horrible ways in which universities practice and profit off bad labor practice, especially when it comes to those to whom they won't give job security. Universities can cultivate and capitalize on their employees' fear of speaking out. Many universities are elitist as fuck. It's a system that was designed to exclude most of the types of people who are faculty, students, and staff at modern-day universities—the public universities, at least. The university system is a juggernaut that needs to change. There are people inside them who are fighting for those changes. I have never worked for a big industry that wasn't treating its workers poorly, that wasn't in need of major changes. Yet I was also excited by the work I was able to do at UCR, and that I hope to do at UBC. I didn't think I would enjoy teaching full-time. In fact, there are aspects of it that are not at all enjoyable. But that "lively exchange of ideas" thing? That satisfaction you feel when a student's world expands a bit? Those are real.

IL: How do your passions for cooking and creative experimentations with sewing and artwork benefit your storytelling?

NH: They're all part of the same thing, except cooking is quicker and has more instant gratification.

IL: How did *The Sandman* gig fall into your lap? Did this experience help with your graphic novel/comic book creation? I find it fascinating that the current big three [Nalo/Nnedi/Nora] have all written in this medium at the same time more or less.

NH: Yes, that's been lovely. As I understand it, Neil Gaiman and DC decided to reboot the Sandman Universe, only this time with four different writers, stories, and artistic teams, rather than Neil being the writer. He jotted down some notes about where he'd left the Sandman Universe, and a new, ominous thing he wanted to set in motion there. He added a new House to the Universe, the House of Whispers, watched over by the Yoruba-originated deity, Erzulie. I'm sure Neil would have given DC some names of writers they might consider, and I'm sure they had their own list as well. In any case, I heard from DC, who told me they were going to do four new stories, and asked whether I'd want to pitch for one of them. I wasn't going to say no! I chose to be one of the writers pitching for the House of Whispers. The Yoruba water deities show up often in my work, so I felt I had a way into the story. So I wrote a pitch, and waited. For two years. Finally, they contacted me, said they'd liked my pitch, and was I still interested. Again, I wasn't going to say no! So I said, "Hell yeah," and there I was, learning how to write comics scripts by working for two years on one of the most popular comics properties ever. It was grueling. It was anxiety-inducing. It was fun. It was quite the learning curve. I rewrote my first two issues of the monthly comic eight times each before the editors declared themselves satisfied. Except perhaps Kat Howard, all the writers, artists, and editors working on all four new Sandman stories had more experience than I did. Thank heaven, because it meant I had a lot of support. I still hate plotting. But I think I got better at it (thank you, frequent cowriter Dan Watters and the DC editors!) You'll see it said in some places that Neil cowrote all four new stories with we four writers. He didn't. He had other things to do than cowrite four comics a month for two years. He invited us to come and play in his sandbox, but the stories we wrote were all ours.

Such an extraordinarily generous thing for a creator to do. I gather he did read all our scripts, and every so often, he'd make a suggestion. I remember him doing so once with mine.

IL: So how does it feel to be the first Black Queer Woman to be named a Grandmaster of Science Fiction? Is it unadulterated joy or some more complex mix of emotions?

NH: Luckily, having complicated feelings doesn't have to dilute the sheer delight I feel at being recognized by my peers for both my writing and my mentorship. It goes a long way towards reducing the weight of the emotional toll I may always carry from the couple of years when I was too sick to work and eventually ended up homeless and couch-surfing. I note that the award has been given thirty-seven times in the past four decades or so, yet I am only the eighth woman of any stripe to receive it. But I also see the work that SFWA's been doing over the past few years to become a more equitable association, and I hope that work will continue. So on balance, I feel great about it.

IL: You and I both love Chip Delany. Aside from his novels, his notion of the "total surround" with respect to race has aided me in academic life if not real life. How about you?

NH: That man is one of my personal heroes. His writing sings, and makes me aim higher. His essay "Racism and Science Fiction" coalesced a bunch of ideas for me that I'd never thought of in that way before. His writing about the craft of writing excites me. His example as a gay Black person, especially since so much of his fiction has been speculative fiction that touches upon the realities of both, has been revelatory and has given me breathing room even back when I still imagined myself to be straight.

IL: You must be flattered by all of the Delany and Butler comparisons, but I wonder how you feel about your own success and that of your own generation's Black leading lights—Nnedi Okorafor, Nisi Shawl, and N. K. Jemisin. So, then, how do you feel?

NH: Is that my generation? Closer to the ground, it's more complicated than that. I encountered Nisi's short story "The Rainses" in *Asimov's* in 1995, which I think is the year I also published my first short story. I first encountered Nnedi when she emailed me to interview me for a newspaper. I don't think she'd published any fiction yet. I don't even remember when/where I first encountered Sheree R. Thomas, and her wonderful writing and editing. And Andrea Hairston, who attended Clarion West in the same year as Sheree. Then Tobias Buckell and Karen Lord. Nora [N. K. Jemisin] was a few years later in my personal memory palace, where I admit that memory screws linearity. Steven Barnes and Tananarive Due were publishing novels before all of us, perhaps contemporaneous with Octavia? Chip [Delany] is my literary lion, always will be. Black and gay and a feminist ally and writing experimental, frank, bawdy science fiction and fantasy and winning awards and taking no fucking prisoners. And, finally, there are more and more names till it's now at the point where I can't name them all: Kiini and Ibi and Rhonda [R.S.A. Garcia] and Cadwell and Roland and Courttia and Rivers— anyway, I'm waffling a bit. I don't know what a leading light should feel like, so I'm not sure how to answer the question. At this point, I think Nnedi and Nora have more public name recognition than I do. But I do have a sense that I was a touchstone for a number of the current generation as they were moving into their own publishing careers. That's a cool feeling, even as I wish my output matched some of theirs. But my brain chemistry and circumstances are what they are, and I'm still making a pretty respectable career. Mostly, I feel caught up in a whirlwind where there are more and more of us, so that the conversations amongst Black SF/F writers about craft, the profession and the industry are beginning to generate their own mass, their own gravitas. In addition, there's just a simultaneous burgeoning of writers of other non-white backgrounds, and we frequently commune with each other, too. One no longer feels quite so much like an anomalous raisin that fell into the pudding. There's much more that needs to happen, but I'm glad to be part of it.

IL: Did you love Jemisin's Hugo speech directed at the rabid/sad puppies or what? That moment of courage reminded me so much of your guest of honor speech at ICFA 2010, "A Reluctant Ambassador from the Planet of Midnight." For me, your talk was one of the great teaching moments in SF con history, just like Chip Delany's classic essay "Racism and Science Fiction."

NH: Nora is graceful forthrightness personified. I still remember her blog post about the ways in which Race/Fail '09 wasn't a failure at all, because people of color in this community began to see that we weren't isolated at all, that we could be a force in each other's support. And because of great initiatives that started, such as publishing ventures and the challenge to read fifty books by authors of color in a year. In fact, I referenced her post in "Reluctant Ambassador." Hers went a long way towards shifting my generalized bad/traumatic feelings about Race/Fail '09 towards one of celebration.

IL: I'm sure you've heard of the attacks on the legal/cultural concept of Critical Race Theory, and I was wondering how you felt and what you thought about this ongoing backlash to the 1619 Project developed by Nikole Hannah-Jones or the global protests last summer during the pandemic. I mean, is it an expression of white guilt and white privilege simultaneously in attempting to shut down this discussion on college campuses, in high schools, and in the general public?

NH: I have heard of it, yeah. Glad I'm getting out of the US. I don't think these kinds of attacks have anything to do with guilt, and everything to do with straight up power consolidation. What's more, I think the left makes a mistake when we assume they come out of sheer stupidity. They don't. They are very cannily thought through, planned and aimed where they will do the most damage in service of fascist ends while pretending the US is a democracy. The people responsible have perfected the technique of misdirection through yelling alarming-sounding lies well enough that they resonate, and people who're inclined to think that way believe them, because America is a country which has steadily—and I suspect deliberately—been undercutting the habits of critical thought in its average citizen. It makes them easier to manipulate.

As to the 1619 Project, I'm confused and suspicious. I haven't been following the controversy and hadn't checked out the website. When I looked it up for this interview, the first link I found was https://www .project1619.org/. Many links were missing, it was poorly copyedited, and some of the claims seemed more inflammatory than factual. I wondered how something like that could have won a Pulitzer and ended up on school curricula. So I dug some more, and found the *New York Times* site "The 1619 Project"; https://www.nytimes.com/interactive/2019/08/14/magazine/1619 -america-slavery.html. But the paywall shows up pretty quickly, seemingly blocking access. True, if you hunt around, you can get to the essays without subscribing, but that information is obscured by fancy site design and lack of clear signage. I almost missed the links to the (professionally researched and written) essays at first, and I'm fairly web savvy. And once I found one essay, it was still a job of work rooting around the site to find the next one. I can totally see many people assuming that project1619.org—the one they can access easily—is the one that won the Pulitzer and got put on school curricula. And I can see why they would be critical of it. I suspect that someone's agenda is being served by this confusion, and that it all helps fuel targeted anti-Black action.

IL: If you wanted to create a label for Black science fiction, what would you call it and why? The reason I ask is that people, largely academics, have caught on to the shortcomings of Afrofuturism while the general public are now embracing the term since the debut of *Black Panther* in 2018. I think it's sell-by date may have expired?

NH: "Afrofuturism" is still a useful filter. I think it's great that the term has escaped academe and gotten out to the general public, because so many people need to know that there is such a thing, need to know that they can find the nourishment of the kinds of stories they crave, and that people of African descent are making those stories. So long as that's still news to anyone and especially to anyone Black, the term has urgent value. What irritates me is that "Afrofuturism" is assumed by so many to be a genre, i.e., what you call it when Black people write science fiction and fantasy. In fact, what it does is to identify particular philosophies and approaches that some speculative fiction artists of African descent bring to our art when we ask our audiences to contemplate centering Africanness. When I write a story about a gay male couple, one white, one First Nations, who live in Toronto and are in a loving 24/7 BDSM relationship, is that Afrofuturism? The only African thing about that story is the author. When I write a novel that's set in an alternate Caribbean past, is that Afrofuturism? There's lots of Africanness, but there's nothing futuristic about it. When we misidentify "Afrofuturism" as a genre, the message many emerging Black spec fic creators get is that they're only allowed to make spec fic a certain way with a certain type of content. It stops being a useful, incisive, and frequently joyful analytical lens and becomes one more way to racialize, limit, and ghettoize Black people. How would I label Black science fiction? Doesn't matter what label I pick; it will always be partial and contextual, and it will always become outdated. That's the nature of labels. Doesn't mean they're not useful. Just that one might need to define the way in which one is using the label in a given instant.

IL: Have racial politics in the genre changed (evolved, regressed) since you've been publishing speculative fiction over the past twenty odd years?

NH: Definitely evolved. More and more editors are developing a sensibility around racism and becoming more pro-active about cultivating a range of voices from multiple racial perspectives. Audiences in privileged places are reading, watching, listening to a wider range of stories. In my twenty-six years in the industry, I've seen the first time a Black man was awarded a Damon Knight Memorial "Grand Master" Award. I've seen the first and second science fiction films from India, and the first Korean science fiction film. Anthologies specifically featuring authors and stories that are culturally specific. More novels—in English—from writers of color. A Black woman author achieving the unthinkable by winning the fan-voted Hugo Award not just once, but thrice in a row. It's rare nowadays that I hear editors saying they don't know why they're not getting more submissions

238 CONVERSATIONS WITH NALO HOPKINSON

from writers of color (the argument used to be "after all, there's nothing stopping them from sending their work!").

Not to say that we've reached the promised land yet. I still hear certain of the opinionati declare that making a point to include authors of color will reduce the quality of anthologies. They're usually smart enough not to say outright that they think our writing sucks. But it's not our inclusion that makes for less rigorous anthologies; it's when we're included at the last minute as a sort of tokenistic anxiety attack by anthologists. What's needed instead is to state up front at submission time that you want to see submissions from authors of color; to include people of color in significant positions on your staff (editorial, marketing, etc.); to educate yourself to the ways in which cultural specificity results in stories being told differently, signifying differently on race, culture, fashion, language, you name it; to recognize that "not seeing race" means that they also can't perceive structural racism; to grasp that racism isn't just a stoned white male musician ranting at his concert that all people of color should be kicked out of the UK. I suspect that only if you do that groundwork will you be able to assess submissions from authors of color on an equal footing with white authors. The Anglophone market is still hugely skewed in overwhelming favor of straight, white, male authors. There are still nowhere near enough translations from other languages into English. Distribution—worldwide access to books—and banking—getting authors paid internationally—are not up to snuff. And racism is finding ways to leverage social media to threaten and attack its targets in force, socially, financially, emotionally, and physically.

I've also noticed a way in which some Anglophone reviewers cloak their racism; they give negative reviews to stories by people of color because (they say) the technology or the folklore undergirding the story has not been explained. So often, that criticism is a veiled way of the reviewer complaining that culturally specific language, history or folklore wasn't instantly legible to them. It's my non-empirical sense that this happens most often with POC writers. There is a very common sfnal technique to which its authors have access; we can create neologisms and new concepts as part of our world-building. Think of the word *mentat* in Frank Herbert's *Dune*, or *whitelighter* in the TV series *Charmed*. The former word makes sense in context; an English speaker can perceive its etymology. Whereas the latter word, which denotes a quasi-angelic helper, doesn't seem to have its meaning embedded in its syllables. The audience learns what it means bit by bit as they watch subsequent episodes. So, common technique, and authors often won't halt the story to explain. You can imagine how doing so might risk destroying the narrative momentum of the piece. Instead, we put the term in context to give the reader a general sense of what the function of the concept is. The reader has to do some mental work. That's one of the joys of SF and F as a reader; employing one's powers of deduction. But when POC authors do it while drawing on our own languages and folklore, some reviewers and readers can find it jarring, even offensive, at which point they blame their sense of cognitive estrangement—something else science fiction and fantasy do deliberately—on the writer. In a conventionally published story, that criticism also indicts the professional editor who chose the story.

Some white folks who are unwilling to recognize their racism can still be very good at weaponizing it. For the TV show *Titans*, Black actress Anna Diop was chosen to play the superhero Starfire, an alien from the comics, typically depicted with orange-ish skin and flowing red hair. Certain fans objected loudly to a Black actress being cast as an orange alien. They wanted a white actress. One fan complained about the tight purple outfits Diop wears. He claimed that the TV Starfire dressed like a hooker, not a superhero. I looked up images of Starfire from the comics. She wears even less clothing than Diop; frequently, thigh-high boots, a bikini bottom that starts barely above her pubes, and a skin-tight, belly-baring top. But a Black woman dressed more modestly is a hooker? What would make you think that, son? Might you be drawing on a particular racialized stereotype of Black women and hoping we don't twig?

So, yeah; racism is alive and well in the industry. But some things are better in ways I would not have thought possible in my lifetime.

IL: Do you feel scholarship is catching up with past, current, and emerging BIPOC writers or is it lagging behind?

NH: You mean, why have things shifted a little? I think that at root it's the vocal, persistent activism of the ones most affected; the people who need positive change. Is scholarship lagging behind? I'm not sure. I'm from the creative practice side of things. My connection to scholarship happens through personal interest. There is some wonderful, synergistic thinking happening out there! If there's lagging behind, it may in part be due to the fact that we generally study something once it's in existence or can be theorized to exist?

IL: Do you have any work in the dust bin that you might dust off and try again?

NH: No, because I don't put things in the dustbin. I mean, there are bits of text I discard permanently in the process of editing a story. But that's in service of polishing that story; it's not whole stories or story ideas. I put things aside sometimes, but I don't trash them. My brain chemistry makes the act of committing words to text a challenge. I struggle constantly with avoidance. I don't churn out hundreds of half-finished ideas every year, so there's not much to throw away. Sometimes when people talk about "trashing" a piece of their writing, you can feel the self-loathing pouring off them. It's like they're trying to reject their own writing before the outside world does it for them. I very much understand where that comes from. And I also understand that not everything that pours out of a writer's pen is a pearl beyond price. I just find that when I value the effort it took me to make any of my writing happen, my brain is more likely to want to try it again. And vice versa.

IL: How important is a sense of location for your writings?

NH: It's world-building, which is environment, culture, language, sensation, history, physical, and social surround. It's integral to the writing.

IL: Do you feel as if you successfully hybridized the genre in your career to date with your complex portrayals of identity?

NH: Lord, who knows? I look to the scholars to do that kind of research. I know I do love it when someone grasps and appreciates what I'm doing when I try not to settle for a singular, expected narrative.

IL: Have you ever thought of doing a critical work of your own; or, is that something you simply don't fancy doing? Something that gathers together your thinking on code-sliding and language, for example?

NH: A book-length one? God, no! Not my training. I'll leave that to experts like you. It's funny; universities talk about creative practice being its own kind of scholarship, yes? But now that I'm a professor of creative writing, I'm getting invitations to submit critical theory pieces to journals, even though that's not my field.

IL: In no small part, your own writing has helped to shape the direction of speculative fiction.

NH: You think so? Thank you. Any effect I might be having on the genre is not something I can easily perceive from within.

IL: Are you excited to see what the next wave of BIPOC writers are doing in speculative fiction?

NH: Always! I don't read as much or as often as I used to in younger days, so I'm behind as well. But I rejoice for every new story or author from a marginalized community that enters the field.

IL: You rock! Thank you.

NH: My pleasure.

Index

Abby (character), 176–80
Acid Queen (character), 105
acrolectal speech, 225–26
Adams, John Joseph, 176, 223
Adisa, Opal Palmer, 71, 83
African American Review, xiv, 12
African cultures, 6, 117, 136, 213
African diaspora, 10, 16, 49–50, 76, 165, 176; effects of, 117; history, 33; languages of, 167; literature of, 14, 70–71, 92, 102, 141–42
African Fractals (Eglash), 171
African languages, 55, 100, 191
African religions. *See* West African religions and belief systems
African sensibility, 81, 119
Afro-Caribbean culture, 31, 174, 219–20. *See also* Caribbean culture
Afro-Caribbean people, depictions of in popular culture, 44, 159–60
Afro-Caribbean religions, 33, 79, 125, 134, 155, 176–77, 184–85, 192, 233. *See also* West African religions and belief systems
Afrofuturism, xiv, 108, 117–18, 125, 236–37
Afrofuturism listserv, 108, 117
Akomfrah, John, 13
Alexandria, Egypt, 54, 62, 136
Alexie, Sherman, 14
aliens, 8, 13–14, 58, 66, 71, 81–82, 98–100, 185–86, 201; as monolith trope, 81–82, 100; colonizing of trope, 13–14, 58, 71, 201; as magical trope, 66; as predatory trope, 66; racialized Other trope, 8, 81–82, 98–99, 185–86
Allen, Lillian, 52, 69, 87, 91, 171
alternative relationship models, 18, 45, 108, 138, 143–44
Always Coming Home (LeGuin), 70
Anansi people and culture, 43, 96
Andromeda Strain, The (1971), 152
Angela Ruskin University, xvi, 214
anime characters with white features, 129–30
Anzaldúa, Gloria, 229
Ariel (character), 170–71
artificial intelligence, 42–43, 93, 160–61
Asimov, Isaac, 48, 196, 198
Astounding Award for Best New Writer, The, xi, xv
Avatar: The Last Airbender (2005), 185
Azania, Malcolm. *See* Faust, Minister

Barnes, Steven, 12–13, 71, 83, 118, 128, 235
basilectal speech, 225–26
Bassett, Angela, 80–81, 128
Baudelaire, Charles, 62, 146, 148–49
Bayou graphic novel series (Love), 168, 187, 209
beauty ideals, culturally prescribed, 141–42

241

242 INDEX

Beloved (Morrison), 58–59, 76
Bennett[-Coverley], Louise, 27, 132, 171, 225
Bes (Egyptian deity), 135
Binti series (Okorafor), 222
BIPOC. *See* Black indigenous people of color
bisexuality, 138–39
Bisson, Terry, 157–75, 183–84
Black Atlantic Speculative Fictions (Thaler), xiii
Black Caribbean people, depictions of in popular culture. *See* Afro-Caribbean people, depictions of in popular culture
Blackheart Man (Hopkinson), 188, 200
Black indigenous people of color (BIPOC), xii–xiii, 239–40
Black Lives Matter protests, 235–36
Black Panther (2018), 236
Black Swan, White Raven (Datlow and Windling), 4, 30
Black Wine (Dorsey), 33, 67
Black Women Writers at Work (Tate), 91
Black writers: challenges getting published, 99, 165–66; limitations imposed on by critics, 15. *See also under* science fiction genre; speculative fiction genre
Blade movies, 118, 127–28
Blank, Hanne, 140
Bodies and/as Technology (Georgi), xiii
Bone Dance (Bull), 110
Bone People, The (Hulme), 18, 34, 229
Borderlands/La Frontera (Anzaldúa), 229
Bradbury, Ray, 18, 44, 174
Brand, Dionne, 28
Brasil, Ione (character), 42
Brathwaite, Edward Kamau, 52, 75, 82, 102, 171, 225

Brer Anansi (character), 42
Briar Rose (Yolen), 14, 35, 209
Bright, Susie, 34, 64, 108–9, 207
British Fantasy Award, xvi, 223
Brown, Charles, 3–11, 60–67, 189–90
Brown Girl in the Ring (Hopkinson), xi, 4–5, 9–10, 14, 21, 24, 27, 31, 44–59, 68, 76, 78–79, 85, 87, 93, 110, 116, 131, 133–34, 138, 142–44, 158, 192–93, 211, 224; film project, 160
Buckell, Tobias, 52, 64, 82–83, 120, 186, 227, 234
Buffy the Vampire Slayer (1997–2003), 159
Butler, Octavia, xi, xiii, 12–13, 18, 20, 33, 60, 71, 74, 77, 88, 101–2, 111–12, 118, 124, 139, 173–74, 186, 190, 234–35

Calamity (character), 149, 198–99
Caliban (character), 170–71
Capek, Karol, 13, 72, 113
Caribbean, fiction set in, 4, 97, 143, 153–54, 215–19, 221
Caribbean culture, xiii, 7, 23, 26–28, 39, 54, 70–72, 77–79, 101, 105, 120, 132, 143, 153–54, 158; diversity of, 116; as exotic, 97. *See also* Afro-Caribbean culture
Caribbean English, 72, 100, 154, 216, 225
Caribbean fabulist fiction, 44, 70–71, 82, 92
Caribbean histories, 19, 42, 77, 101, 220–21
Caribbean Quarterly, 39
Carl Brandon Society, xii, xv, 75, 103–4, 114–15, 122; Carl Brandon Kindred Award, 135; Carl Brandon Parallax Award, 135
carnival celebrations, 42–45, 65
Carr, Terry, 103
Catholicism, 25, 62, 97, 147

Chaos, The (Hopkinson), xvi, 172, 180–81, 189, 191, 224
Charnas, Suzy McKee, 33, 88
Cherryh, C. J., 5, 78, 104
Chestnutt, Charles, 228–29
childbirth. *See* pregnancy and childbirth
children's challenge games, 7, 134, 158
Chopstix in Mauby (maxwell), 33
Christianity, 6, 147
Clara's Heart (1988), 44
Clarion Science Fiction and Fantasy Writers' Workshop, xi, xv, 4, 6, 20, 30–31, 47, 50–51, 53, 63–64, 78, 83, 87, 89–90, 96, 109–10, 134, 153, 155, 182, 211–12, 215, 227, 234; increasing number of writers of color, 121, 124
classical literature, 3, 12, 48, 96, 132, 171, 194
Cleve (character), 138
Clute, John, 173–74
"Code Sliding" (Hopkinson), xii
code switching, xii–xiv, 25–28, 71–72, 120, 227–28
colonialism, 8–9, 48, 77, 99, 113, 117; effects of, 16, 28, 41, 48, 113, 201, 217–19, 203–4; resistance to, 76
color-blindness. *See* race blindness
Constantine, Storm, 33, 139
"Crate" (Sturgeon), 151–52
creole languages, 10, 26–29, 41, 54–55, 64, 71, 75, 99–100; Caribbean, xiii, 23, 27–28, 41, 154; orality of, xi, 27, 100, 216; subversiveness of, 71–73, 100
Crichton, Michael, 152, 198
critical race theory, 22, 235–36
Cube (Natali), 128
cyberpunk style, xi, 98, 149

Damon Knight Memorial Grand Master, xii, xvi, 234, 237
dance, 3, 10, 20, 24, 26, 56, 86, 197
Dark Dreams (Massey), 118

Dark Matter (Thomas), 32, 64, 73, 75, 101–2, 107, 228
"Darmok" episode (*Star Trek: The Next Generation*), 101
Dash, Julie, 81, 125, 129
Datlow, Ellen, 4, 30, 33, 63
Daughters of the Dust (Dash), 81, 125, 129
Davis, Tiffany, 211–15
Davis, Wade, 7
DC Comics, 209, 233
Dean, Pamela, 227
Delany, Samuel L. (Chip), xii–xv, 3–4, 6, 9, 12–14, 17, 20–21, 28, 32, 38, 52, 57, 64, 70–75, 87, 94, 101–2, 107–9, 111–12, 114–16, 118, 124, 134, 139, 155, 163, 173–74, 187–88, 197, 215, 227, 234–35
Dhalgren (Delany), 32, 107
dialects, 26–28; Jamaican, 27–28, 55, 72, 75, 100, 225; Trinidadian, 27–28, 55, 72, 75, 100, 225
Díaz, Junot, 125–26, 182
Dillion, Diane, 32, 65, 98
Dillon, Leo, 32, 65, 98
Diop, Anna, 239
Donkey (Hopkinson), 179–80, 189. *See also Sister Mine* (Hopkinson)
Dorsey, Candas Jane, 18, 33, 57, 139
Drown (Díaz), 182
Du Bois, W. E. B., 25, 102
dub poetry, 39, 171. *See also* poetry
Due, Tananarive, 12, 71, 118, 235
Dukan, Asli, 159–60
Duncan, Andy, 113
dusky saint, the. *See* Gypsy Mary
Duval, Jeanne, 62, 138, 145–49
Duval, Mer (character), 138, 145
Dykes to Watch Out For (Bechdel), 168
dystopia, 152, 217–18, 221

Eaton Collection, 182, 195, 197–98, 232
Eaton Conference, 195

244 INDEX

Egyptian artifacts, 136–37
Elliott, Missy, 80–81
Ellison, Harland, 3, 198
Emerge (magazine), 8
English, standard, 27–28, 72–73, 225–29. *See also* Caribbean English
epic allegorical tales, 96, 101
erotica, 64–65, 107–9, 172, 207; difference from pornography, 141
Eshu (deity), 48, 72, 79
exile, trope of, 40–41, 49

fabulist fiction, Caribbean, 36, 44, 51–53, 62, 70, 82, 92, 96, 102, 111–16, 119, 133, 224
fairy tales, 33, 96, 101, 209–10
Falling in Love with Hominids (Hopkinson), xvi, 213, 220, 224, 230
fantastic fiction, 3, 12, 16, 32, 37, 48, 52–53, 63, 71, 82, 95–96, 110, 125, 141, 158, 168, 209; definitions of, 58–59; disdain for, 193–95, 197; lack of diversity in, 8–10, 13–15; storytelling possibilities of, 98
fantasy genre, xi–xii, 12–16, 23, 32–34, 38, 44, 48, 54, 58–59, 62–63, 65–66, 70–71, 75, 77, 92, 93, 95, 102, 105, 107–10, 120, 126–27, 130–32, 137, 141–42, 150, 153, 156, 159–62, 167–72, 177, 182, 191–201, 223, 228, 235, 237; contemporary retellings of ancient folktales, 37; conventions of, 125, 168, 203–5, 239; difference from science fiction, 96–97; disdain for, 157, 209; racism in, 186; readership, 194–95, 200, 208; respect from mainstream literary community, 131, 197, 199; subversiveness of, 37, 98–99, 149, 157, 222; writing in, 203–6, 209. *See also under* young adult fiction
fat-positive fiction, 37, 74, 94, 222
Faust, Minister, 126

feminist science fiction community, xii, 3, 18, 33–34, 70, 75, 103, 149, 199, 202; importance of, 87–94, 103–4; intergenerational, 93. *See also* WisCon: The Feminist Science Fiction Conference
Fifty Book Challenge, 186–87, 235
Findlay, David, 41–42, 99–100
"Fisherman" (Hopkinson), 140
FitzPatrick, Jessica, 201–10
Flesh of the Spirit: African and Afro-American Art and Philosophy (Thompson), 34
folklore, xi–xii, 12, 93, 101, 192, 238; African American, 209, 239; African diasporic, 191; Caribbean, xi–xii, 6, 31, 34, 37–38, 48, 132, 167, 191, 238–39; Euro-Celtic, 31–32, 101, 191
folktales, 19, 31, 43, 50, 95–96, 159, 209–10; African American, 12; African diasporic, 142; Caribbean, 32, 34, 37, 42, 49, 101; contemporary retellings of, 37–38; Euro-Celtic, 35
Fowler, Karen Joy, 4, 34, 87, 97
Frakes, Jonathan, 23–24
Frankenstein (Shelley), 13, 182
Free Within Ourselves (Rhodes), 91

Gaiman, Neil, xi, xvi, 172, 185, 233–34
"Ganger (Ball Lightening)" (Hopkinson), 64, 107–8, 138
Garvey, Marcus, 9–10
Gaylactic Spectrum Award, xi, xvi
Geek's Guide to the Galaxy, The (podcast), 176
gender, 11, 26, 57, 69, 108–10, 112–13, 117, 121, 138–40, 148; nonbinary representations of, 139–40; women as experts on, 121
gender bending, 40, 108–10, 139–40, 151, 174
gender roles, queering, 108–10, 139–40

INDEX 245

gender theory, 122

General Gun (character), 177

genre fiction, 22, 66, 76, 131, 157, 196–97, 224; distinctions among genres, 76; as formulaic, 22; as limiting, 66, 196–97; prejudice against, 66, 131, 157. *See also* fantastic fiction: disdain for

Ghost in the Shell (2007), 129–30

Gibson, William, 34, 39, 159

Glave, Dianne D., 68–83

globalization, effects of, 218–19

"Goblin Market" (Rossetti), 176, 179

Godbody (Sturgeon), 151

Goldberg, Whoopi, 44

Gomoll, Jenny, 75

"Goophered Grapevine, The" (Chestnutt), 228–29

Gordon, Joan, xiv, 138–50

Grande Nanotech Sentient Interface. *See* Granny Nanny (fictional technology)

grandmother healers, 6–7, 92–93, 176–77

Grandmother Ocean (character), 176

Granny Nanny (fictional technology), 42–43, 96, 167

"Granny Rumple" (Yolen), 35

graphic novels, 168, 187, 208, 209, 222, 231, 233

"Greedy Choke Puppy" (Hopkinson), 93, 170

Green Grass, Running Water (King), 34, 58, 71, 187

Griffone (Hopkinson), 44, 62, 83, 88, 134. See also *Salt Roads, The* (Hopkinson)

Gulliver's Travels (Swift), 3, 48, 194

GUT Symmetries (Winterson), 33

Guyana, 20–21, 31, 84, 109, 175, 192, 213

Gypsy Mary, 62, 147

"Habit of Waste, A" (Hopkinson), 45, 130, 133, 141, 153; as autobiographical, 133

Haiti, 6–7, 25, 54–55, 62, 207

Haldeman, Gay, 4, 90, 126

Haldeman, Joe, 4, 90, 126, 182

Hamilton, Virginia, 12–13

Hanna, Mary, 40, 193

Hannah-Jones, Nikole, 235–36

Harris, Wilson, 52, 64, 82, 155

Harry Potter series (Rowling), 191

Heinlein, Robert, 174, 196, 198

Hendrix, Jimi, 177–78

herbal lore/medicine, 6–7, 79, 92

Hernandez Brothers, 168, 187

Hill, Walter, 80–81, 128

Hines, Gregory, 87

historical fiction, 62, 83, 88, 199

Hollinger, Veronica, xiv, 138–50

Holocaust, 14, 16

Homer, 12, 96, 132, 171

hoodoo, 177

hooks, bell, 108, 174

Hopkinson, Freda, xv, 20–21, 37, 61, 68, 77, 79, 84–85, 88, 90, 132, 152, 162–63, 174, 192–93, 197–98

Hopkinson, Keïta, 68, 87, 192

Hopkinson, [Muhammad Abdur-Rahman] Slade, xv, 12, 19–21, 24–25, 30, 37, 40, 49–52, 63, 68, 77–78, 105, 155, 158, 171, 175, 192–94, 197–98, 216, 226; death of, 84–85, 87, 90, 132, 178

Hopkinson, Nalo: ADHD, 162, 173, 178, 183; ancestry, 10, 26, 31; Canadian identity, 14, 107, 160, 192–93; Caribbean identity, 31, 55, 71, 76, 92, 97, 107, 132, 160, 174, 192–93, 203, 219–20; challenges of making a living as a writer, 35–36, 78, 85, 88, 120, 152–54, 183, 190–91, 232–33; chronology, xv–xvii; cooking, 163, 212–13, 233; digital collage project, 221–22; dislike of

horror, 81, 128, 131–32, 198; early life, 3, 13–15, 18, 20–21, 30, 37, 49, 51, 68, 77–78, 84–85, 105, 132, 163, 192–94, 197–98; editing, 51–54, 62–67, 82, 111–13, 119–20, 132, 165–67, 200, 202, 211–12, 223; education, 20–21, 30–31, 50, 60, 68–70, 78, 84–90, 94–95, 100, 109, 194, 197–98, 211, 227; fabric and fashion designer, 161–63, 212, 222, 233; fitness instructor, 50, 57, 86, 134; fostering diversity in literature, 163–67, 187, 198, 201–2, 211–12; health challenges, 169–73, 178, 183, 189–90; homelessness, xvi, 169, 183–84, 234; honorary doctorate, xvi, 214; identity as a writer, 50, 53, 85–87, 152–54, 169–70; immigration to Canada, 21, 31, 68–69, 84, 104, 192; influences on her writing, 17–19, 32, 68–70, 81, 91, 93–94, 107–9, 114, 138–39, 155, 157–59, 163, 167–68, 193–94, 197–98, 203; reader feedback, 8, 155–56, 181–82; readership, 14, 65, 93, 138, 144, 146, 215; reading tastes, 12–13, 32–34, 48, 57, 132, 152, 167, 209–10, 222–23; research for her writing, 101, 132, 180, 204, 221; scholarly work about, xiii, 193; sexuality, 138–39; teaching career, 57, 110, 123–24, 132, 152, 169–70, 175, 182, 190, 194–95, 202–6, 209, 211, 214, 225, 227, 230, 232–33; television and film viewing habits, 23, 80, 105, 127–29, 170, 197; writing process, 17–19, 30–34, 38–39, 43, 45–48, 50, 54–56, 61–67, 77–79, 87–90, 99, 103, 156, 170, 172–73, 177–78, 199, 202–8, 213, 217, 227–29, 233, 239–40
horror genre, 6, 12, 58, 64, 71, 75, 95–96, 109–10, 118, 126, 128, 131–32, 150, 198, 232
House of Whispers (Gaiman), xi, xvi, 233
Hugo Awards, xii, xv, 60, 235, 237

Hulme, Keri, 18, 34, 229
human, definitions of, 187–88
hybrid genres, xii, 10, 25–26, 48, 52–53, 71, 83, 92–93, 95–110, 196–97, 240

Iliad (Homer), 3, 12, 96, 132, 171, 194
Imaro trilogy (Saunders), 12, 118
imperialism, 76–77, 113; resistance to, 76. *See also* colonialism
In Another Place, Not Here (Brand), 28
indentured laborers, 77, 221
Independence Day (1996), 81, 128
indigenous peoples, 42, 99
Inferno (Dante), 171
International Conference of the Fantastic in the Arts (ICFA), xii–xiii, 51, 62, 82, 111, 113, 119, 133, 170, 183–85, 235
intersectionality, 112–16
Invisible Cities Press, 62, 82, 119, 133
Invisibles, The (Morrison), 168, 209
"I Shall Do Thee Mischief in the Wood" (Koja), 210
IT (King), 132

Jackson, Shelley, 213
Jama-Everett, Ayizé, 108, 117, 163
Jamaica, xv, 3, 20–21, 31, 39, 152, 167, 191–92, 198, 213; Kingston, xv, 3, 198
Jar Jar Binks (character), 127, 159
Jarvey, Paul, 151–56
Jemisin, Nora (N. K.), xiii, 187, 223, 233–35; Hugo Award speech, 235
"Johnny Mnemonic" (Gibson), 159
Johnson, Charles, 18, 79
Johnston, Nancy, 138–50

Kelly (character), 140
Keyes, Daniel, 195
Kincaid, Jamacia, 82–83, 102
Kindred (Butler), 18, 71
King, Martin Luther, Jr., 106, 128
King, Thomas, 34, 58, 71, 187

INDEX **247**

Kirtley, David Barr, 176–88
Klages, Ellen, 34, 113, 180
Kress, Nancy, 4, 87

Lai, Larissa, xiii, 58, 132, 210
language, power of, xii–xiii, 29, 41, 49,
   54–55, 71–73
LaValle, Victor, 223
Laveau, Marie, 91
Lavender, Isiah, III, 111–30, 232–40
Le Chat du Rabbin (Sfar), 168, 208–9
Le Guin, Urusla, 14, 18, 33, 70, 91, 126,
   163, 173–74, 196–97, 223, 228
Lewis, Sharon, 160
Levine, Jamie, 199
libraries, importance of, 3, 8, 13, 20, 37,
   49, 68, 76–77, 85, 109, 132, 149, 152,
   155, 173, 198, 221, 230
Lightspeed (Hopkinson), 211, 223
Link, Kelly, 18, 34, 69, 132, 155, 197
Lion, the Witch and the Wardrobe, The
   (Lewis), 197
Lion's Blood (Barnes), 83
literary canon, 22, 48, 193–94, 197
Little Mermaid, The (1989), 159
Locus, xiv, 3–11, 60, 64, 189–90
Locus Award for Best First Novel, xi,
   xv
Lohr, Michael, 131–37
Lord, Karen, 187, 197, 234
Lord of the Flies (Golding), 152
Lot to Share, A (documentary), 192
Love, Jeremy, 168, 187, 209
Love and Rockets (Hernandez Brothers),
   168, 187
Lovecraft, H. P., 172, 223
Lynn, Elizabeth, 3, 18, 34, 108, 139

Maass, Don, 61–62, 200
Mackandal, François, 207
Maerlande Chronicles, The (Vonar-
   burg), 57

magical realism, xi, 12–13, 18, 54, 63, 75,
   81, 83, 92, 96, 102, 168, 193
mainstream literature, 22, 66, 83, 95,
   102, 194, 199, 224
Makeda (character), 176–80
Mama Day (Naylor), 58, 76
manual labor, mechanization of, 160–61
marronage, 42, 221
McBride, Rita, xvi
McDonald, Ian, 53, 97
McHugh, Maureen, 33, 71
Mehan, Uppinder, xii, xvi, 48, 116, 126,
   163, 201, 211, 224
Merril, Judith, 4, 50, 66, 85, 89, 134, 173
mesolectal speech, 225–26
Met (character), 145
Middle Passage, 77, 117
Middle Passage (Johnson), 18, 79
Midnight Robber (character), 9, 39–40,
   43, 49
Midnight Robber (Hopkinson), xi, xiii,
   xv, 9, 28, 31–32, 37–45, 47, 49, 54, 60,
   72, 75, 77, 79, 81, 93, 96–101, 138, 140,
   142–43, 153–55, 160–61, 167, 200, 206,
   208, 211, 224, 227
Miéville, China, 163, 197, 215
Miguel Street (Naipaul), 168–69
Millie Christine, 180
Milstead, John W., 125
mimetic fiction, 15–16, 95–96, 98, 194,
   205; limitations of, 16
Mitchell, Betsy, 62, 70, 76
Mohanraj, Mary Anne, 30–36, 224–31
Mojo (Hopkinson), xvi, 113, 116, 119, 122,
   126, 163, 165–66, 177, 211, 224
Mootoo, James, 18, 58, 134
More, Thomas, 182, 214
Moreno-Garcia, Sylvia, 215
Morrison, Grant, 168, 209
Morrison, Toni, 58–59, 76
Morrow, James, 18, 58, 134
Mosley, Walter, 13, 15–16

248 INDEX

Motion of Light in Water, The (Delany), 107
Mumbo Jumbo (Reed), 33
Murphy, Pat, 4, 34, 87
Muslim, Kristine Ong, xii

Naipaul, V. S., 168–69
Nanny (character), 42–43, 101
Nanny of the Maroons, 42–43, 167
Native Tongue (Elgin), 57
Naylor, Gloria, 58, 76
Nebula Award for Best Novel, xv–xvi, 60; Andre Norton Nebula Award for Middle Grade and Young Adult Fiction, xvi
Nelson, Alondra, 95–110, 118
Neverÿona series (Delany), 71, 107
New Half-Way Tree (fictional location), 31, 39–40, 42, 225
New Moon's Arms, The (Hopkinson), xvi, 149, 160, 198, 224; film project, 160
Nichols, Nichelle, 82, 105–6
nkyimkyim symbol, 213–14
Nobel Prize winners, 158, 174, 193
Noon, Jeff, 10, 14
Norman, John, 104
Notkin, Debbie, 75
Nu Wah (deity), 210

Odyssey (Homer), 171
Ogoun (deity), 177
Okorafor, Nnedi[mma], xiii, 120, 172, 222, 233–34
Once upon an Elephant (Mathur), 58
"Once on the Shores of the Stream Senegambia" (Mordecai), 63
orality, xii, 49, 100, 216–17
Orisha (Afro-Caribbean belief system), 6, 79, 92, 97, 110, 125, 155
Orwell, George, 8
Oshun (deity), 176–77

"Ours Is the Prettiest" (Hopkinson), 170
Outspoken Authors series (Bisson), 157–75, 183

Pacific Edge (Robinson), 18, 39
Papiamento, 97, 100
Particulates (Hopkinson and McBride), xvi
Patrice (character), 145
Pearson, Wendy Gay, xiv, 138–50
People of Colo(u)r Destroy Science Fiction! (Hopkinson and Muslim), xii, xvi, 211
Playboy, 198
poetry, 3, 27, 41–42, 49, 52, 54, 63, 69–70, 72, 84, 99, 158, 171, 176, 179, 197. *See also* dub poetry
Pohl, Fred, 173
Pohl-Weary, Emily, 173
polygamy/polyandry, 139, 143, 145
popular culture as "low culture," 196–97
possession, 184–85
postcolonialism, xii, xiv, 65, 71, 89, 193, 201, 218, 224. *See also under* science fiction genre
postmodernism, 65, 89
post-race world trope, 122
Powers, Tim, 4, 87
"Precious" (Hopkinson), 4
pregnancy and childbirth, 41, 64
publishing industry, 34–35, 113–14, 118–19, 184–86, 239; consolidation of, 34–35; electronic production and distribution of work, 35; lack of diversity, 113–14, 118–19, 238; racism in, 118–19, 184–86

Queen Nanny. *See* Nanny of the Maroons
queerness, 14, 17, 32, 70, 80, 107–9, 117, 138–39, 144; fatal love trope,

INDEX **249**

144; negative representations of, 80; queerphobia, 117

queer rights, stories about, 151

Queer Universes (Pearson, Hollinger, and Gordon), xiv, 138–50

Quilombo (Diegues), 170

Rabbi's Cat, The (Sfar). See *Le Chat du Rabbin* (Sfar)

race, 15, 120–22; American concept of, 120; Caribbean concept of, 15, 120; as social construct, xiii, 121–22

race blindness, 9, 74, 80–82, 111–30, 164, 184–86, 238; breaking the illusion of, 81–82, 184–86; in popular culture, 127

raced future, 123

RaceFail, 184–86, 235

race theory. See critical race theory

racism, 70–71, 73–77, 81–82, 98–99, 103, 107, 118–19, 223, 234–36; institutionalized, 164–67, 184–86, 238; internalized, 15–16, 28, 127, 141–42; reluctance to openly discuss, 111–17

"Racism and Science Fiction" (Delany), 73, 114, 234–35

"Rainses, The" (Shawl), 234

Rastafarian "dread talk," 27, 73

ReaderCon conferences, 73–74, 114–15, 137, 151

realist fiction. See mimetic fiction

Reed, Ishmael, 33, 71

"Reluctant Ambassador from the Planet of Midnight, A" (Hopkinson), xii–xiii, 184, 235

Report from Planet Midnight (Hopkinson), xvi, 157, 183–84

Rhodes, Jewell Parker, 91

"Riding the Red" (Hopkinson), 30, 93, 142

"R Is for Rocket" (Bradbury), 174

Robber Queen (character), 39–40

Robinson, Kim Stanley, 18, 34, 39, 163

Roddenberry, Gene, 82, 106

Rossetti, Christina, 176, 179

Royal Ontario Museum, 135–37

Rudy (character), 21, 46–47

R.U.R. (Capek), 13, 72, 113

Russell, Mary Dorin, 60

Rutledge, Gregory E., 12–29

Ryerson, 47, 50

Ryman, Geoff, xvi, 120, 175

Saint Mary of Egypt. See Gypsy Mary

Salt Eaters, The (Bambara), 76

Salt Roads, The (Hopkinson), xi, xvi, 134, 136, 138, 143, 145–46, 149, 199, 213, 224

same-sex relationships, 140–41, 145–46, 149

Sandman universe (Gaiman), xi, xvi, 231, 233

Sarah Canary (Fowler), 97

Saunders, Charles, 12–13, 71, 118, 121, 187

Sayers, Dorothy, 229–30

Scheier, Libby, 69

Schellenberg, James, 46–59

schizophrenia, incidents of in male immigrants from the Caribbean, 5, 134

"Schooner *Flight*, The" (Walcott), 158

Schuyler, George, 102

science, language of. See technology and science, language of

Science Fiction and Fantasy Writers of America, xii, 234

science fiction community, 38, 61, 64, 106, 124–25, 137, 160, 183, 201, 205–6; closed-minded, 116, 150; diversity of, 66; racism in, 73–75, 103, 107, 111–17, 184–87, 223, 234–35, 238–39; reluctance to discuss race, 111–17, 122, 184–87; willingness to discuss sexuality, 122

250 INDEX

science fiction genre, 38, 65–66, 69–77, 88, 95–101, 105–12, 118–19, 123–24, 137, 151–53, 160, 162, 184–87, 203–6, 209, 226, 228, 235; Black science fiction, 72, 78, 101–2, 118, 236–38; Black writers, 60, 78, 87, 101–2, 186, 211, 215, 222–23, 232, 234, 236–37; definitions and conventions of, 41, 62–63, 96, 110, 125, 129, 132, 139, 141–42, 170, 177, 184–85, 201, 203–5, 239; difference from fantasy, 48, 96–97; diversity of expression, 35, 107, 197–98, 220–21, 237–38; feminist, 3, 18, 33–34, 70–71, 85, 103, 149, 199, 202; film, 44, 126–28, 185, 237; Golden Age, 174, 199; lack of diversity in, 74, 102–3, 110, 201–2; lack of respect from mainstream literary community, 131, 157–59; as "low culture," 197; marketing, 22, 199–200, 238; New Wave, 3, 149, 174, 198; over-representation of Western middle-class perspective, 35, 70–71, 118–19, 196, 201–2, 216–18; post-colonial, xii, xiv, 201, 218, 224; Pulp Era, 70–71; queer, 87, 202, 211, 215, 222–23, 232, 234; racism in, 71, 73, 75, 81–82, 98–99, 113, 167, 234–35; representations of women in, 34, 71; scholarship, 12–25, 67, 117, 122, 125, 182–83, 198, 201, 211, 232, 239; sexism in, 167; subversiveness of, 14, 37, 92, 98–99, 149–50, 202; writers of color, 31–32, 57–58, 70, 73–75, 82, 120, 126, 149, 196, 202, 211, 235; women writers, 34, 78, 93, 125, 186, 196, 211, 222–23; young adult, xvi, 12

science fiction readership, 194–95; aging of, 22; readers of color, 8, 13, 71; readership, 38, 65–66, 88, 100, 125, 174, 194–95, 228

"SF Writers of Color" (Hopkinson), 149

Sebastian the crab (character), 159

Sejpal, Avni, 216–23

Serpent and the Rainbow, The (Davis), 7

Seton Hill University, 134, 194

sex, graphic depictions of, 140–41, 143, 146–69, 179, 181–82, 207–8, 237

sexism: institutionalized, 164–67; internalized, 15–16, 141–42. *See also under* science fiction genre

sex-positive writing, 14, 17, 32, 64, 107–9, 138–50, 238

sexual abuse/violence, 40–41, 206–7; writing about, 206–7

sex workers, 62, 146–49

Sfar, Joann, 168, 208–9

Shakespeare, William, 18, 167, 170–71, 229

"Shattered Like a Glass Goblin" (Ellison), 3, 198

Shawl, Nisi, 71, 163, 234

Sheier, Libby, 91

Sheldon, Alice Bradley. *See* Tiptree, James, Jr.

Shelley, Mary, 13, 182

Sherman, Josepha, 5

"Shift" (Hopkinson), 170–71

Silverberg, Robert, 164

Sister Mine (Hopkinson), xvi, 176, 179, 181, 189, 191–92, 198, 200, 224

sisters, 176–88

1619 Project (Hannah-Jones), 235–36

"Skin" (Jackson), 213

Skin Folk (Hopkinson), xi, xv–xvi, 64, 97–98, 109, 140, 142, 224; movie project, 159

slavery, 16, 49, 76–77, 113, 117, 149, 160, 211; in the Caribbean, 77, 83; effects of, 16, 77, 160, 203–4

slipstream fiction, 53, 62

Smith, Will, 81, 128

Snipes, Wesley, 126, 128

Social Problems Through Science Fiction (Greenberg), 125

INDEX **251**

social realism. *See* mimetic fiction
Social Text, xiv, 95
sociolects, 26–28
Solomon, Frances Anne, 160
So Long Been Dreaming (Hopkinson
and Mehan), xii, xvi, 116, 126, 163, 201,
211, 224
Something Wicked This Way Comes
(Bradbury), 44
Speculative Fiction Foundation, 135,
224–31
speculative fiction genre, xi–xii, xvi,
15–16, 20, 22, 34–35, 62–63, 70–76,
95–111, 118, 120, 123, 130, 135–38, 149,
168, 224–31, 240; Black writers of,
xii, 12–14, 32, 71, 74–75, 92, 101–2,
228–29, 234, 237; cyberpunk, 137;
definitions and conventions of, 12,
22, 72, 95–96, 98, 149, 168; diversity
of expression in, 35; feminist, 70, 137;
film and television, 80–81; marketing, 22, 34–35; New Wave, 149; queer
writers, 137, 234; scholarship, 101–2,
224–31; subversiveness, 149–50;
vs. science fiction, 95–110; women
writers of, 12–14; writers of color, xii,
12–14, 111, 120, 135, 137, 240; under-
representation of women writers,
110; under-representation of writers
of color, 102–3, 110, 118, 137. *See also*
science fiction genre
speculative fiction readership, 22, 102;
aging of, 22
Sperandei, William, 24
Spirited Away (2001), 129–30
Spoonflower, 162, 212, 222
Starfire (character), 239
Starr, Belle, 39
Star Trek franchise, 23, 81–82, 101, 105,
106
Star Wars franchise, racist stereotypes
in, 127–29, 159

steampunk genre, 173–74
Steering the Craft (Le Guin), 228
"Stolen Song" (Findlay), 41–42, 99–100
storytelling, 43, 95–110, 126, 153, 159;
importance of, 126; for political ends,
43; power of, 49, 95–110
Strahan, Jonathan, 189–200
Sturgeon, Noël, 151
Sturgeon, Theodore, 139, 151–52, 199
Supernova (Hill), 80–81, 128
"Survivor's Ball" (Link), 155
Swift, Jonathan, 3, 48, 194
Switzer, David M., 46–59

Taíno people, 221
Taint (Hopkinson), 156, 180–81, 191
Tam Lin (Dean), 227
Tan, Shaun, 197
Tan-Tan (character), 39–42, 44, 49, 77,
96, 140, 206, 224
Taylor, Laurel, 88
technology and science, language of,
48, 72
Tempest, The (Shakespeare), 170–71
Ten Monkeys, Ten Minutes (Watts), 57
Terminal Café, The (McDonald), 97
Tesseracts Nine (Hopkinson and
Ryman), xvi, 120, 175
Thieves' World series, 144
Thomas, Sheree (Renee), 32, 64, 71, 73,
75, 92, 101–2, 228, 234
Ti-Jean and His Brothers (Walcott),
24–25; influence on *Brown Girl in the
Ring*, 25
Ti-Jeanne (character), 18, 25, 76, 133–34,
158
Tipingee (character), 145
Tiptree, James, Jr., 18, 34, 64, 103–4, 164
Tiptree Awards, 56, 63–64, 83
Titans (2018–present), 239
tokenism, 8, 124
Tommy (1975), 105

252 INDEX

Tom Swift series, 71
Toronto, Canada, xv–xvi, 3–4, 10, 21, 23, 26, 48, 50–52, 56–57, 69, 85, 87, 91, 100, 104–5, 108, 134, 153–54, 160, 169, 173, 179, 182–83; cultural diversity of, 25, 192; as setting in Hopkinson's fiction, xi, 7–8, 25, 31, 47, 97–98, 192, 237
Toronto Arts Council (TAC), 56, 153
Toussaint (planet), xi, 31, 39–43, 160–61, 206; government of, 43
Trinidad, xv, 9, 18, 20–21, 31, 49, 65, 84, 105, 158, 193, 197, 213
Trinidadian Carnival, 9, 18, 39–45, 49, 105
Trinidad Theatre Workshop, 24, 49, 158, 193
Trollope, Frances, 132
Tucker, Chris, 80
Turing threshold, 160
Tutuola, Amos, 28
twins, conjoined, 176–88

Uhura, Lieutenant (character), 82, 105–6
University of British Columbia, xi, xvii, 232–33
University of California, Riverside, xvi–xvii, 169, 182, 190, 195, 225, 232
University of Toronto, 48, 57
unwed motherhood, 18, 41
Utopia (More), 182, 214
utopian fiction, 38–39, 125, 160

vampires, Black, 118, 127–28
vampire tropes, 7, 66, 105, 118, 159
vernaculars, 203, 227–30; Black, 27–28, 75; Caribbean, 27, 100, 132, 154, 191, 203, 216–19, 225–27
Vonarburg, Élizabeth, 33, 57, 139
voodoo, 177
Voodoo Dreams (Rhodes), 91

Walcott, Derek, 24–25, 158–59, 174, 193
Walden Pond, skinny dipping in, 137

Warner Aspect, 13–14, 28, 46, 52, 61–62, 104; attempts to increase offerings by writers of color, 70; First Novel Contest, xv, 4–5, 9, 21, 46, 61, 70, 78, 104, 153, 211
Watson-Aifah, Jené, 84–94
Watters, Dan, 233
Watts, Peter, 57, 69, 153
"Waving at Trains" (Hopkinson), 216–19
Welcome to the Monkey House (Vonnegut), 198
West African religions and belief systems, xii, 6, 8, 72, 76–77, 79, 113, 147, 176, 233
When Fox Is a Thousand (Lai), 58
Whispers from the Cotton Tree Root (Hopkinson), xii, xv, 51, 62, 64, 82, 96, 102, 116, 133, 224
white reluctance to openly discuss race and racism, 111–17, 184–86, 235–36
white resistance to diversity, 114–17
Wild, Wild West (1999), 81
Williams, Hype, 80
Willis, Bruce, 80
Wilson, Gahan, 172
Windling, Terri, 4, 30, 33, 209
Winfield, Paul, 101
WisCon: The Feminist Science Fiction Conference, xii, xv, 75, 103–4, 114–15, 122
Wole Soyinka prize for literature, 222
Wolfe, Gary K., 189–200
Wolfe, Gene, 18, 34, 163
Wolff, Christian, 37–45
women's hesitancy to write, 89; due to family responsibilities, 91
Wooden Sea, The (Carroll), 57
world-building, 16, 31, 35, 98, 203–4, 238, 240
World Fantasy Award, xi, xvi, 64, 83, 159, 172, 224
World Fantasy Convention, 224

World Science Fiction Convention, xii, xvi, 219

Wright, Ronald, 18

writers of color: racialization of, 111, 122–23, 129, 131; reluctance to have work identified as science fiction or fantasy, 58; under-representation of, 113–15; work not represented in bookstores, 58. *See also under* science fiction genre; speculative fiction genre

Xenogenesis series (Butler), 33

X-Men, The (2000), 80

Yale (character), 160

Year's Best Erotica, The (Bright), 108

Yolen, Jane, 14, 33, 35, 209

Yoruba English, 28

Young, Kendra (character), 159

young adult fiction, 12, 180–81, 189, 191, 224; fantasy, xvi, 120, 156, 172

About the Editor

Isiah Lavender III is Sterling-Goodman Professor of English at the University of Georgia, where he researches and teaches courses in African American literature and science fiction. His most recent books include *Afrofuturism Rising: The Literary Prehistory of a Movement* (2019) and *Literary Afrofuturism in the Twenty-First Century*, coedited with Lisa Yaszek (2020).